OCT 1986

OBJECTIVITY AND HUMAN PERCEPTION

BOOKS BY M. D. FABER

Suicide and Greek Tragedy

The Design Within: Psychoanalytic Approaches to Shakespeare (editor and contributor)

A New Anatomy of Melancholy: Patterns of Self-Aggression among Authors (co-editor and contributor)

Culture and Consciousness: The Social Meaning of Altered Awareness

Objectivity and Human Perception: Revisions and Crossroads in Psychoanalysis and Philosophy

M. D. Faber

OBJECTIVITY AND HUMAN PERCEPTION:
REVISIONS AND CROSSROADS IN PSYCHOANALYSIS AND PHILOSOPHY

 The University of Alberta Press

First published by
The University of Alberta Press
Athabasca Hall
Edmonton, Alberta, Canada

Copyright © The University of Alberta Press 1985

ISBN 0-88864-083-8

Canadian Cataloguing in Publication Data

Faber, M. D. (Mel D.)
   Objectivity and human perception

ISBN 0-88864-083-8

1. Integration (Theory of knowledge)
2. Objectivity.   3. Perception.   I. Title.
BD218.F32 1985   121   C84-091504-7

Typesetting by The Typeworks, Vancouver, British Columbia, Canada.
Printed by D. W. Friesen & Sons Ltd., Altona, Manitoba, Canada

CONTENTS

PREFACE

This book has been growing within me for some time. Indeed, I believe I was preparing to write it several years ago as I researched various topics far removed from those with which I deal here. If there is a lesson in that it probably has something to do with the motto E. M. Forster appended to the title-page of his novel, *Howards End*: "only connect." Which brings me directly to the nature of my present undertaking.

I strive in the following pages to synthesize certain important aspects of psychology and philosophy, and, having done that, to employ the resulting synthesis toward a better understanding of our protracted obsession with scientific or "objective" thinking. My chapters deal with such diverse subjects as mysticism, economics, epistemology, politics, and the rearing of children because I have discovered these areas of human activity to be vitally, even fundamentally related. In Chapters 2 and 3 I refine a model of perceptual development originally set forth in *Hartford Studies in Literature* (1973) and in my book, *Culture and Consciousness* (1981). My present purpose has been to bring this model into line with the most recent psychoanalytic discoveries in the area of human mentation and to add to it a critique of what has come to be known as "ego psychology," and an informational approach to the problem of altered awareness. Also, by placing the model in an explicitly epistemological context, and by giving it an explicitly epistemological slant, I mean to alter the ideational implications which surround its principal features. Readers who wish to familiarize themselves thoroughly with the growth and the nature of my model might take up the earlier works before turning to this one.

In Chapters 1, 4, 5, and 6, I wed innovative psychoanalytic concepts to the mainstream of modern philosophical thought, including several phenomenological works of this century. It is there that I develop a new approach to Freud's last writings that breaks ground with regard to the application of psychoanalysis to the philosophical and psychological understanding of man as a perceptual being. And it is there that I strive to indicate the relevance of all this specialized thinking to the political, economic, and technological world we currently inhabit. A large order, to be sure. Yet, I will be satisfied if my efforts succeed in merely opening a direction of enquiry which proves fruitful to those who come after, seeking to comprehend the full unconscious nature of what we have been doing, and are doing, on this planet.

A final prefatory observation: at no point in this book am I suggesting that altered states of consciousness, or what is popularly known as "mysticism," comprise the only real answer to psychological dilemmas of an individual and/or social nature, or to the problems that emerge from philosophical and religious debate. To the extent that this book employs words to indicate issues, it falls on the side of reason. I personally regard it as a modest exemplification of reason's ability to find fresh approaches to age-old, and urgent, concerns. At the same time, it should be remembered that the words themselves are not the pay-off. One uses them to discover what might be called an intuitive or paradoxical methodology in which exists the potential for genuine change at the deep mind-body level, where much of the world's madness resides, and for enriched experiential understanding of the religious and philosophical questions that underlie the enterprise as a whole. I am offering, in short, a kind of dialectical mix that charts a rational course into and through the irrational, suggesting along the way concrete physical practices, intuitive or paradoxical in themselves, that may actually *increase* the rationality to which one finally returns. Indeed, an overriding purpose of this volume is to recommend that we stop thinking in terms of the old dichotomy, rational vs. irrational, and begin to appreciate, and to act upon, the flow that is always occurring between these supposedly disparate facets of our being.

ACKNOWLEDGEMENTS

Portions of Chapters 6 originally appeared in the *Psychoanalytic Review* under the title, "The Computer, the Technological Order, and Psychoanalysis." I am grateful to the editors of the *Review* for permission to use those materials here. The Canadian Federation for the Humanities generously assisted me (both financially and intellectually) along the way, and I am deeply appreciative of that assistance. This book has been published with the help of a grant from the Canadian Federation for the Humanities using funds provided by the Social Sciences and Humanities Research Council of Canada. The skill and professionalism of Mrs. Norma Gutteridge of the University of Alberta Press facilitated the completion of the job, as did the fine copy-editing of Ms. Jean Wilson. Finally, I wish to express my appreciation of the outstanding secretarial skills of Ms. Colleen Donnelly of the English Department, University of Victoria.

ABBREVIATIONS

AI   *American Imago*
IJP   *International Journal of Psychoanalysis*
JAPA   *Journal of the American Psychoanalytic Association*
JTP   *Journal of Transpersonal Psychology*
PQ   *Psychoanalytic Quarterly*
PR   *Psychoanalytic Review*

1
PSYCHOANALYSIS AND THE CENTRAL PROBLEM OF PHILOSOPHY

INTRODUCTORY OBSERVATIONS

This book may be regarded as a psychoanalytic meditation on several crucial topics. By crucial I mean topics that bear directly upon our understanding of ourselves as perceiving animals, as creatures who are given to cultural modes of organization, and as members of a species that is coming perilously close to destroying itself through the despoliation of its environment and the deployment of nuclear weapons.

One thing that should be mentioned immediately about the topics I mean to treat is their very close interconnection. Here I must confess a certain despair about the necessities and rigors of exposition. Forced to begin somewhere, I offer my initial observations stripped of their rich relation to matters that are subsequently explored. In a future age, perhaps, books will emerge whole on some sort of cybernetic screen, and "readers" will be touched as by a single chord. It is precisely because I confront a linear development that I choose to present my topics, including their relations to one another, in a brief, preliminary way.

The Rootedness of Human Confusion

During the past 100 years our recognition of the extent to which "the irrational" informs our perception, loads our "reason," guides our judgement, finds its way into every aspect of our behavior, has grown enormously. I would characterize the strange, somewhat disturbing plateau we have reached in the following manner: we are on the verge of realizing fully that everything which is a source of good for us is also a source

1

of bad, that everything we rely on in a fundamental way to bring us inner richness and contentment, to ameliorate our condition in the world, and even to distinguish us as a form of life is also that to which we must trace our disruptive, aggressive behaviors, our self-inimical, self-destructive tendencies, and our neurotic, miserable inner condition generally. Let me stress that when I say the source of everything good is the source of everything bad and imply thereby a dreadful "double bind," I am not referring to items at the surface of life, to such things as political parties, daiquiris, automobiles, and engagement rings. I am suggesting, rather, that we are "double-bound" and confused in a basic, structural way that touches upon our very organization as perceivers, our deepest mental and emotional make-up, our *nature,* including of course our propensity to organize ourselves into societal groups. Two examples will suffice.

As everyone knows, it is our verbal-symbolic capacity which distinguishes us from the beasts, which allows us to explore, indeed to *grasp* not only the universe within us but the earthly and heavenly environments in which we reside. The acquisition and growth of language, the employment of the symbolic in the widest communicative sense, not only stands behind the wonders of human culture—art, music, literature, philosophy, science, government, law—but also behind the evolution of human awareness itself, "the light." At the same time, words and symbols have long been recognized by philosophical and religious thinkers in both the east and the west as that which comes *between* the user and his keen apprehension of "the facts." Words in this regard become a kind of mentalistic filter which impedes direct contact, clarity of vision, *awareness.* The incessant inward babble that comprises our ordinary consciousness, the mental "place" in which we live as we go about our affairs, must, say the sages, be shut off or we never escape the realms of illusion, a second-hand relation with the world, or, as Aldous Huxley once expressed it, "the *ersatz* of Suchness."

Yet even at a much more mundane level we easily grasp the two-sidedness of language, the power of the symbol to mobilize not only our capacity for "objective" thought and behavior but also our capacity for ugly, irrational conduct, for passion in the most pejorative sense of the term, for duplicity and blindness. Because the development of language and symbol is rooted in the development of personality generally, with all its ambivalence, its unconscious conflict, its anxiety and aggression and envy and disappointment, the symbolic realm is of necessity

2

fraught with the most *objectionable* as opposed to *objective* human tendencies. When one thinks of the abominations that have been committed in the name of "God" or "Fatherland," or in the shadow of such symbols as the swastika or the burning cross, one recognizes at once the madness that resides in our capacity for words, the agony that resides in our attachment to symbols. And one is tempted to ask, if only for the adventure of asking, would it not be better to be *without* that, for some time at least? Would it not be a relief to put that *off* occasionally, to get *away* from that occasionally? And would not the ability to *do* that, to gain distance and detachment from symbol and word, be of therapeutic value to the species as a whole?

The second example is just as basic and disquieting as the first. When we find ourselves in crises, "up against it," in trouble, we look within to those parental figures, those deeply internalized sources of support, which became for us, long ago, the foundation of our personality, of our resiliency and strength. Parental figures do not constitute merely the source of our biological development, our mental and sensorial participation in life, they constitute the source of our ontological development, our moral and emotive participation in the world, our "courage to be." At the same time, those deeply internalized parental figures become a major source of our difficulties, even our woes, as we go about the business of living. When we look within during periods of trouble or crisis, when we turn inward to the "trace" of the parental figure for support, we often discover not a positive inner world of benign presences but a kind of wax museum of negative attitudes, blindness, fecklessness, stubbornness, indifference, and sometimes downright injustice and humiliation. For most of us, the major source of our strength is the major source of our weakness. The parental figures upon whom we base our lives and through whom we come eventually to realize ourselves are the same figures who prevent us from living fully, from becoming truly centred in ourselves, from actualizing in a concrete, unmistakable way who we really are. Just as language comprises a blessing and a curse, and in this sense, ultimately, a human confusion, so the parental influence comprises a blessing and a curse, and in this sense, too, a source of confusion — perhaps the greatest and most persistent source of all.

This is not, let me stress again, simply a way of declaring life is hard. One is of course tempted to adopt that attitude and to brave it out. But one must be very alert to "character armor" here, to the ultimate hollowness of the stoical attitude, its ability to persuade us to persist in our dilemma and never to change and grow. One must also be alert to the tendency of such an attitude to fill us with a certain contempt for others, a belief that one has "grown up" if others haven't, when in fact one has merely hardened his defences. The confusion I am addressing goes very, very deep, to the structural level itself. It constitutes a genuine danger, to us, to our children, and to theirs. It should not be shrugged off with a "life is hard" attitude but faced and tackled. Encouraging in all of this is something to which I referred earlier, namely the extent to which our grasp of the unconscious has grown during the past 100 years. It may just be possible, now, to lessen our confusion and our danger. Such a development would, in my view, comprise an evolutionary break-through on the part of a mixed-up animal that is openly confronted, in the midst of a nuclear age, with the very real possibility of its fiery extir-pation.

Two Kinds of Philosophical Objects

The "quest for certainty," for "objectivity," for unmediated contact with "the truth," has been with us for perhaps 2,000 years. Eventually, in an effort to demonstrate the roots of our current epistemological di-lemma (the so-called mind-body problem), I will explore meticulously, and from a psychoanalytic angle, the way in which this obsessional pur-suit has expressed itself in the work of several modern philosophers. What I wish to emphasize here is the close association that exists be-tween the old philosophical search for the truth and the rise of modern, scientific thought.

It was Descartes who offered the infant world of science a detailed procedure for the attainment of "certainty." I will deal with Descartes fully in the subsequent section to which I just referred. Let it suffice at this point to suggest that Descartes, by "detaching his mind from his sense," by relying solely upon "mathematics, logic, and reason" as trustworthy tools of enquiry, and by concentrating upon "only those objects" to the "sure and indubitable knowledge of which our mental powers seem to be adequate," believed he could discover his way to a perception of things as they are (Descartes 1969, pp. 37, 40, 194). "No direct experience can ever deceive the understanding," he wrote, "if it restrict its attention accurately to the object presented to it" (1969, p. 132). Here, precisely, is the gist of the scientific attitude, and, of scientific methodology. I am not suggesting, of course, that scientific thought remained philosophically and theoretically stagnant between the seventeenth and early twentieth centuries, or that a later, pivotal figure such as Ernst Mach was not considerably more alert to perceptual issues than was Descartes. Nor am I unaware of what has been occurring recently. I am simply maintaining that Descartes' position is the essential one, that it underlies the scientific beliefs of the last three centuries, and that it is *still* very influential even among scientists who are intellectually aware of its limitations. "When pressed," writes the physicist Roger Jones, "most scientists will concede that all physical theories are tentative and approximate and that there is no clear conception of physical reality in modern quantum theory." Such "disclaimers," however, are made in the interest of "fair play." They do *not,* says Jones, "characterize the way scientists behave and think in their everyday activities of research and teaching nor in their conversations with each other" (Jones 1982, p. 206). There, the Cartesian belief in an "objective" realm, and the one methodological way to it, reigns supreme.

Among the key expressions in all of this are, of course, "objects" and "objectivity." These are the terms around which the controversy swirls. These are the terms that have, through Heisenberg and the Copenhagen school on the one hand and Popper and the positivist school on the other, split the scientific community in our time, particularly with reference to theoretical problems arising from the subatomic realm where "objects," as Roger Jones has just indicated, fail to meet rigorous requirements of definition, and where "objectivity" is of the strange sort that includes the observer in the "objective" part of the observation.

Now, while all of this was going on, another discussion of "objects" was emerging from a discipline that, at first glance, appears to have no connection whatever to the "objects" and "objectivity" of the scientific-philosophic debate. As we shall see, however, this emergent discussion from this apparently unrelated discipline bears on that debate in a vital, even decisive way.

From the inception of his career Freud was scornful of philosophy's readiness to deal with *only* the phenomena of consciousness. He regarded the "psychoanalytic assumption of unconscious mental activity" as an "extension of the corrections begun by Kant in regard to our views on external perception." Just as Kant "warned us not to overlook the fact that our perception is subjectively conditioned and must not be regarded as identical with the phenomena perceived," so psychoanalysis

5

"bids us not to set conscious perception in the place of the unconscious mental process which is its object." The "mental," like the "physical," is "not necessarily in reality just what it appears to us to be." Still, Freud concluded, it is gratifying to discover that the "correction of inner perception" does not "present difficulties so great as that of outer perception," that the "inner object" is "less hard to discern truly than is the outside world" (Freud [1915] 1971, p. 104). Freud gives us here, for the first time in western intellectual history, not merely two kinds of philosophical objects, those of the inner and those of the outer world, but an *inner object with an unconscious, dynamic, perceptual dimension.* Thus he points the way toward an epistemological synthesis, toward a unified philosophic and psychoanalytic model of our characteristic modes of "discerning" the universe.

The Internalizing Body-Mind

Psychoanalysis, as an originator of knowledge and understanding, culminates in our full appreciation of the significance of *internalization* in human life. It has long been stressed, perhaps to the point of becoming a cliché, that man is distinguished from the other animals by his proclivity to create and to dwell within a world of symbols, that his existence must not be regarded dualistically as of the mind over here and of the body over there but must be grasped in terms of his psychobiological propensity to unite mind and feeling in a symbolic mode of expression. Indeed, the entire shape of modern philosophy, anthropology, and to some extent sociology, is importantly determined by its concentration upon the symbolic style of social and individual organization. Yet to stress this aspect of our behavior is to stress what is merely a visible, "higher" manifestation of a considerably more basic human tendency. As we concentrate upon the nature of internalization we find ourselves in possession of a more powerful analytic instrument than that which inheres in the symbolistic approach—which deals, if the truth were told, with materials that have taken shape *after* the elemental events of our lives have transpired. I do not believe we can genuinely grasp the symbolic—including the symbols of science—without first having grasped the psychoanalytic, and by psychoanalytic I do not mean the libido theory, the Oedipus complex, the classical "Freudian" scheme. I mean, rather, those close, "neo-Freudian" investigations of the infant-mother symbiosis which have occurred within the past four decades.

Virtually none of that has found its way to the scientific and humanistic disciplines to which it so urgently applies.

To underscore the basic role of internalization in human life means to synthesize recent psychoanalytic discoveries which bear upon the development of our sense of time, our sense of space, our relationship with the parental figures, our acquisition of language — in a word, the development of our primary universe of feeling and perceiving. I want to indicate the raw, psychodynamic nature of the earliest affective, perceptual worlds that we fashion out of our biological tendencies and our interactions with the environment. I want to shift psychoanalytic discussion away from its absorption in repression, adaptation, narcissism, and transference, toward an absorption in the onset of ordinary awareness, an absorption which recognizes above all that "reality" is made, not given, that the open, volitional "system" which *is* the human organism is open in an explicitly perceptual way that obliges us to reconsider all the central features of our traditional theoretical models. I say this fully apprised that psychoanalysis is, ultimately, a therapeutic discipline and that its official epistemology has been developed along lines which are to aid the doctor in his treatment of the disturbed individual. To concentrate upon the psychodynamics of ordinary perception, I am convinced, is actually to discover new therapeutic possibilities for a healing practice that has become notorious for its failure to heal. It may well be that the problem of "cure" in psychoanalysis is rooted in the discipline's inclination naïvely to take "reality" for granted — in its failure to focus closely upon how that "reality" comes about.

Concentration upon key perceptual features of our development, including the crucial role of internalization therein, will result in a wholesale redefinition of the terms "object" and "objective." I hope to demonstrate that we must start using these words in a radically new way, that they are presently fraught with misunderstandings and difficulties which may have grave, even fatal consequences for us as an evolving species.

Psychological Objects

The human infant, perhaps from the inception of his extrauterine life, evinces a powerful urge to internalize the universe around him, to take in and to retain a sizeable portion of the materials with which he comes into contact during the long course of his development toward childhood. It is customary in psychoanalytic circles to approach the problem of internalization by referring to introjection, incorporation, and identification. We do not have to worry too much about these terms here, but it is probably a good idea to mention that introjection and incorporation are generally regarded as the kinds of "primitive" or pre-cognitive internalizing processes that are employed by the infant and the pre-Oedipal child of three to four years, and identification as the kind of internalizing activity that is characteristic of the Oedipal child, the adolescent, and the adult. I say "generally regarded" because the child, the adolescent, and the adult retain (and often express) the capacity to incorporate and introject other persons and things in a deep, tenacious, "primitive" way when circumstances provoke intense psychological pressure and recall the aims and disappointments of life's early stages. "All those processes" by which we "transform real or imagined interactions" with the environment, and "real or imagined characteristics of the environment" into *inner* relationships and *inner* characteristics might be thought of as that to which the term *internalization* refers (Schafer 1968, pp. 8–9).

We must also note in this connection that the tendency to internalize the environment is prompted by *both* the developing cortex *and* the growing organism's *defensive needs*. It is the infant's helpless condition, his long period of dependency, his anxiety over separation and loss, along with his accompanying urge to master, to control, a world that is frequently at odds with his wishes and threatening in itself, that goads the internalizing process into life. What we have here is in large measure a kind of "magical" activity based on the feeling-belief that one is safe only when vital external objects and relationships (including paradoxically "bad" objects and relationships) are *taken and held inside*. Of paramount importance in all of this, of course, is the *caretaker*.

That the child's interaction with the parent is the foundation of human psychology everyone appreciates in a "soft," general way. What I wish to emphasize here, and what I will demonstrate in detail later, is that the child's interaction with the parent is the foundation of human *perception* in a "hard," specific, structural sense that has yet to be recognized by large numbers of people. Internalization transpires at the sensorial, bodily level. The materials that are taken in — and these are largely aspects of the caretaker — are taken into the child's *perceiving organism*. It is there that they root themselves, and it is there that they remain, for the duration of the individual's life. In the remarks of Freud cited earlier, Kant was explicitly called to mind. We must call him to mind again here by declaring that the very temporal and spatial cognition which serves as the "a priori" ground of our perceptual participation in the world is connected inextricably to the internalizations of the early period in which the parental object functions as the dynamic, emotive centre of the neonate's existence. It is in this perceptual-structural context, in this foundational context, that I may suggest what the psychoanalytic term "object" refers to.

It is employed to indicate the child's "care-giver," the individual who accompanies the child "through all the successive stages of development." This person is, first of all, a "partner" in a "complex totality of biological reflex mechanisms"; she/he is then "somebody" who can be "distinguished, recognized, and represented," as well as "needed, respected, feared, hated, confided in and finally loved" (de Levita 1983, p. 277). With regard to the phenomenal complexity embedded in this general picture, "object" may refer to the "thing" (breast) that provides "organ pleasure" or "organ frustration"; the person who provides the "thing"; the "percept thereof"; or the "psychical representation of the percept" (Compton 1983, pp. 420–21). In subsequent paragraphs and chapters I will range among these distinctions. The extent to which such "objects," through the process of internalization, come to be integrally bound up with the individual's existence is captured dramatically by the current trend in psychoanalysis to refer to a person's "self-objects" when probing into issues of identity formation and into conflict-inducing situations (Miller 1981, p. 62). It is precisely here that we find the deepest meaning of the psychoanalytic commonplace that virtually all relationships between human beings contain an element of the transference, that is, an unconscious element tied developmentally to significant figures of the past. Behind the transference stand the primary internalizations of the early period. What I will strive to establish in this book as a whole is that *all* our relationships—to things, creatures, ideas, fields of knowledge, the world itself in the most inclusive sense, and not just to other people—are colored by the "objects" with which we have come into contact during the formative years.

Which calls to mind the following: after a debate of several decades over the nature of psychological objects and the process of internalization, psychoanalysis is coming finally to recognize and to admit that "objects" are best understood as "split-off aspects of the ego" which have been "projected into" mental representations (Ogden 1983,

p. 234). What this boils down to may be appreciated fully when we re-call that the term "ego" in psychoanalysis designates the "perceptual ap-paratus." Thus psychoanalysis is coming to recognize that our percep-tion of objects in the world "out there" is, *generally,* determined by our perception of objects in the world "in here." Accordingly, when we hear the word "object," or "objective," we must begin to discern its *double* meaning, its *active, relational* nature, and we must do this in the fresh, original way implied by the context. Rather than dwell on the old, shopworn notion of the choiceless "subjectivity" of experience, we must alert ourselves to the *dynamic, unconscious materials* on the "sub-jective" side of the equation.

Conceptual Dangers

From the many conceptual dangers hovering about the attempt to rede-fine the terms "object" and "objective" two must be singled out. First, there is the danger of reification, of regarding psychological objects much as we regard sticks and stones — as "there" in a simplistic, empiri-cal sense which reflects our ordinary attitude toward the "things" of the world. While my view of psychological objects will only emerge fully from subsequent material, and while I must, of course, be held account-able for that view, I have no intention of fashioning a daemonology, of creating the impression in the reader's mind that a surgical incision into the human abdomen would permit one or more psychological objects to step forth onto the stage of life. Psychological objects are as "real" as stones but only in the special sense I will develop as the discussion pro-ceeds.

The second danger is rather more methodological than theoretical and resides at the opposite extreme from the first. It may be illustrated by discussing briefly a recent psychoanalytic reaction to the many reifi-cations inherent in Freud's topography of the mind. Finding it impos-sible to accept the existence of the "id," the "libido," "psychic energy," and similar "Freudian" items which cannot be perceived in any accept-able scientific sense ("acceptable scientific" here = "positivistic empiri-cal"), such writers as Peterfreund (1971) and Wilden (1972) have chosen to develop a psychoanalytic model along informational (or cy-bernetic) lines. They regard the human animal as essentially an infor-mation processing entity and view psychological disturbance as arising from the vicissitudes of the processing procedure itself. Gregory Bate-

son's now famous essay on schizophrenia and the "double bind" provoked considerable interest in this approach and still serves as a good
example of its effectiveness (Bateson [1956] 1972). What is of particular importance to us here, however, is that within this "school of
thought" the psychological object — far from being reified into a "thing"
— becomes a kind of informational "trace" or psychic "echo" abiding in
the "mental apparatus." Wilden tells us, for example, that an "object"
important to the child "is the constitution of information out of *noise*"
and that "it will be integrated into the system as *trace.*" It is thus "a sign
(a symbol in the Saussurean sense)... which has been chosen to emerge
from [an] infinite multiplicity of signals" (Wilden 1972, p. 438).

Apart from the difficulties inherent in the notion that infants and children choose what to internalize, the chief problem with this passage is
its tendency to play down *the body's role* in the development of the
inner world. While I cannot, strictly speaking, quarrel with the theoretical emphasis, with the "primacy of perception" implied in such a passage — and indeed, while I will sometimes adopt an informational viewpoint myself in order to support my own contentions, I can assert that a
radical mentalism will lead to methodological inadequacies serious
enough to cripple the psychoanalytic enterprise. It is just not possible to
liberate the individual from the harmful effects of his internalizations
without engaging *his body* in a concrete way, without treating psychological entities as more than mere "informational trace," without according the significant "signs" and "symbols" the *thingness* their nature
requires. The psychological object of the early period roots itself in the
biological organism as an ever-present psycho-physical entity influencing not only our perception of the world but our bodily orientation,
physical disposition, musculature, chemistry, and "length of blood and
bone."

In this way, those "inner objects" of Freud's essay are not entirely "inner" or "mental" in the customary sense, the sense he had in mind. They
have a kind of physical or "objective" existence in the body. As for the
"objects" of the "outside world" also mentioned by Freud, they themselves are not entirely external or "physical" — again in the sense he had
in mind, for they are "colored" or projectively "touched" by the perceiving organism with which they come into contact. Notably, the theoretical and methodological perspective I am developing here does not
simply leave Freud's dualism behind (inner vs. outer), it reflects the
most recent models of the physical universe in which the interactions of

the forces under investigation (the relational field) contribute over-whelmingly to the "reality," and in which the observer's participation in the "event," as mentioned earlier, comprises an integral part of the picture. "The given object is an element of interactions on various levels," writes Antal Müller, "and is characterized on every interaction level by different laws and properties." That the "measuring instrument" is the "extension of our senses" does not mean the "epistemological boundary between consciousness and the external world" should be placed "outside man," but that it "forms a connecting link between the human sense organs, which are adapted for macroscopic conditions, and the microphysical processes" (Müller 1974, pp. 27, 54). Psychological objects must be regarded accordingly. They are no more and no less "real" than anything else in this new, fluid universe of ours. Most of all, their existence within, and their effect upon, the actual, sensatory human body must not be ignored in the effort to serve the logical requirements of some theoretical position. What is human is often contradictory. Indeed, opposition and contradiction enter integrally into the growth of our awareness as an evolving form of life.

As for the physiological characteristics of internalization, while they are still in large measure a mystery (just as the processes of thought themselves are a mystery), they undoubtedly occur as a facet of the neuronic, "microphysical" activity which comprises the material expression of our development, including the material expression of the *constraint* which that development invariably entails in culture. I will return to this notion later, during my discussion of altered states.

The Mind-Body Dichotomy and Psychoanalysis

All of this, I realize, lands me in the middle of the "central problem in the philosophy of mind," to wit, the ancient "mind-body dichotomy" (Wilson 1979, p. 47). Concentrating explicitly upon that troublesome business, I will put forth two related statements which characterize my overall position in the chapters to follow. First, I consider human feelings to be a real aspect of bodily existence — and I mean by that a real, physical aspect. It is a tenet of my approach that emotion is an aspect of perception, as much an event, a bodily event, as noticing the rain, preparing lunch, or scratching. Now, that the internalized, emotive material of life's first years becomes a major component of our perception, that we look out at the universe through, as it were, the eyes of our internalizations, is also fundamental to my discussion, and in this sense I regard "the mental" as "physical" and designate as "object" that which we "take in" during the early period.

My second statement has methodological as well as theoretical implications. Of the many procedures employed by thinkers to answer the mind-body question, there is one which seeks "to dissolve the problem by deeming it to be in some way misconceived" (Wilson 1979, p. 48). At both the epistemological and psychoanalytic levels my argument reflects this view. Not only do I regard the mind-body dichotomy (and the related internal-external dichotomy) as a feature of ordinary awareness, as a problem the conceptual nature of which stems directly from the perceptual tie to the internalizations of infancy and childhood, I believe that people "get better"—more fully in touch with themselves and their environment—when they achieve the ability in mind and body to moderate, or relax, the tie to the internalized object, actually to alter their perception in a concrete, physical way. Thus, I aim to establish that philosophy's quest for "the truth" and psychoanalysis's quest for human actualization are not distinct, isolated endeavors, that they meet right here, where our tendency to internalize the world makes its mark on our perceptual endowment.

This does not mean that philosophy is destined to be absorbed into the world of psychological exploration. On the contrary, the philosopher will always have a role to play in formulating fresh epistemological, ethical, and aesthetic views, as well as in dissecting the assumptions which underlie existing views. Nor should the importance of the shrewd, logical critique be minimized in a world as given as ours is to following the leader, to swallowing the latest myth from the latest "expert" or guru. What it does mean is that philosophy is obligated to recognize the all-encompassing significance of psychoanalytic insight into the nature of our perceptual behavior, particularly as that behavior derives from the internalizing activities of life's first years. While the philosopher may dispute the notion that there is nothing in our minds that was not first in our senses, he must also appreciate that what *does* get into our minds through our senses is not only quantitatively enormous but crucially affected by those psychological objects which the child encounters and takes deep into his sensorial being.

My position here, remarkably enough, bears directly on the materialist objection to philosophy promulgated by Marxist theoreticians such as Lenin who are fond of declaring that philosophy is a nebulous, use-

13

less discipline because, strictly speaking, "it has no object, in the sense that a science has an object." If something "actually does happen" in the sciences, it is because "they do have an object, knowledge of which they can increase." This gives the sciences a "history." Because philosophy "has no object, nothing can happen in it." The "nothing of its history simply repeats the nothing of its object" (Althusser 1971, pp. 56–57). What I wish to suggest, without agreeing necessarily with these Leninist views, is that psychoanalytic exploration of the "inner world" may well provide philosophy with a direction from which it can derive, and have, its "object." It has been remarked that "transformations of philosophy" are often "rebounds" from "great scientific discoveries" (Althusser 1971, p. 15). Surely the psychoanalytic discovery of the unconscious as it bears upon the development of our perception from infancy to adulthood must eventually effect such a "transformation." I do not see any reason why it should not begin now, as we discuss the foundational "objects" of our early experience in conjunction with the traditional "objects" of philosophical discourse. The pedants and purists will, of course, balk at this, preferring to continue with their naïve discussions of "raw feels" and similar homespun items. One hopes they will not prevail.

The Issue of Liberation

The transformation I have in mind, because it is related so integrally to the body into which the object of the early period is taken, involves still another ingredient, namely those mind-body practices which for thousands of years have striven to guide the human creature toward an alteration of awareness capable of lessening the stressful effects of his perceptual habits. I mean to discuss such practices for their epistemological implications as well as for their therapeutic significance. Equally, I mean to discuss the way in which psychoanalysis (and to a lesser extent philosophy) helps us to grasp certain misconceptions and dangers that attend the so-called mystical realm.

We live in an age which is prone to believe that liberation from ordinary, egotic consciousness with its attendant discomfort and strain can be achieved by a simple act of will. Bent upon a "transcendent breakthrough" and the "new consciousness" that ostensibly comes with it, the individual makes up his mind that his "neurosis" is an "illusion," adopts a "fresh perspective" on the world, and commits himself to an occasional meditation, or yogic exercise, or glance into a "sacred" piece of literature. Far from doing the job, this sort of thing will merely stiffen one's defences or prompt a mild regression to an earlier stage of development. The deep and tenacious influence of our foundational objects cannot be offset by "decisions" in the usual sense or by half-hearted activities which provide a "break" from one's customary routine. While I do believe that positive, fundamental change can occur, I also believe that it will depend upon commitment to a scrupulous, long-term, knowledgeable program which engages the mind and the body in a concerted way. As I suggested in the preface, and as I wish to re-emphasize here, my discussion of altered states is designed to facilitate a dialectical flow between "paradoxical" or "intuitive" methodologies capable of transforming ordinary perception and felt analytical insights without which our subsurface powers cannot achieve their richest potential. Such a program might lead to the kind of enlightened, perceptual *play* that would mark a genuine reorientation of being.

Admittedly, a faint-sounding optimistic (Utopian?) note may be detected in this aspect of the discussion. Still, I believe I can say with assurance that I have no illusions. I am perfectly aware of the degree to which we are "hooked" on our reckless, self-destructive styles of individual and social conduct. I realize how difficult it is—how anxiety-inducing it is—to change. I appreciate the strange, circuitous gratifications that egoism and narcissism can bring. Nor am I blind to the manifold alienations that are spawned each week and month and year by our ubiquitous, implacable technology. In a word, I see the gulf that separates our present psychic shores from the fragrant coasts of Utopia. I also see, however, the danger of ceasing our efforts to get there. It is not simply, as the old cliché has it, that a little genuine change can make a difference; on the contrary, it is that our desperate situation, as we teeter at the edge of nuclear confrontation and despoliation of the environment, demands a wholesale shift in the way we perceive ourselves and the world around us. The more joltingly we come to confront the disturbed, neurotic side of what we take to be our "normal" awareness, the more eagerly we may begin to work toward an evolutionary transformation of our perceptual habits.

2
THE PSYCHODYNAMIC ORIGINS OF HUMAN PERCEPTION

MIRRORING, SEPARATION, AND THE WORD

For all the rich insight modern psychology has afforded people into their "condition," it has failed to make plain what may well be the most crucial psychological fact of all, namely that what we take to be our ordinary consciousness, our ordinary way of perceiving and being-in the world, is itself a disturbance, a state of imbalance and tension so serious as to virtually negate the possibility of achieving our full potential as living creatures. I want to express the thesis of this chapter in as forceful and dramatic a way as I can by declaring that our ordinary awareness constitutes a "conversion."

This term, introduced into psychoanalysis by Freud toward the turn of the century, denotes the capacity of the human animal to "transmute" or "convert" traumatic "ideas" into "bodily forms of expression" in a defensive attempt to "render" such ideas harmless (Freud [1894] 1959, p. 63). For example, one of Freud's (and Breuer's) earliest patients, Anna O, underwent a paralysis of the arm whenever her buried feelings toward her father were aroused. The paralysis desisted as the unconscious materials were brought to light. The "conversion," wrote Freud, may be "partial" or "total," and it proceeded "along the line of the sensory innervation" that was "more or less intimately related to the traumatic experience." In this way, although the individual succeeded "in resolving the incompatibility within himself," he also succeeded in "burdening" himself with a kind of "memory-symbol" or "parasite" in the "form of a persistent motor innervation" (Freud [1894] 1959, p. 63). Freud's interests eventually led him away from strict concentration on the bodily registration of emotional disorders. A number of his followers, however, pursued the matter vigorously.

What they concluded has been generally accepted by the psychological community and may be summarized as follows. There are no purely somatic processes in human life, even from the beginning. At every stage of development the human creature is a "psycho-physical entity" in which "bodily and emotional processes" are "fused" (Mushatt 1975, p. 85). To speak of the mind apart from the body is as incorrect as to speak of the body apart from the mind. This means that psychic stress, whatever its origin, will leave its mark upon the body. Freud's "conversion process" is a universal aspect of human development because human development always involves emotional stress and because emotional stress always begets physiological expression. It is not only the neurotic symptom of the disturbed individual that we must regard as a "compromise formation" (Freud [1896] 1959, p. 163), as a method of fending off anxiety, of coping with psychological tension. The behavior of every person reveals "compromise formations" and attests to his having answered the anxieties and tensions of his life through the conversion process. Neurosis is simply an exaggerated version of what we take to be "normal" conduct. Now, when one considers that perception is as much a behavior as maintaining a certain posture, or eating, or making love, when one returns, in short, to the basic premise that the human creature is a "psycho-physical entity," one confronts the contention set forth earlier: our ordinary consciousness, our ordinary way of perceiving and being-in the world, may well evince features of the conversion process, may well be a sort of compromise formation, a symptom of our past and present life with its inevitable strains and imperfections.

Structuring in the Infantile Period

Psychoanalysis, during the first two decades of this century, concentrated its efforts primarily upon repression, and upon the relation of repression to the dynamic unconscious. As Freud viewed the matter, the requirements of civilized existence obliged the individual's sexual and aggressive tendencies, or more correctly, the individual's sexual and aggressive "drives," to "go under," to manifest themselves but partially, in an "inhibited" way. The tension between one's urgent instinctual demands and their truncated expression in culture led in a good many instances to "neurotic" disorders with repression at their centre, and in *all* instances, for *all* people, to a life of "discontent" and conflict. It was through slips of the tongue, free associations, organic and behavioral symptoms, and above all through dreams that such conflicts and dis-contentments revealed themselves to the "analyst of the psyche." As he continued to work with people, however, Freud came increasingly to recognize the extent to which the problem of "neurosis" involved not merely the "repression" of "instinct," the struggle between nature and culture, unconscious and conscious experience, but the extent to which one's *conscious life,* lived primarily at the level of "ego processes," was itself a vehicle for the expression of unconscious aims. In short, he came to recognize our potential for living a *split* existence at the level of our ordinary, everyday awareness.

Internalizing activities resulted in formation of the "superego," or that part of the ego which observed the individual as he went about his business, and this agency impelled the ego to perceive the environment, actually to perceive the external world, in a way that loaded the percep-tual life with anxieties, demands, and restrictions of an unconscious na-ture. What was "underneath," in other words, was not merely "id," but the regulations of conduct which we have made a part of our percep-tion.

The poor ego was suddenly discerned by Freud as residing between two enormous psychical agencies — the id on the one hand and the su-perego on the other — and attempting to negotiate between them (Freud [1923] 1974). Thus the accent of Freud's writings began to fall on the ego's "mechanisms" of "defence," on the ways in which the ego at-tempted to give "instinct" its due and, at the same time, to fulfil the re-quirements of conscience. As we shall see, the perceptual implications of Freud's work became more and more compelling to many of his fol-lowers, but with developing emphases that aroused in Freud a certain measure of resistance.

Throughout his career Freud avoided close, persistent enquiry into the early stages of human existence, and particularly into the mother-infant bond. He regarded the infant's tie to the mother as "cathectic," not "structural"; that is to say, he considered it an emotional attach-ment that did not shape the actual mental make-up of the individual in a foundational way (Freud [1923] 1974, p. 21). I will explore this problem rigorously in Chapter 4. Here it is sufficient to note that for Freud the structuring of the psyche occurred after the first four or five years of life as the child identified with the *father* in an effort to resolve the Oedipal struggle.

Freud's tendency to play down the mother's influence is captured unforgettably by his remarkable statement, made at the height of his powers, that the greatest need in childhood is the need for a "father's protection." As Freud expressed it, "I cannot think of any need in childhood as strong as the need for a father's protection" (Freud [1930] 1975, p. 9). I do not believe there would be very many who would quarrel with the exact opposite of this notion, namely that the greatest need in childhood is the need for the satisfaction and security that derives from the primary relationship to the maternal caretaker. Of late it has been realized that Freud's resistance to such matters may well have been rooted in his own intense, highly ambivalent relationship to his own demanding, doting mother, a relationship that persisted into his seventy-fifth year, and that left him exhausted, depressed, and finally unable to attend his mother's funeral (Abraham 1982).

What is especially important for us to remember is that Freud's conflict in this area not only made him sceptical of the many theoretical advances which were taking place all around him toward the close of his career (those of Melanie Klein, for example), but also made him suspicious of therapeutic techniques that stressed the patient's need to regress to the pre-Oedipal period and to "abreact," or work through, the primary traumas arising therefrom. Such deep regression, to be facilitated by a caring attitude on the part of the therapist (something Freud also found objectionable), became the goal of one of Freud's closest and most admired associates, Sandor Ferenczi, and the tension that grew between the men because of this dispute nearly led to a breach on Freud's part. As everyone knows who has read even a little about him, Freud was prone to detach himself radically when he became convinced of irrevocable disagreement on theoretical or clinical issues. In this case, the disagreement touched a sore spot that plagued Freud all his life.

It boils down, then, to the following: as Freud came to see the perceptual split in the ego and the psychodynamics of development which led to the formation of conscience, he wrote in a monumental utterance with enormous philosophical and evolutional significance: "A portion of the external world has, at least partially, been abandoned as an *object* and has instead, by identification, been taken into the ego and thus be-

19

come an integral part of the internal world. This new psychical agency continues to carry on the functions which have hitherto been performed by people in the external world." (Freud [1940] 1964, p. 205; emphasis added). What Freud's followers came increasingly to recognize is that this internalizing or "taking in" activity is occurring within the individual long before Freud believed it was, and that it was *structuring* the individual in a hard, perceptual way long before Freud believed the individual was capable of such structuring. As Rheingold expresses it, the *object,* specifically the mother, "enters" the infant's "dawning psyche" as the "deep introjection" of the earliest phase of development, and she persists there as a "presence," later to become an "image" during the symbolic phase. This early interplay between mother and infant is directly involved in the "structuring" of the infant's "personality" (Rheingold 1964, p. 30). Again according to Rheingold, "intuitive or feeling perception" begins with "maximal intensity" at birth when the infant becomes "immediately subject . . . in a structuring way" to the maternal attitude, and this is attested to by virtually every leading expert in the field of child psychiatry including, as Rheingold cites them, "Deutsch, H. S. Sullivan, Spitz, Benedek, Fries, Mahler, and Sperling" (Rheingold 1964, p. 31). It is precisely the details of this structural event which must be explicated now.

The Origins of Self

Where do we come from? This fundamental question has intrigued the human animal since the inception of genuine self-awareness 10,000 or 15,000 years ago. With the rapid evolutional development of the "big brain," of those cortical regions capable of sustaining abstractions, it became possible for man to behold in the representational "mirror" of his mind both the environment of which he forms a part and, most compellingly and conflictually, himself. I say "conflictually" because of the following consideration: to become aware of oneself as an object, as a creature more or less differentiated in space from other objects and creatures, is to confront not merely the question of origin but the question of destiny as well. What appears in the "mirror" may disappear. Invariably, at some level, the problem of the beginning poses the problem of the end. We must keep this in mind from this point forward.

One can, of course, reply from a variety of perspectives when asked, "where do we come from?". The question touches on the origin of the universe itself, on the putative "big bang" which stands at the opposite, macrocosmic extreme from the sexual, reproductive actions that catalyze our beginnings at the microcosmic, individual level. And there are, needless to say, a thousand variables relating to the history of the earth and human society which may be brought to bear in a significant way upon the issue. Here, I want to focus on the problem of origins from a psychodynamic angle. I want to create a generalized, developmental model that can help us to understand the perceptual nature of our beginnings as members of modern western culture. With the content of the last two paragraphs in our minds, it is interesting to note that at the centre of this model is a peculiar, indeed a unique kind of *mirroring* experience.

During life's first weeks and months the infant and its caretaker are locked in a symbiotic relationship the intensity of which can hardly be overstated. True, we come naked and separate into this world, unattached to others of our kind except in the very rare instance of Siamese twins. But this, our primal condition, is belied by the relational field, the field of *objects,* in which we discover ourselves from the moment of our birth. From a psychological angle, in fact, we leave the total maternal symbiosis of the womb to enter the almost total symbiosis of the first relationship. In contrast to the African wildebeest, which is on its feet and perhaps running for its life only hours after emerging from its mother, the human infant enters the scene in a totally helpless, dependent condition, and he remains in that condition for a considerable period, far, far longer than any other mammal on the planet. In a very real way, he is nurtured into existence as a person through his intensive symbiotic contact with his caretaker. Thus our separateness, our sense of ourselves as individual creatures is something that we gradually *achieve* over a relatively long period of between four and six years. So intense, pervasive, and basic is this interaction between mother and child that we would do well to regard the mother herself not as a distinct entity but as a kind of "organ" of the baby, an actual "separate" *part* of the actual "separate" newcomer (Lichtenstein 1961, p. 202). It is precisely here, in the growth or processing of this unique, combinatory union that we find the "nucleus" of "human identity" (Lichtenstein 1961, p. 208).

The "genesis" and "formation" of the self, writes Esther Menaker (1978, p. 621), derive from the "initial mirroring experience with the mother." For the past three decades this unique, remarkable aspect of our origins has been studied intensively by observers both within and without the psychoanalytic community and has come to be regarded generally as a central structural occurrence of our normal development (McCall 1980, p. 70). The investigations of Spitz during the 1950s and 1960s established at the clinical level the baby's inclination to concentrate upon the mother's face—and in particular upon her eyes—during periods of feeding. For three, or perhaps four or five months the nursing infant does not look at the mother's breast (or at the bottle held close to her breast) but at her face. The baby "does not look at the breast" when his mother approaches, when he grasps the nipple, when he manipulates the breast, or when he feeds. "From the moment the mother comes into the room to the end of nursing he stares at [her] face" (Spitz 1965, p. 81). What is especially interesting in this regard is the inextricable connection between such primal gazing and the oral cavity.

While the child takes into his mouth and body his physical nourishment, he takes into his dawning awareness, his "visceral brain," his earliest perceptual registration of stimuli, the affective, psychological materials that he discovers in the physiognomy, the eyes, and the entire bodily attitude of the mother, or feeder. It is often remarked that the first ego is a body ego and that our later life is influenced at the egotic or perceptual level by the foundational experiences which our bodies undergo as the "perceptual apparatus" awakens. We have here an arresting instance of how this works. When Spitz calls the oral cavity in its conjunction with the mother's body "the cradle of human perception" (Spitz 1965, p. 82), he reminds us that sucking in and spitting out are the first, most basic, and most persistent perceptual behaviors among humans. They underlie at the bodily level our subsequent rejections and acceptances, negations and celebrations, of experience. Moreover, they regularly turn up in their most primitive expression (and thus reveal their pervasive effect) when patients regress to the early levels of psychosexual development during therapy.

Although Spitz established the baby's proclivity to stare at the mother's face, he did not state that mother and infant spend *considerable* time looking at each other, nor did he contend that such looking, along with the mother imitating the infant's facial expressions and sounds, provided the means for the baby to regard the mother's face and sounds as his own (Southwood 1973, p. 235). The essence of the matter may be presented succinctly by calling to mind key discussions in the literature.

An inborn tendency on the part of the infant, writes Southwood, prompts him "to seek out his mother's gaze" and to do so regularly and for extended periods. The mother, because of tendencies developed during the course of her relationship with her own mother, "sets about exploiting" this mutual face-gazing activity. As the eye-to-eye contact becomes frequent, and easily observed by the investigator, the mother's continual inclination to change her facial expression, as well as the quality of her vocalizing, emerges with striking clarity. Usually she smiles, and nods, and coos; sometimes in response to an infant frown she frowns. In virtually every instance, the mother's facial and vocal behavior comprises an imitation of the baby's. Thus, as the mother "descends" to the infant's level she provides him with a particular kind of human mirror. She does not simply give the baby back his own "self"; she reinforces a portion of the baby's behavior in comparison with another portion. She gives the baby back not merely a part of what he is doing but, in addition, "something of her own" (Southwood 1973, p. 238). As Winnicott expresses the matter, "in individual . . . development *the precursor of the mirror is the mother's face*" (Winnicott 1971, p. 130). The upshot may be stated as follows: the kind of behavior we connect with the "ego" — and we must recall once again that "ego" in psychoanalysis refers to the "perceptual apparatus" in an inclusive, general way — derives in large measure from the behavior of the mother. Not only does she trigger and enhance the ego's formation, she determines the *kind* of stimuli to which the child will attend, including the eventual stimuli that will come through the introduction to language.

The entire developmental sequence is captured in painstaking detail by Daniel Stern. As we move through the following material we must keep several things firmly in mind. First, by ten to twelve weeks the normal infant's memory is "robust" (Fagan and Rovee-Collier 1982, p. 93). Infants only four weeks old, in fact, consistently demonstrate preferential choice with regard to proffered visual items, choosing to gaze on depictions of the human face rather than on abstract designs (Dowling 1981, p. 291). Again, during psychotherapy, materials which are clearly related to the deep "imprinting" that human beings undergo as infants turn up with arresting regularity (Almansi 1983, p. 391). While we must not "adultomorphize" the baby, we must also not fail to recognize his capacity to respond in a vital, enduring way to the events taking place around him. The initial mirroring experience with the mother is the first truly *social* interaction in which the baby participates, and one that will powerfully influence his subsequent conduct. The events of the mirror phase are deeply internalized by the developing child to become structural features at the "ground level" of his perceptual existence.

The social interactions (sometimes called "free play") which transpire between the mother and the baby, Stern declares, "are among the most crucial experiences in the infant's first phase of learning and participating in human events." By the time the baby has reached the age of six or seven months the "work" of this "phase" has been completed, and it is "considerable." The baby has developed "schemes" of the "human face, voice, and touch," and, within these "categories," he knows the specific face, voice, touch, and movement of his "primary caregiver." The infant, Stern writes, possesses the "foundation" of an "internal, composite picture" of the caretaker such that, a few months after the completion of the primary phase, we may speak of his having established "object permanence," that is, a lasting representation of the mother which he can carry around "on the inside" with or without "the mother's presence" (Stern 1977, pp. 5–6). But what precisely is the actual, "mechanistic" nature of this "interchange," this primary "social" experience from which we "arise" as perceivers?

It consists for the infant of "hundreds of . . . experiential units" which are strung together, and which occur over and over again during each interaction, every day. The infant has the opportunity to "internalize" each unit as a separate "representation." At the level of neuronic processes, of course, we do not know how such internalization occurs, any more than we know what a thought is. All that we can say is that these "experiential units" precipitate memory traces in the total mind-body of the infant; in other words, they get formed and they get stored. For a "unit" to become internalized, Stern maintains, regarding the matter once again from a clinical angle and employing a key-lock figure, four items are required. The "key" is the "sensori-motor-affective unit of experience" itself. The lock that opens the way to the internalization, or to the "encoding," consists of "three tumblers," one sensory, one motor, and one affective. When each of these is "turned into place" the key works and the unit is assimilated (Stern 1975, p. 105). A critical point in Stern's discussion, and one to which we will frequently return, is that *affective* components are essential to the establishment of "representations." At the foundational level of our perceptual nature cognition and emotion cannot be treated dichotomously, separated, compartmentalized. We begin and we continue as human beings to "see the world feelingly," as Gloucester puts it in *King Lear*. Although such feeling may be scarcely discernible, or even totally concealed by one's attitude toward the world, it is there.

The most dramatic shift in psychoanalytic theory to have occurred within the past half century is called to mind by these materials. "Sexual theory has moved away from the confines of a theory of energic discharge," writes Meissner (1976, p. 130); "the experiencing of sensual pleasure... has a directional component which involves intentions, purposes, meanings, and motives." And then, in a crucial statement, "the developmental process is not envisioned primarily in terms of the predetermined unfolding of genetically embedded biological potentials, but in terms of the interaction and intermeshing of innate maturational factors with experiential components derived from the interaction with objects." Our mental make-up, then, is significantly shaped by those with whom we entered into "object relationships" during the early phases of our development. Our earliest "objects" become dynamic parts of our personality structure and continue to influence us in all that we do long after the specific objects who were the aim of our internalizing tendency have ceased to exist "in reality." By the time we have reached adulthood there exists within us an "inner world," a kind of psychic universe which is "inhabited" by the "objects" that have entered us, or, more properly, that we have taken into ourselves, along the maturational way. *We live in two worlds,* from the beginning, and our *perceptual life* must be regarded as a function of the *interaction* of these worlds *which continually impinge upon one another.*

Good and Bad Objects

We are beginning to understand where we "come from." To do this more fully, however, we must grasp the two-sided, or "split," nature of our early, foundational experience. On the one hand, many of the "representational units" which are taken in by the baby contribute to his contentment. The mother gives him a positive, nurturing introduction to existence. She soothes him, reassures him, delights him; she develops his confidence, enthusiasm, "joy in life"; in a word, she triggers his internalizing participation in "good" materials. On the other hand, many of the "units" that are assimilated by the growing child are disruptive or, in a very special sense, *negative* in their qualitative importance. This becomes particularly true as the mirror phase gives way to the phase in which the child is able to recognize himself as a separate creature, separate that is from the caretaking parent with whom he is so entirely bound up and upon whom his existence so entirely depends. Needless to say, this phase is essential to our actualization as higher organisms, for it is "only with the development of . . . the capacity to create a mental representation of the absent object" that the child progresses from the immediate, "sensory-motor response" to the "delayed, conceptualized response that is characteristically human" (Beres 1960, p. 334). Just as the occurrence of birth involves trauma, trauma that some believe permanently marks the organism (Rank 1929), so does the early "object relation" with the mother. "It seems inherent in the human condition," writes Margaret Mahler, "that not even the most normally endowed child, with the most optimally available mother, is able to weather the separation . . . process without crisis, come out unscathed by the . . . struggle, and enter the oedipal phase without developmental difficulty" (Mahler, Pine, and Bergman 1975, p. 227). I will concentrate in what follows on the manner in which the "anxiety-units" of the early time find their way to the ground of our perception and thus precipitate the "conversion" described in the opening paragraphs of this chapter.

As the child goes about building up his good maternal representation, as he gradually enlarges and schematizes those aspects of the caretaker that will serve as the perceptual basis for his positive participation in the world, he confronts of necessity the imperfections of the symbiotic relationship in which he is involved. No matter how solicitous the mother is, the infant is fated to undergo tension, frustration, discomfort, and even a certain amount of pain. Such experiences mobilize anxiety. Indeed, "very young infants" manifest "grossly identical patterns" of anxious behavior when they discover themselves in "frightening situations," and when they are in contact with the caretaker during a period in which she is tense, angry, disquieted, or anxious herself (Rheingold 1964, p. 162). Repeated, inescapable exposure to inconsistent conduct prompts the developing baby to *split* the caretaker into what are customarily called in psychoanalytic circles a "good" and a "bad object" and to *internalize* these "objects" into a part or aspect of his perceiving self. The "complement" of "people" which each of us harbors within, carries about, and projects into our "reality," reaches back "in every instance" to the "first pair of our personifications: the good mother and the bad or evil mother." With the passage of time these early, primitive "personifications" get transmuted into the "good me," the "bad me," and the ambiguous, frightful "not me" (Rheingold 1964, p. 162).

26

We must remember here that the mother's inconsistency is a grave, disruptive event for the child, that it corresponds to his worst imaginings, his worst inchoate fears (Ross and Dunn 1980, p. 342). The infant's "postponement of gratification from its mother's supplies" constitutes a "trauma," writes Schiffer (1978, pp. 11–12), and "residues" of the infant's "reaction to this trauma" can be "found in the psychology of later years." Because he is simply not able to *integrate* the mother's "two sides," her "bad" and "good" facets, the infants attempts to "co-ordinate" them by splitting *and then dealing with the splits* (Melito 1983, p. 531). He declares, in effect, "*mother* is not bad. There just happens to be this bad mother who appears once in a while. She and mother are not really the same person, for *mother* is always good and will never hurt and disappoint. I am obliged to interact with both *mother,* and the other one" (the author's quotation). Only later, when the child matures, will he be able to accept goodness and badness in the same person. Thus "threats" to the "narcissistic cathexis of the self exist from the moment of birth" and "stem from the interaction of the child's libidinal and aggressive drives" with the "demands, frustrations, and gratifications" of the external world. Such "narcissistic hurts" may "evoke feelings of depression" and a "growing sense of perplexity" that is sometimes answered with "aggressive behavior" (Lax 1977, pp. 289, 293). The infant's mere inability to "influence, predict, or comprehend an event which the infant expected on the basis of previous experience to be able to control or understand" is registered as "trauma" (Broucek 1979, p. 315). Indeed, we now realize that the parent's very power over the life and death of the child is perceived as "threatening" and internalized to become a part of everyone's susceptibility to nightmare, everyone's residual paranoia (Bloch 1979).

The Jungian researches of Erich Neumann (1970, pp. 148–49) are helpful on this score. The symbolism of the "Terrible Mother," he writes, "draws its images predominantly from the inside." That is, the "negative elementary character of the Feminine" expresses itself in "fantastic, chimerical images" that do not originate in the environment. The "dark side" of the maternal presence takes the form of "monsters," whether in "Egypt or India, Mexico or Etruria, Bali or Rome." In the tales and myths of "all peoples, ages, and countries," as well as in our own nightmares, "witches, vampires, ghouls and spectres, assail us, all terrifyingly alike." It is the internalizing of this "bad object" that explains our emotional fear of death. At issue here is not death as the adult "conceives" it, but a "threat of a quality and magnitude beyond the adult's imagination." We get a glimpse of it in "panic states" and in "the momentary probe into infancy" that some individuals experience in therapy. Thus the struggle between the "forces of life and death" which is "inherent in the biologically precarious infantile condition" becomes involved in the infant's response to the mother that protects and satisfies and to the mother that frustrates and deprives (Rheingold 1964, p. 148). Where the fear of death is concerned, it is the "uncertain ties" to the living world "at all ages" that "shake us more than the awareness of biological mortality" (Steinzor 1979, p. 118).

What I am maintaining here is that we cannot understand the "complex symbol" that death comprises for the human creature (Becker 1973, p. 19) if we exclude from the discussion the primal anxiety that characterizes the early period. Because the mother's impact on the child is pre-verbal, because her presence is internalized before "higher" conceptualization begins, it is very, very difficult to subject our split foundations to "reason" (Dinnerstein 1977, p. 84). Our anxious obsession with death, as well as our dangerous indulgence in rigid, dichotomous views of the world, with the "good guys" over here and the "bad guys" over there, is rooted largely in a primitive defensive technique (splitting) that leaves perdurable traces on our "normal" perception.

Pains of Growth

As the child begins to separate from the parent in earnest, further splitting, further enhancement of the "bad object" occurs. The symbiosis of the very early period may have been imperfect, but it was there, and it reassured the baby in his "precarious biological condition." Now that is taken away. In grasping the affective meaning of this major developmental occurrence we must bear in mind that for the infant the repeated association of the perception of the mother and the relief of tension creates, of itself, an emotive investment, or a "drive investment," in the mother (Compton 1980, p. 760). Separation involves trauma because the maternal object is discerned as separate *only* as the infant experiences frustration and need (Coen 1981, p. 339). In this way, separation comes to "mean" disappointment.

To express the matter from another angle, because the infant's attachment is "there" before the other is experienced as other, the growing awareness of the caretaker as a "differentiated" being is itself "experienced as a loss" (Pine 1979, p. 226). True, there is an "objective" gain in "cognitive comprehension" as this process transpires. At the same time, however, there is the awareness "that certain treasured sensations are not part of the self but can come and go" (Pine 1979, p. 226). Thus the presence of the early, powerful attachment both "facilitates" and "complicates" our movement away from the mother, our growth as separate, differentiated creatures. It facilitates by providing us with a stable, loving internalization, a "good object" that endures and that leads us toward positive attachment to other people and to the "objects" of culture (the so-called transitional phenomena of Winnicott [1953]). It complicates because the experience of loss permanently "endows" the relationship to the mother with "painful undercurrents" and sets up a "developmental pathway" that can be "traversed" in "both directions," that is, toward progression and selfhood, or toward regression and pathogenic absorption in the "objects" of the past (Pine 1979, p. 226). Here is the "dichotomous human condition" (Neubauer 1980, p. 139), the forward maturational pulls and the backward neurotic attractions which all of us feel to one degree or another at various times in our lives. In subsequent passages, and particularly in Chapters 5, 6, and the Conclusion, I will strive to indicate the manner in which this material bears upon our current "scientific" attitude. Here I will make only the following brief observation.

What occurs as the infant undergoes separation has been described as a "life-long mourning process," a process that triggers an endless search for "replacement" which is tied integrally to our participation in the symbolic realm (Rizzuto 1979, p. 49). Every new step that we take toward autonomy holds the threat of loss. We *agonize* as we come to differentiate ourselves from the other, to learn in our body-minds what separation means. We pay for our new cognitive powers in "blood, sweat, and tears" (Katan 1979, p. 170). In this way, our very ability to conceive of "objects" as *separate in space,* an ability which underlies the "scientific" view of the world (Jones 1982, p. 17), is awakened early in life in inextricable association to the emotive dilemma of separation from the caregiver. Our persistent tendency toward dualistic conceptualization, our curious ability to exist *in* a world that is also at the same time, somehow, *out there,* is itself an expression of the manner in which we go *inward* with internalization as separation transpires and *outward* through "cognitive growth."

We must recall, in all of this, the overwhelming extent to which the limbic system, or that portion of the brain which catalyzes our *emotive*

29

interaction with objects, is involved in mental functioning during the early time (Taylor 1981, p. 110). What is internalized as differentiation takes place, as the ability to represent the absent object (and by extrapolation all future objects) increases, is internalized movingly, affectively, with love and hate and fear. The "objective" thought, or approach to creation, that comes later through cortical development sits as it were on top of this primal condition and is always influenced by it, either directly through passionate, "irrational" behavior that seeks union with or destruction of the "object," or more invidiously through the disguised madness, mixed with "reason," that characterizes so much of our "normal" activity at both the individual and social levels. Every evolving conception of the "outer" universe comes into contact with and emanates from the bodily world, the world that is permanently loaded with the frustration and desire, longing and disappointment, that entered it during the "separation-individuation" phase. The development of our temporal consciousness gives additional, striking expression to these points.

Time

The "awareness of change" is the most rudimentary or primitive condition "on which our perception of time flow depends" (James 1890, p. 620), and the awareness of change, again from the most rudimentary perspective, entails a relationship between the registrator of stimuli and the environment in which he exists. The "present," which separates "past" from "future," indicates the instant in which the "undetermined" happens and thereby becomes "fixed in time" as the "determined." If our experience transpires in the "present," every time we perform a thinking act we create a point of reference in time. Freud maintained along these lines that our notion of time begins with our primitive body perception, or auto-perception, of the unconscious energy that enables our "perceptual apparatus" to register stimuli. This energy, when placed and withdrawn rhythmically from the unconscious on to the "perceptual apparatus," creates a "link" between our own biological time rhythms and those of "nature" generally (Dupont 1974, p. 483).

What is crucial to remember in this regard is the inextricable "link" between the needy infant's posture of anticipation, the environmental change that posture induces, the stimulation that accompanies such change, and the development of temporal awareness. The agreement on this among depth psychologists is remarkable. Hartocollis (1974, p. 248) has gathered these views together, and I draw now upon his work. According to Hartmann, the "danger signal" and the "mental function of anticipation" are the "precursors of the time sense." Arieti "explicitly attributes the evolution of anxiety and of symbolic processes to expectancy and anticipation." Rapoport points out that the "notion of anticipation is intimately related to time experience and, in particular, to time perspective." Fraser concludes that "anxiety and the time sense are mutually generated modalities of the mind." Spitz indicates that "affect is the element responsible for the acquisition of the notion of time" and cites "anticipation" as the principal "affect" involved. Schiffer (1978, p. 12) summarizes the matter when he writes that "time is subjectively experienced in terms of man's separation from the nourishing object, a traumatic event that dictates his defensive projections." I am not suggesting that the infant possesses an organized time sense. I am suggesting, rather, that immediately after his emergence "innate factors" become "subsumed" in the "mother-child dialogue" (Colarusso 1979, p. 244) and hence colored by the powerful emotions which dominate that dialogue. "What was biological becomes psychological" (Colarusso 1979, p. 244), experienced in the child's developing "ego" as part of the "link" to the gradually emerging "object." Thus the infant attempts to protect himself from traumatic experiences of frustration by anticipating the fulfilment of his needs, and such anticipation is integrally tied to his primitive, bodily awareness of change. The stimuli that derive from the very processes which keep us alive become the foundation of our temporal awareness.

Here is a typical sequence. Once again I draw upon the work of Hartocollis (1974, p. 250). As "tension rises" and the caretaker is not "there," the good image of the object emerges in fantasy and unites with the self-image to protect the child. We have here a kind of "need-fulfilling hallucinatory experience." If the caretaker's arrival is delayed further, however, this experience rapidly "fades." The infant's displeasure grows, and the "uncertain" good object begins to get transformed into the "bad" one. It is precisely in the child's attempt to maintain or "hold onto" the good object and to eject the bad one that his ability to anticipate the future is strengthened. While tension is "tolerable" the "situation" is "anxious." But as tension mounts the bad object begins to dominate the good. Anxiety "gives way to fear," and then to "rage" in which anticipation and future are obliterated. Further delay "floods" the baby with "excitation" and prompts him to regress to the level of "undifferentiated bad object" and self-image. Such an experience would be both "catastrophic" and "timeless." Eventually, what Hartocollis calls "object constancy" develops in the maturing infant. The early hallucinatory process is replaced by the ability to anticipate the fulfilment of need. And as the fused "good" and "bad" maternal figures are internalized or set up within as the scaffolding for "normal" character development, a relatively trustful tendency to believe in good outcomes is projected into the environment, which begins to be experienced as continuous, as possessing the attribute of duration. At the same time, the rather tense, anxious proclivity to believe in the good outcome is attached to the child's growing representation of himself, one that he projects beyond the confines of his immediate environment. Time becomes perspective; the "future" is born.

Clearly then, if our perception is tied "categorically" (Kant) to our sense of duration, and if our sense of duration is tied psychologically to motivational processes involving the caregiver, then time and the caregiver, time and the internalized object, are not merely connected at the deepest level of our being but connected in a *conflictual* way. For the infant to experience time as such it is necessary that he go through a process in which he experiences the mother as both need-fulfilling and frustrating. These are the foundational facts which underlie our symbolic notions of infinity—infinite bliss, infinite woe, and all the variations and nuances we encounter in the realms of ordinary and non-ordinary reality, including mathematics. The atomistic time of the physicist is fashioned "above" this emotive material in what may be an effort to suppress its existence. The unconscious mental activity that is always occurring "beneath" our conscious and preconscious operations has at its core a powerful intentionality—desires, feelings, aims—which cannot be dissociated from the temporal awareness that dawns with the first, ambivalent relationship. The clock-like regularities of the scientific, technological order are not simply "at odds with our natural rhythms," as the modern cliché has it; they continuously reactivate our deepest, most pervasive sources of anger and frustration. In short, they are *at war* with the human body.

Space

I mentioned toward the close of "Pains of Growth" (pp. 28–30) that our ability to conceive of objects as separate in space is tied inextricably to the separation-individuation phase of our infantile experience. I want now to say more about space in an effort to indicate its tight, *epistemic* connection to the earliest internalizing processes that are the basis of our normative perception. Like time, space is "categorically" associated with the "objects" of the first relationship.

"Psychic space," writes Grotstein (1978, pp. 55–56), comprises a kind of "container" which can be "originally associated with the maternal caretaking functions" and with the absorption of "infantile projections." He goes on, "the capacity to experience space" is a "primary apparatus" of the "ego" which "seems to have emerged from the inchoate sensations upon the foetal skin at birth, thereby 'awakening' the skin with its sense receptors into its function as a surface, as a boundary between self and non-self, and as a container of self." Without the development of such a "psychic space" there can be, quite simply, "no perception." In a more recent discussion, Dinora Pines (1980, p. 315) focuses the role of the skin still further. The baby's "non-verbalized affects" often discover their expression "through the skin" which may "itch . . . weep . . . [or] rage." Such exigencies will be "dealt with by the mother" according to her ability to "accept and soothe" the "blemished" infant who will, in turn, "internalize" the experience. The mother demonstrates how the "containing object," herself, is "experienced concretely as a skin." It is precisely this "function" that precipitates the rudimentary idea of external and internal "space" (see Hagglund 1980).

With regard more specifically to the relationship between space and the separation phase discussed earlier, Roth and Blatt (1974, p. 871) remind us that "spatial representations" are an "integral part of the individual's attempt to understand and organize reality and to achieve . . . differentiation." The growth of "object relations," as well as "advances" in "object constancy," occurs "with progress in the separation of the self from objects and with increased . . . articulation of the self and objects." Such "advances" can be "evaluated" by the "cognitive development of spatial representations." Thus the "self," as we usually conceive of it, needs some *place* to live and to perceive. When we speak of the "breathing room" which individuals require to maintain their existence in the world we recapitulate unconsciously the whole struggle of the human being to escape the womb which crushes and expels him, to cope with the appearance of the "bad" maternal object whose imperfect care makes him choke with rage, and to survive the loss of the "good" maternal figure who breathes his very life into his mouth. The defensive strategies of the early time are formed within levels of spatial representation. Indeed, spatial representation is the cognitive matrix out of which defensive strategies arise. When we withdraw, we withdraw to some place, some psychic place, which allows us to withdraw there. We split the maternal figure off to another place which permits us to split it off. We reduce the world to a space in which we dwell securely, our substitute womb of enumerated types. The very notion of separateness implies exclusion, boundaries which establish the "end" of one individual and the "beginning" of another. When Bachelard (1969, p. 5) reminds us that "all really inhabited space bears the essence of the notion of home," he only calls to mind the inextricable connection between spatial representation and the problems of separation and mothering, for all notions of home bear the essence of the notion of mother. The German biologist Jakob von Uexkull once observed that we go about as human perceivers with a kind of umbrella of sky spread out over our heads, a phenomenological feature of our normative "reality" which is not shared by, let us say, a worm. We might suggest from a psychodynamic angle that the ribs of this umbrella are forged in the primary relation to the caregiver.

The problem of *causality* must be seen in a similar light, for the very conception of "cause and effect" cannot be grasped apart from its spatial and temporal parameters. As the child comes to develop a sense of duration, as he grows toward the conviction that relief with the "good" mother will soon come, he begins to "intend" the future, to actively await gratification. Now according to Piaget (1968, pp. 13–15) and others, the idea of "cause" develops directly out of the child's expectation of the environment. Indeed, the notions of causality and space (encompassing succession, simultaneity, and velocity) are, in Piaget's view, necessary psycho-physical determinants of the time sense which, as we have seen, is firmly connected with the problem of maternal care. While the idea of "cause" may be, in the Kantian meaning, a necessary dimension of human consciousness, just as space and time are, the manner in which we come to that idea, as well as the particular version of it that we have, cannot be accurately understood apart from its affective roots, its psychodynamic significance.

Words

The processes I have been describing are primarily pre-verbal, pre-symbolic ones. I want now to discuss the nature of human perception as it develops into the symbolic phase, in which internalization meets and combines with the individual's linguistic capacity.

By the time this developmental phase has concluded, the individual will have set up within himself a world of mental pictures and ideas which discovers its full expression in employment of the sounds we call "language." However, as a bridge between the "splitting" of the early period and the later development of symbolic mentation I would concentrate briefly upon another aspect of the first relationship (hinted at earlier in "The Origins of Self," pp. 20–25) that sheds important light upon the manner in which the human animal comes to associate the internalized object with the whole process of bodily and emotive stimulation.

The function of mothering is to a significant degree protective. Not only does the caretaker avoid the dangers of the outside world, she also attempts to protect the infant from sheer over-stimulation. Indeed, the management of stimulation is by and large what mothering is. I do not mean that mother simply avoids loud sounds and bright lights, for the matter goes deeper than this and bears upon the entire question of the child's growth and development. "An essential feature of mothering," writes Gruen (1974, p. 560), entails the mother's ability to "screen" the "stimuli" that "impinge" upon her child in a way that makes it possible for him to develop "connections" between "relevant stimuli" and his own "inner readiness" to respond to them. "Good mothering" furthers "appropriate learning" precisely through the "screening" of the "stimulus field." When Piaget reminds us that stimuli are meaningful only as they fit the schema of inner processes he calls to mind another vital fact, namely that interference with the formation of connections impedes development and forces the child to continue his dependence on the mother. In this way, if the caregiver fails to protect the child from over-stimulation, he becomes "handicapped in learning to differentiate and to link outer and inner schemas." Moreover, exposure to an "undifferentiated stimulus" can make stimulation itself seem "threatening."

Although the mother who neglects her baby does not, at least, contribute to over-stimulation, her neglect may, in itself, create "a situation in which the environment becomes disturbing" (Gruen 1974, p. 561). The point is, "whichever way" the development takes place, "the child's experience of himself and the world is mediated through the tactual, visual, and kinaesthetic contact with the mother. His initial intake of the world comes through her and with her" (Gruen 1974, p. 561). This "passive-receptiveness" in which the caretaker teaches the child to "touch" the world with his "probing senses" has been called by Erik Erikson (1956, p. 208) the "oldest" and "most neglected mode of our experiencing." What is the upshot? Clearly, that the object of the inner world will be integrally conjoined with the human creature's reception of stimuli and hence with his perception of the environment. "The child's perception is the mother's perception," declares Gruen (1974, p. 562) in a statement the epistemological implications of which cannot easily be missed.

As indicated at the outset of this chapter, by the time the child is experiencing his ability to retain the image of the object in his mind and to attach it to a verbal equivalent, by the time his brain has developed to that point, the more "primitive" process of internalization has already been at work for many months. At the level of emotive, pre-verbal awareness, the child has actualized his need to take the mother in, and even to split or divide her in an effort to cope with the anxiety that arises from her "bad" or discomfiting behavior. As indicated subsequently, a considerable amount of tension and a posture of anticipation result from the child harboring the "bad object" within himself. However, it is not an "image" or a "picture" of the mothering figure which enters the child during the early period; relationships, not pictures, are internalized. And even later, when the ability to retain pictures is there, the internalization of relationships predominates. Indeed, the mental image of the caretaker is always a projective version of the primary relational attitude. Thus, by the age of two-and-a-half, the child has experienced and has learned to cope with a series of traumatic separations. He has separated from his mother at birth; he has been weaned; and he has been confronted on a daily basis with the mother's coming and going and with the anxiety that this can engender. From one perspective the whole task of infancy and childhood is getting separate, getting "independent" or "autonomous," and as we all know, many human beings struggle and stumble toward that condition throughout their lives.

During the phase of separation-individuation, described in "Pains of Growth" (pp. 28–30), the struggles of the early time become especially intense. More and more the child must learn to survive without the mother. Increasingly it dawns upon him that mother must eventually be relinquished. The result may be described as follows: the tendency to cope with separation through the processes of internalization and splitting is reinforced, or buttressed, by the ability to create an entire symbolical universe and to have it "inside," in a "space" that Winnicott (1966, p. 371) calls "transitional"—the word "transition" indicating, of course, the movement *away* from the caregiver. He writes: "In favorable circumstances [and by that he means in more or less "normal" circumstances where "mothering" is "good enough" to prompt "ordinary" development] the potential space becomes filled with the products of the baby's own creative imagination." If he is "given the chance," the baby will begin "to live creatively," and "to use actual objects to be creative into." If he is not given the chance "then there is no area in which the baby may have play, or may have cultural experience; then there is no link with the cultural inheritance, and there will be no contribution to the cultural pool." On the one hand, then, our ability to make symbols, to imagine, to create, to *use* our powerful brains, is an innate ability that is nourished into production by "good enough" maternal care. On the other hand, however, that ability is prodded into action by the very real problem of maternal separation. In the development of symbolic mentation, and in the perceptual behaviors which arise therefrom, there is an element of that "conversion," that rooted discontentment of body and of mind, to which I made earlier reference.

The Unconscious in Ordinary Mentation

As the pioneering investigations of Vygotsky ([1934] 1979) began to make clear half a century ago, the development of language is not primarily a cognitive process (Piaget) but an interactive, social process loaded with affective, bodily components from the pre-verbal stage. Because "thought" and "speech" do *not* develop in a *meshed* but in a *parallel, reciprocal* fashion (this is perhaps Vygotsky's major insight), we must ultimately think of language as a "dynamic system of meaning" in which "the affective and the intellectual *unite*" ([1934] 1979, p. 8; emphasis added). Piaget is simply wrong to maintain that the "egocentric" speech of three or four years "disappears" as the child reaches seven or eight. Instead of "atrophying," writes Vygotsky ([1934] 1979, p. 18), such "egocentric" speech "goes underground"; that is to say, it "turns into inner speech" and forms the foundation of that "inward babble" which, joined to "higher" cognitive components, comes eventually to comprise a sizeable measure of our ordinary mentation. In this way, the development of thinking is not from the individual to the social but from the social to the individual. "The child starts conversing with himself as he has been doing with others" ([1934] 1979, pp. 19–20).

As for the *spoken word,* it is initially "a substitute for the gesture," for the bodily attitude and bodily expression which precede the truly verbalized sound ([1934] 1979, p. 30). When the child says "mama" it is not merely the word that means, say, put me in the chair but "the child's whole behavior at that moment, his reaching out for the chair, trying to hold onto it, etc." ([1934] 1979, p. 30). In contrast to "egocentric" speech, which goes inward, "verbalized" speech goes outward; the child uses it as a method of "pointing" ([1934] 1979, p. 31). It is the fusion of this "inward speech" and developing "outward speech" that finally comprises human "thought" in its basic, foundational significance ([1934] 1979, p. 112). We appreciate from this perspective the growing psychoanalytic realization, based explicitly upon Vygotsky's work, that "thinking" is an "unconscious process in the first instance" (Basch 1981, p. 163). Even our "conscious speech," the analytic community has come to recognize, is "pervaded" by "unconscious mechanisms" to the degree that it is tied to our "thinking" (Roustang 1976, p. 63). This means that our "thinking," our "stream of consciousness" itself in the most general, all-inclusive sense, is the source of those "slips of the tongue" upon which Freud stumbled eight decades ago. With regard more specifically to the role of separation in all of this, it is underscored sharply in a seminal paper by David Bleich.

After declaring that cognitive and affective development cannot be disassociated, Bleich (1970, p. 8) reminds us that symbol formation arises from the infant's sharing experience with the mother. "The common act of referential pointing starts with the invitation by the mother, but soon eventuates in the child inviting the mother to contemplate some object together." This marks the inception of what Bleich calls "intellectual stereoscopy, the start of the schemata of objectification as being dependent upon social interaction." The child "develops a schema of naming things *to* someone," and the "love and attention" he receives "becomes the motive for his naming further things." It is precisely the "attention and love" *of* the caretaker *to* this procedure of naming that "deposits the schemata of mutuality to be later incorporated in the important step of conceptualizing the whole idea of twoness and separateness" (Bleich 1970, p. 9). Thus the presence and absence of the mother, and of important physical objects or "things" in the child's world, play motivational roles in the development of representational thought. Indeed—and we reach here the heart of the matter—"the cognitive component of the ability to recognize mother," that is, to conceptualize her, is "goaded into existence . . . at the onset of representational thought and language . . . by the need to cope with . . . affective loss." The "feeling of affective loss" becomes "the motive for acquiring the capacity to represent absent objects" or to represent objects "regardless of their presence or absence" (Bleich 1970, p. 9). When the baby names the "absent object" he "predicates" it on the basis of its former "presence"; thus, "mommy gone." The "same act" can "predicate" a "subsequent presence" on a "current absence." Bleich writes: "The schema 'gone' and the schema 'mommy' are independently linked and placed in relation to one another. Chomsky's major insight . . . is his discovery that all languages . . . are built on transformations of a simple . . . act of predication" (Bleich 1970, p. 9). Such "predication," then, is inextricably associated with the not so "simple act" of separation from the maternal figure, the major, and universal, "transformation" of infantile experience.

There is another vital aspect to Bleich's discussion, for "when the child links up 'mommy' and 'gone' he creates a dependent relationship between two ideas which substitutes for each idea's dependency on real experience" (Bleich 1970, p. 10). Piaget calls this action "reciprocal assimilation" and employs it to describe the child's capacity to "invent new means to cope with a new problem in the sixth sensorimotor stage" (Bleich 1970, p. 10). This new "representational capability" gives the child "power" to recall the mother "at will." In this way, representation comprises a "way back" to the "missing libidinal object" (Bleich 1970, p. 10). Gruen (1974, p. 563) expresses the problem somewhat differently when he writes that "The child's sense of cohesion, of meaning, of order . . . is threatened by the [mother's] disappearance or emotional withdrawal." The first "discontinuity" in the development of the self "is the transition from a self that is the other's—from a state wherein the order of things is attained through the other's order—through a frightening state of chaos and aloneness to an order of one's own." It is, of course, the symbolical world, the world of one's own "representations," the world developed in Winnicott's "transitional space," that comes to comprise one's own "order."

The implications of these findings are crucial, and strikingly clear. Because the verbal representation of the thing is the culmination of the symbolic process, the word is the magical tie that reunites us with the all-important figure(s) of infancy and childhood. It is not merely that

39

"maternal stimulation during the critical period of language development is necessary for the fulfillment of the child's neurophysiological
potential" (Weil 1978, p. 480); our symbolic seeing is actually charged
with the emotive energy that went into our life-and-death struggle to
maintain our connection with the caregiver at the same time we were
giving her up. Through the early imperfections of mothering, we learn
to grip the world with our bodies, with our tense anticipation, as we
have seen. Through the crises of separation which continue to transpire
after the early time, we learn to grip the world with our minds, symbols, and words. The "mirror phase" of infancy eventually gives way to
the representational "mirror" of a mind that has separation on its mind.
Nor is it verbalization alone that magically summons the object. Our
"thinking" itself, the "stream" of our inner babble, performs the same
task. The "egocentric" speech that goes inward, notes Andresen (1980,
p. 515), recreates the "parental presence." Although it may sound odd
at first glance to put it this way, the very running on of our thoughts in
ordinary consciousness is a "link" to the figures of the past.

The problem is, of course, that these "figures" recall not only the
"good" side of our early existence but the "bad" side as well, the side
that is replete with frustration, rage, envy, anxiety, and disappointment, that speaks for the ambivalence of the primary years. Moreover,
no matter how "bad" the internalized object is, the wish for reunion
persists. Indeed, the internalization of particularly "bad" materials customarily and paradoxically increases the intensity of that wish. Here is
the source not merely of the "conversion elements" in language; here
also is the source of the deep-seated malaise that resides in our "normal"
awareness generally, in what we take to be our normative perception.

There is both accuracy and profundity, then, in Roheim's contention
that culture itself, at the deepest psychological level, is a way back to
the object, a symbolic connection with the early time, a creative manifestation through which separation is overcome and security maintained, however precariously. "We suggest," writes Roheim (1962, p.
203), "that thinking, which at its apex is very much an ego activity, is
deeply rooted in the libido, and that between the two we must place the
mental image as magic. It means both 'away from the object' and (by
means of the image) 'back to the object'." And again: "It would seem
that the function of the word as a cultural object is to link the internal to
the external world—in other words, to summon the mother when the
child is hungry." And finally, "civilization originates in delayed infancy

and its function is security. It is a huge network of more or less successful attempts to protect mankind against the danger of object-loss, the colossal efforts made by a baby who is afraid of being left alone in the dark" (Roheim 1971, p. 131). Thus, while it is important to bear in mind that language is not a system for the "transmission of truth" but for the "creation of belief" (Reynolds 1981, p. 233), it is equally important to remember that such "belief" has its rooted, unconscious aspect at the centre of which resides the longing for the absent object. As for the languages of science and philosophy, with their commitment to the notions of space, time, causality, and number, they are no exception. When western Europe, during the eighteenth century, went "collectively out of its mind" (Berman 1981, p. 121) through its "objective," Newtonian belief in a totally desensualized cosmos consisting entirely of matter and motion, it may well have been denying on a massive scale, unique in history, its origins in the mother's body. The languages of science and philosophy provide people with an opportunity to obliterate their connection to the living, and dying, flesh.

Thinking specifically about the "mechanisms of defence" uncovered by psychoanalysis, I would suggest that the life of ordinary consciousness is not merely a "dream" but a projective dream which at all times—most noticeably at the crucial, dynamic times (when some people decide to drop bombs on other people, for example)—projects the object of the inner world upon the objects of the external environment. As hinted earlier, we do not perceive "subjectively"—the customary claim—but objectively, objectively in an unconscious manner that begins in infancy, persists into "adulthood," and determines the whole nature of our struggle on the planet. Not only do we recognize currently that projection is a feature of infantile existence (Katan 1979, p. 168), we recognize as well the full signification of Freud's insight that projection is a feature of "everyday" awareness. While it is often "turned to abuse... for purposes of defence," it is also a "psychical mechanism... commonly employed in normal life" (Freud [1895] 1950, p. 209). Indeed, writes Darius Ornston (1978, pp. 129–30), Freud may be said to have developed generally "a projective point of view," one in which "all mental presentations" are not only "perceptual," but "active " as well: "attention" meets the sense-impression "half-way." From early infancy on, Freud proposed, "whenever we mentally attend or tentatively classify, whenever we orient or organize, whenever we anticipate or understand, we project" (Ornston 1978, p. 154). Because he failed to recog-

41

nize the degree to which the object of our early period, the internalized object of infancy and childhood, became connected inextricably with our perceptual behavior, Freud failed to recognize that our "normal" projections, our "everyday," active perceptions of the world, were fraught with the defensive, pathological requirements engendered by the imperfections of the mother-infant symbiosis, and by the subsequent threat of separation and loss.

Eventually, as promised, I will apply these conclusions rigorously to major trends in philosophic and scientific thought. Too, I will explore the question of whether or not we can do anything to ameliorate our "projective" mode of awareness, our "normal" pathogenic perception. Now, however, I must examine the depiction of human behavior at the heart of our current "ego psychology," the theoretical offspring of the "Freudian" revisionists (most notably Dr. Heinz Hartmann) and a going psychoanalytic concern in our day (particularly in North America). To do this will not only clarify further the analytic import of the discussion thus far, it also will adumbrate the direction in which depth psychology must now go if it is to fulfil, or even begin to fulfil, its promise as an aid to healthy human development. For I would contend that this functional, adaptational "ego psychology," in spite of certain clinical contributions that it has made of late to our understanding of infancy and childhood,[1] burdens us with both an outmoded, inadequate model of personality and an emphatically dangerous method of dealing with people that can only impede whatever evolutional advancement the species is capable of achieving. As for the epistemological implications of ego psychology, they will also emerge sharply from the following material.

Ego Psychology: A Brief Critique

Ego psychology takes its inspiration from the tendency in Freud's later writings to concentrate less upon the problems of instinct and repression and more upon the problems of ego development and anxiety. The psychological growth of the individual in general, and his struggle to achieve a relatively successful adaptation to his environment in particular, come to be the therapist's principal concerns. "The history of the development of psychoanalytic psychology," writes Hartmann ([1939] 1958, p. 6),[2] "explains why we understand as yet relatively little about those processes and working methods of the mental apparatus which lead to *adapted achievements.* We cannot simply contrast the ego as the non-biological part of the personality with the id as its biological part; the very problem of adaptation warns agains such a division" (p. 8). Hartmann then goes on, in one of his key utterances, to "propose that we adopt the . . . term *conflict-free ego sphere* for that ensemble of functions which at any given time exert their effects outside the region of mental conflicts" (p. 9). But with the context of our discussion in mind, especially that part of the discussion which demonstrates the degree to which the ego, from its inception, harbors the ambivalent object, indeed, internalizes the object into its very perceptual activities, we recognize that there is no "conflict-free sphere," that there is no behavior in ordinary consciousness which fails to reflect the stress of the early period. Herbert Marcuse, in *Eros and Civilization,* has established unforgettably, and in my view irrefutably, the conformist, reactionary tendencies of ego psychology with regard to the political sphere. The critique of this "school" must now, however, move to the perceptual sphere, a sphere that is more tightly bound up with politics than one might at first imagine.

To suggest as a key theoretical postulate that specific human "perceptions" transpire "outside of conflict" (p. 8) is to doom the analytic enterprise from the outset, *for our perception itself is the chief carrier of our conflict.* It must be directly addressed for any *good* adaptation to occur. The kind of "adaptation" which Hartmann and his followers offers us means, quite simply, more ordinary consciousness, more projection of the internalized object into the objects of the environment, more irrationality parading as rationality—in a word, more tension, more misery, more woe. No wonder Dr. Gedo (1979, p. 34) informs us that psychoanalysis (read ego psychology) considers the actual liberation of the individual from his psychological problems to be an unattainable "ideal." There is not a word in his book, or in any other book written by an ego psychologist, which regards the "perceptual apparatus," the ego's very domain, as a constructed, interactional system in a hard, physical way, a way that is sensitive to the possibility of a modal shift in the apparatus's functioning. Not only does Hartmann continually talk about "reality" as if it were there, as if it were given, not made (pp. 16, 18, 66, 91), not only does he reveal thereby what can only be termed an epistemological naïveté, he also presents us with a therapeutic program that is ultimately dualistic in nature—one that attempts to leave the "conflict-free" half of us over here as the basis of our "adaptation" to (or

43

absorption of) the conflictual half over there, that splits us apart for the purpose of putting us back together again. But we are one perceiving organism, and the "part" which is supposed to be "free of conflict" also holds the internalized object, also attests to the disturbances of the early period which have been internalized into our perceiving bodies.

However, ego psychology is not merely a dead end with regard to human evolution, to the kind of behavioral change that might foster an ability to perceive the environment in a manner that is less stressful and more joyous than our present one. As suggested, ego psychology actually harbors an evolutionary danger in that it encourages persistence of transitional aims which are expressed "automatically" through the perceptual system, in that it lulls us to sleep in a projective "reality" which is "fated" to reflect the unconscious inclinations of the culture. Can it be without significance in our competitive, patriarchal world that Hartmann talks of "mastering" the "environment" (p. 70) rather than achieving an harmonious relationship with it, that he refers to new "divisions of labor" in psychoanalysis (p. 55) which will permit the ego to operate more "effectively" in the world, that he elevates "science" as the "highest" form of "thinking" (p. 59)—one that is supposed to "free" us from our "perceptual situation" (pp. 59, 64), and that he characterizes religion as a "tradition-saturated institution" (p. 79) capable of "integrating" people into the communal order? By making "irrational forces" *equal* "instinctual drives" (p. 87) Hartmann not only discourages discovery of the irrational in the way we perceive the world, he discourages discovery of the way culture establishes itself at the level of the so-called ego processes themselves. By asserting that our perceptions "rest on constitutional givens" (p. 101) Hartmann not only guides us away from grasping the role of the internalized object in the development of ordinary consciousness, he also guides us away from recognizing the role of internalization, with all its irrational, defensive features, in the perpetuation of cultural traditions which are, ultimately, perceived by individuals and groups.

When Hartmann maintains that "adaptation" in "man" is "guaranteed" by his "primary equipment" and "maturation" (p. 25), or that the newborn infant and his environment are "adapted" to each other "from the first moment" (p. 51), we gasp, and wonder whether or not we are supposed to take him seriously. Shall I simply cite here recent statistics on infant and child abuse, an enormous, tragic problem for both children and "adults" in our happy social order? (Korbin, 1981). As Philip

Slater (1974, pp. 40–41) points out, the human organism experiences more danger from its "adaptive reactions" than from its instinctual endowments or the "external agencies" it encounters. Yet Hartmann's *Ego Psychology* continues to serve as a bible for the community of psychoanalytic professionals that flourishes today. Gertrude and Robin Blanck, with their *Ego Psychology II* (1979), emerge as prime examples. Not only do these authors accept Hartmann's theoretics absolutely, they are still writing about "reality" (1979, p. 217) as if it were somehow given, not made. They are still working to get the patient to see the validity of *the therapist's* "philosophy" (1979, p. 124). They are still unable to recognize the ego's irrationality at the level of perception itself (1979, pp. 216–17). They still consider "mental health" to be an optimal adjustment in ordinary awareness (1979, p. 245). Between the appearance of Hartmann's treatise and the most recent publications, nothing has really changed. The next chapter of this book, I hope, will offer new directions for theory and practice.

3
PERCEPTIVE MIND-REST

TRANSFORMATIONS OF ORDINARY CONSCIOUSNESS

There is a "particular need," Norman O. Brown (1957, p. 320) once remarked, for psychoanalysis "to become conscious of the mystical stream that runs in its blood." My purpose in this chapter is to demonstrate the accuracy of this notion, not merely with regard to the "consciousness" of psychoanalysis but also with regard to the philosophical problem of "objectivity." By concentrating upon the realms of altered awareness in a fresh way, a way that is sensitive to the conflicted nature of our "normal" mentation, I believe it may be possible to suggest procedures for diminishing considerably the perceptual distortions of the infantile years. Such diminishment, in turn, may lead to a new epistemic mode of *knowing* the world around us, and to a joy in existence, a "liberation" in simply being sentient, that is at odds with the troubled sleep which comprises so much of our "waking" life.

No question but this kind of thinking places me outside the orthodox stream of psychoanalytic opinion, which has little good to say about anything associated with mystical practice. To partake of such activity means, quite simply, to withdraw, to deny, to isolate unconscious materials—in a word, to *regress* to a kind of behavior that is generally characterized as "schizoid." The conventional analytic attitude derives mainly from Freud's *Civilization and Its Discontents* ([1930] 1975, pp. 1–2), where the transcendent moment is "traced back" to the "oceanic feeling" one has in the "early phase" of ego development, the phase in which union with the mother predominates. The longing for this "earlier stage" is, at one time or another, experienced by most human beings. The "mystic" is inclined to indulge it. As for the epistemic notion that "immediate feeling" can give one a reliable knowledge of his "connection with the world," it "fits in" very "badly," says Freud, with the "fabric" of scientific psychology.

Not only has Freud's attitude persisted to the present day, it has hardened. Mystics are "immature, retrograde, escapist" (Fisher 1976, p. 37) and may be lumped together with "Jesus freaks," drug addicts, solipsists, and weaklings in general (Wangh and Galef 1983, p. 322). As for the "knowledge" mysticism offers us, it is both unreliable and dangerous (Fisher 1976, p. 37). At the very best, an active interest in this "path" speaks for a relatively harmless attempt to "adapt" to the "real world" on the part of poor souls who have not achieved "integration" and "harmony" in their lives (GAP 1976, p. 189). This last estimation exudes the influence of "ego psychology," that is to say, the influence of those psychoanalytic theorizers who have not faced up to the splitting inherent in ordinary, "adapted" consciousness, to the ego's delusional side, to the distorted perception and "neurotic" discontent that even Freud, their master, declared repeatedly to be the lot of just about everyone. When it comes to the issue of altered states, psychoanalysis has a curious penchant for using one aspect of Freud and ignoring another.

However, my aim here is not to confute the orthodox analytic position on these matters. It is, rather, to suggest that "mystical" practice, with its accent on introspection and relaxation, is by no means incompatible with the therapeutic enterprise as a whole. Indeed, once we leave behind our small but influential band of traditionalists (the devotees of Heinz Hartmann and, more recently, Charles Brenner, based mainly in New York) we discover that practices such as meditation and biofeedback have become an important adjunctive facet of psychological programs designed to enhance both the insight and the inner contentment of the individual (Carrington 1982; Speeth 1982). Which brings me to a central contention: no matter how such techniques have been used in the past, no matter by how many regressives, psychotics, solipsists, shamans, and Aztec priests, we are now in a position to utilize their positive, self-transformative potential. *We can get from them what we wish.* Setting aside the spiritual implications for a moment, we can regard the mind-altering methodologies which have been passed down to us, and to which we are currently adding our investigatory, empirical knowledge, as practical processes (dare I say technologies?)

for moderating the psychobiological stress accumulated during the early period of our development.

Needless to say, as the pervasive effects of infantile "conversion" subside, the quality of our lives, of our interactions with other people and with the "objects" of the environment, improves. Simply to sit back and contend that attempts to modify everyday, egotic consciousness and to achieve thereby new phenomenological "realities" are *perforce* "escapist" or "retrograde" or "schizoid" is not only to assume implicitly that "reality" is somehow *fixed*—given as opposed to made—it is to shun possibilities for growth and change, to languish in the analytic past, to serve those familiar forces of reaction which are invariably hostile to the disruption of perceptual habits. It is time for psychoanalytic writers to stop referring to "objective reality" in a way that recalls the world of nineteenth-century physics (Treurniet 1980, p. 325). Equally, it is time for psychoanalysis as a collective discipline to stop assuming that all "religious" activity is regressive. Procedures embedded in the transformational religions of higher awareness may well comprise the human species' deep, biological, intuitive effort to offset the deleterious consequences of internalization, the projective, transitional mode of individual and social organization which characterizes the present stage of our evolutional history.

Breaks

"Breaks" with ordinary consciousness may be achieved by a wide variety of methods including concentration, self-hypnosis, meditation, physical exercise, teaching stories, fasting, chanting, dancing, drugs, and countless others. On occasion such "breaks" occur quite spontaneously, without the obvious prodding of specific activities or external agencies. My aim in exploring these "mystical" events in the next few paragraphs is to intimate the phenomenological and psychoanalytic nature of that "perceptive mind-rest" which is my ultimate concern in this chapter as a whole.

Several points must be established at the outset. First, the achievement of a "break" may be partial or total, superficial or profound, joyous or mildly gratifying. One may discover oneself in a "new" condition, in a "new" relationship with the world, or one may simply have an inkling of such things. Additionally, the achievement of a break may be illusory, genuine, or somewhere in between; it may indicate an actual disruption of the stressful psychobiological ties that bind one to the inner world, or it may indicate stiffening defences, a denial of internal conflict, a narcissistic withdrawal and alienation from others which all too frequently passes for sublime detachment. Second, understanding of a "break" cannot be complete apart from an understanding of the method employed to achieve it. Indeed, the distinction I make in writing that statement is misleading. What one does in accomplishing the alteration, or truncation, largely will determine what one "is" in the realization of it. Again, because "breaks" frequently involve contact, or better, recontact, with the "good objects" of infancy and childhood, they also involve the presence at the phenomenological level of what might be termed good time, good space, good imagery and symbolification, as well as feelings of security, well-being, and closeness to other people and things.

James's *Varieties of Religious Experience* ([1902] 1958, pp. 302–5) provides us with several prototypical examples. One concerns a "police officer" who, "many times when off duty and on his way home in the evening," experiences a "vivid and vital realization of his oneness" with the universe, as well as a "spirit of infinite peace" that so "takes hold" of him "that it seems as if his feet could hardly keep to the pavement." What is described as his "inflowing tide" produces a profound "exhilaration." Another instance involves a "gentleman" who has spent the evening discussing philosophy and poetry with his friends. While riding home alone in a cab, he discovers himself in a state of "quiet, almost passive" enjoyment, letting his "ideas, images, and emotions flow of themselves." Suddenly, "without warning," he is "wrapped in a flame-colored cloud." For an instant he thinks of fire; then he realizes the fire is within. "Directly" there comes upon him "a sense of exultation, of immense joyousness accompanied . . . by an intellectual illumination impossible to describe." Finally from James, we are introduced to a man who finds it "impossible" to accompany his wife and children to chapel one Sunday. Leaving them on the road, he strolls through the surrounding hills and valleys. "On the way back," and again "without warning," he feels he is in "heaven," an "inward state of peace and joy" together with the "sense of being bathed in a warm glow of light." The objects around him at this moment undergo a perceptive alteration. They "stand out more clearly," as if "nearer" to him than "before." The experience as a whole comprises an "illumination."

A more recent and strikingly similar account may be gleaned from a psychoanalytic case history presented by Horton (1974, p. 368). It concerns a patient who attends church one morning after having fasted the previous day. Upon entering she feels "scared" but soon finds herself quietly praying amidst the other worshippers. "Suddenly" a "brilliant white light" begins to "shine" within her—she *is* the light. Her whole body feels "radiant"; she is "overcome with love and joy ... ecstatic." A few moments later the transport subsides. Ordinary consciousness, along with a certain sensation of "dullness" and "misery," commences once more. Yet she "knows" that what has just happened to her is the "most real" event she has ever experienced. Horton maintains of this material that it evinces a "distortion of reality" insofar as the patient's break tends to "transmute outer events into inner experiences," a tendency which comprises for psychoanalysis the essence of "mystical" distortion in general (Horton 1974, p. 377). As he views the matter, such distortion is affectively accompanied by "regression," while the occurrence in its totality is ultimately "transitional" in nature: hungry, scared, and then "filled with light," the patient rediscovers the "good object."

I will not argue with Horton here. After all, the patient was his, and he offers a meticulous, "scientific" analysis of her "case." But I do feel it worth mentioning, particularly with Chapter 2 of this book fresh in our minds, that we are psychophysical organisms who always perceive and feel at the same time. Everyone "transmutes the external event into the internal feeling." To do this is to be human. It is that simple. However, most individuals, by the time they have reached "adulthood" and fully endured the unconscious effects of infantile "conversion," have very nearly *lost* this natural tendency. What passes for "objectivity," "detachment," adherence to the "reality principle," is actually the deadening of one's sensitivity to the world, the lessening of one's potential to participate fully in the sensorial universe, to indulge feelingly in the experience of living, to *play*. What Horton's patient undergoes as she sits "radiant" in church may contain not simply "distortion" but an element of integration; it may speak for an awakening capacity to attain an "objectivity" considerably more in touch with the "reality" of our emotive-perceptive "style" of existing than the constricted everyday awareness customarily regarded as "normal."

It is also important to note in this connection James's attitude toward such events. He writes that the "incommunicableness of the transport" is its "keynote." The "truth" of the mystical moment "exists for the individual" who experiences it, and "for no one else" (James [1902] 1958, p. 311). As for the epistemological implications, James (ibid.) declares that "knowledge" afforded us by this means "resembles the knowledge given to us in sensations more than that given by conceptual thought." Unlike the analyst, James is very sensitive to the philosophical questions that swirl about "transcendence." More than that, he recognizes the inseparableness of philosophical and psychological issues. Skilful phenomenologist that he is, he grants the experience to the person who is having it. He refuses to translate the "inside story" into "data" which are but another person's description of an occurrence that he has not undergone directly. As Herrick (1949, p. 180) expresses it, the "bias" that develops from one's "unrecognized personal attitudes, interests, and preconceptions" comprises the most "treacherous" of the "enemies" of "scientific progress." At the same time, such "attitudes and interests" are the most crucial items in "all original scientific investigation." This "issue," states Herrick, must be confronted "courageously." To take the "easy way out" and maintain that science has no concern with "troublesome personal ingredients" is not merely unwise, it "cannot actually be done." The "whole course of investigation" is "shaped" by the "inquirer's attitudes."

Blackburn (1973, pp. 31–35), discussing the "sensuous-intellectual complementarity in science," reminds us that "a single phenomenon (for example, light or matter) manifests itself to the observer in conflicting modes." The "description or model" that "fits" the event "depends on the mode of observation." Thus the notion of "objectivity" is "somewhat broadened" but not "eliminated." As for the "expert," he is "highly suspect." His "expertise" is apt to be limited to "distractions," and "there is [also] a danger he will project sensitive and complex problems onto some underdimensioned space where he feels less involved and more in control." Cognizant of all this long before others who claimed to be scientists had even begun to examine their assumptions, James realized that knowledge in the body is no less knowledge than knowledge in the mind. Hence to suggest as Horton (1974, p. 372) does that "mystical experiences" are "transitional phenomena," that they entail the rediscovery of one's "good objects," the benign presences of one's inner world, is acceptable only if one makes clear, as Horton does not,[1] that the experiences cannot be *equated* with such a rediscovery.

Depending upon the methods employed and the character of the experiencer, the ultimate result of "transport" may be increased integration and heightened awareness of all levels of personality.

Touching the Deep Sources of Being

To maintain that breaks are transitional, that they invariably entail the refinding of the "good object," not only presents us with the danger of reductionism, it also presents us with the danger of analytical misemphasis, an even more serious error. While "transport" may well involve fresh contact with the good presences within, that contact may actually be minimal in any given instance. Indeed — and here we reach a crucial point in the discussion — the quality of a break is frequently determined not by the degree to which the individual reparticipates in the "good object," but by the degree to which he "breaks free" of internalized objects, good ones as well as bad ones. The question arises, how can this be? If the individual lessens or even severs the tie to internalized materials, what is the source of his positive emotion? What is it that he recontacts? Surely his good feelings must originate somewhere; they do not "come from the void." But in a very real sense, that is precisely where they come from. They are the result of the person approaching what is sometimes called his "original nature," his "being" as it is given to him by those natural forces which created him. While the influence of the "environment" is, as we have seen, hugely significant, there is a "genetical" aspect of existence over which environmental influences are laid. In this way, there is an aspect of the break which is not derived from the world of the internalized other but which goes beyond or behind that world to a realm of experience in which vibrating atoms evolve along an infinite continuum of structural possibilities.

The relative presence or the relative absence of the "good object" in any given break will be determined, among other things, by the extent to which the individual who is having the "transport" experiences the diminution of time and space as we usually conceive of them, and the disappearance of symbols, or symbolical thoughts, as we usually conceive of them. One of James's subjects, for example, describes her "mystical interlude" as taking place during a solitary walk along the seashore. She feels liberated, reconciled with former enemies, closer to present friends, and impelled to kneel down before the "illimitable ocean," the "symbol of the infinite." The "earth," the "heavens," and the "sea," all "resound" as with "one vast... harmony" (James [1902] 1958, p. 304). It is the conspicuous presence of the ocean as symbol which indicates the relative presence of the "good object" in this "transport." The tie to the benign internalization is strengthened, renewed. The boundaries of the inner landscape shift in a positive way. Another instance in James is accompanied by a description which states, "there is no feeling, and yet the mind works, desireless, free from restlessness, objectless, bodiless." The "alteration" stems "from the perception of forms and figures to a degree which escapes all expression" (James [1902] 1958, pp. 304, 311). Or again, from a related account, "the soul finds no terms, no means, no comparison whereby to render the sublimity." One receives this "knowledge... clothed in none of the kinds of images... which our minds make use of in other circumstances" (James [1902] 1948, p. 312). Here we have, above all, the relative absence of the object. The tie to the inner world diminishes. One's perception is no longer "objective" in the double sense I am developing in this book.

Such an experience, at first glance, might appear to resemble psychosis. But psychosis does not involve the radical diminution or severing of ties to the inner world, as is sometimes thought to be the case. It involves, rather, the diminution or severing of only the good ties. The bad ones remain, as they do for J. A. Symonds, who describes a spontaneous "trance" as consisting of a "gradual but swiftly progressive obliteration of space, time, sensation, and the multitudinous factors of experience... the apprehension of a coming dissolution... the abyss" (James [1902] 1958, p. 296). To put it somewhat differently, psychosis does not occur when the individual loses his connection with "reality" and cannot, therefore, discover his way back to the "ordinary universe," as the orthodox ego psychologist would be inclined to say. It occurs when the individual becomes absorbed into the "bad object," when nothing remains but an inimical, persecuting presence (Aronson 1977, p. 15).

The meditator who sits contentedly in a deep, contemplative trance may resemble the psychotic in that he has detached himself from "ordinary objects." But he is different from the psychotic in that his detachment stems from wilful renunciation of perceptual links to the inner world, rather than from a tragic, hopeless sense of rejection, of narcissistic injury. The meditator knows at the bodily, emotional level that "the world" is forged in the conflicts and terrors of the early period and

53

therefore contributes to his discontent; he has survived that period and wants to modify the "ordinary reality" which is its result. The psychotic is still struggling to *gain* "the world." He has not survived the splitting and confusion of his primary interactions with people. As for the "mystical interlude," it consists in the instinctive or "sudden" expression of what the meditator has raised to the level of diurnal practice. In this way, to determine the relative presence or absence of the object in the "break" is to determine its peculiar, "inner" quality, its place among the many examples of this kind of emotive, psychical experience. Earlier I indicated that "breaks" offer an enormous variety, an enormous range. With regard to further investigation, we are now in a position to grasp one direction from which that range and variety derive. Our next job is to grasp, first, why the fading off of ordinary consciousness—time, space, cause, symbol—should produce good, even joyous feelings, and second, how diminution of these items may be triggered in the human organism.

Psychoanalytic Passage through the Doors of Perception

I will rely here upon the most vivid and influential account of a break precipitated by the use of an hallucinogen, namely Huxley's *Doors of Perception* (1974, pp. 16–26), and I will stress two points as I do so. First, Huxley's report is, in respect to its chief phenomenological features, identical with other vivid, influential accounts by such writers as Havelock Ellis ([1898] 1961) and Christopher Mayhew ([1956] 1961). Second, Huxley's pages look forward, once again in respect to phenomenological items, to philosophical and religious utterances which stand at the centre of the "mystical" tradition.

Shortly after taking his "pill," Huxley finds himself sitting quietly in his study and staring at a "small glass vase" that contains "three flowers—a full-blown Bell of Portugal rose, shell pink . . . a large magenta and cream-colored carnation; and, pale purple at the end of its broken stalk, the bold heraldic blossom of an iris." Earlier that morning, "at breakfast," Huxley had been "struck" by what he calls the "lively dissonance" of the flowers' hues. Now, however, he beholds something quite different, namely "what Adam had seen on the morning of his creation—the miracle, moment by moment, of naked existence." Continuing to behold the blooms in their "living light," Huxley "seem[s] to detect the qualitative equivalent of breathing—but of a breathing without returns to a starting-point, with no recurrent ebbs but only a repeated flow from beauty to heightened beauty, from deeper to even deeper meaning." Words such as "grace" and "transfiguration" come to his mind, for as he perceives it, the experience he is undergoing indicates what such words "stand for." Yet the "really important fact"—and here we reach the phenomenology with its tie to the infantile period—is that "spatial relationships" among objects suddenly cease to "matter." The mind begins to apprehend in other than spatial categories. Instead of place and distance, "intensity of existence, profundity of significance," and "pattern" become paramount. Everything simply "glows" with a "living light."

After shifting his gaze to other objects and discovering their won-drousness—the "miraculous tubularity" of a nearby chair's legs, for ex-ample—Huxley concludes from his "journey" that symbolic expression of the world's objects can only take one in the direction of "Suchness," never *to* it. An "emblem" such as Van Gogh's chair in the famous paint-ing of his room is a "source of true knowledge about the Nature of Things, and this true knowledge may serve to prepare the mind which accepts it for immediate insights on its own account. But that is all." No matter how "expressive" they are, "symbols can never be the things they stand for." Art, then, "is only for beginners" or "for those resolute deadenders, who have made up their minds to be content with the *ersatz* of Suchness." Finally, one experiences in the "break," in addition to the lessening of the ordinary sense of space, "some of the perceptual innocence of childhood when the sensum was not... automatically subordinated to the concept," as well as a diminution of the ordinary sense of time. As Huxley states it, "interest in time" falls "almost to zero."

The "equation" of a break, then, is clear: removed from ordinary space and time, as well as from symbolified thinking, the organism is suddenly filled with feelings of knowingness, wonder, and bliss, feel-ings that arise from a new, or altered, mode of perception. What under-lies this process may be expressed this way: because symbolical sight de-pends upon a translation of the particular "thing" into an instance of the class of things to which it belongs in ordinary perception, symboli-cal sight perforce requires *duration*. There can be no translation with-out time. For example, in Kleitman's classic paper on dreaming we are reminded that the "cortex" subjects the "impulses" that "stream toward it from the various receptor organs" to a particular kind of "analysis." It "refers the present moment of experience to its memory of the past and projects past and present into the future, weighing the consequences of action not yet taken." When a "decision is reached," the cortex "generates an integrated response" which is "manifested in the action of the effector organs . . . or in the deliberate inhibition of action" (Kleitman [1960] 1972, p. 46). Lashley ([1951] 1969, p. 515) renders the matter by noting that "input is never into a quiescent or static system, but always into a system which is already excited and organized." Behavior "is the result of interaction of background . . . with input." It is only when one can "state the characteristics" of "background" that one can "understand the effects" of "input." Neisser (1973, p. 205) puts it even more succinctly: "perceiving involves a memory that is not representational but schematic."

The implications are evident. The diminution of time which occurs in a break—linear time as we usually apprehend it—precludes or "inhibits" the formation of symbols. The "thing" which comes into the ken of the perceiver is apprehended *directly* rather than "schematically." We must recall here, of course, that "schematically" in psychology or "structurally" in psychoanalysis designates the reception of current feelings and/or events into perceptual sets which have been laid down during the early period, the period in which the object is internalized in close and conflictual association to the development of temporal and spatial perception. A chair, a vase, a flower, or a mountain is not unconsciously translated, in an instantaneous quantum burst of cerebral energy, into an example of the species "chair," "vase," "flower," or "mountain." It becomes instead the "creature" that it simply is. Thus, without categories within which to fit items, the world is suddenly "there," fresh, new, pristine, with each perception of it. The habitual, frustrating "alienation" that resides at the ground of our ordinary consciousness subsides.

Again, because symbols "live" or exist in time, the time which permits the translation to occur, the apprehension of timelessness or the feeling of "eternity" will ordinarily increase with diminution of symbolical sight. What I am describing is a kind of pulsation, a kind of reinforcing give and take, between the cessation of linear time and the direct perception of objects. As the "items" which comprise the "external universe" are reborn, over and over again, "forever," eternity becomes "real" to the perceiver, as real as his own being, the organismic "unit" through which his perception transpires. "Believe it or not," declares Huxley, "eternity is real." It is as real as the contents of the human body (cf. Huxley, Laura 1971, p. 132).

However, if symbolical sight depends upon linear time for its existence, linear time, in turn, depends for its existence upon the continuous generation of cerebral or perceptual energy. "Perceptions are in quanta," says James (cf. Eisendrath 1971, pp. 143, 264); "the concept of time as duration develops out of incessant impulses of voluntary reinforcement in maintaining attention with effort." Hence, "experience comes in quanta," and it is the "intellect only" that "makes it continuous." Freud's conclusions are virtually identical with James's: "the attention we bestow upon objects" results from "rapid but successive cathexes which might be regarded in a sense as quanta issuing from the ego." Inner perceptual action makes a "continuity" of such cathexes only "later." The "prototype of time" is found precisely here (cf. Bonaparte 1940, p. 467). Clearly then, the translation of "thing" into "member of class of things," a translation that is grounded in linear time and that constitutes the essence of ordinary awareness, is a particular kind of behavior, of projective action, a specialized mental and emotive performance on the part of the human organism. As that behavior subsides, as that performance ends, the organism is suddenly charged with the very energy, the very "quanta," that formerly went into the translation, making, and maintaining of the temporal world and its symbolified inhabitants, the "items" of "ordinary awareness." When Freud writes of "the attention" we "bestow" upon "objects," and when James writes of the "experience" we daily undergo, each neglects to specify that it is our *ordinary attention,* or *ordinary experience,* which is at issue.

"The ubiquitous use of light as a metaphor for mystic experience . . . may not be just a metaphor," suggests Deikman (1973, pp. 227–28). "'Illumination' may be derived from an actual sensory experience" involving the "liberation of energy." With the energic connection between time and symbol firmly established in our minds, we are able to perceive the source of this "liberation." I am not implying, of course, that the entire store of the organism's energy is consumed in the moment of "illumination." Obviously a portion of that power is involved in the individual's positive sensorial experience. Reminding us that "entrancing displays of imagery of great beauty and clarity can be experienced by ordinary people under the influence of hallucinogenic drugs such as mescaline," Eccles (1972, p. 39) declares that "the cortex under these conditions tends to develop ever more complex and effectively interlocked patterns of neuronal activity involving large fractions of its neuronal population." It is precisely those "large fractions" of the "neuronal population" which are customarily devoted to the preservation of ordinary reality that are freed to create such "entrancing displays."

To stress the liberation of neurons, the redistribution of quantified impulses emanating from the cerebral cortex, is to stress what might be termed a physiological side of a break. To stress how such phenomena bear upon the internalized conflicts of the early period is to stress what might be termed a psychological side. Once again it is James and Freud who point us toward a synthesis. For when James writes that time as duration develops out of "incessant impulses" of "voluntary reinforcement," and when Freud writes of the "successive cathexes" which we "bestow upon objects," each reminds us that ordinary awareness fulfils a *need* within the individual which cannot be understood apart from its connection to the whole development of the person as a psychophysical organism. The voluntary maintenance of time as duration is rooted in the individual's need to translate the thing into the symbol and hence to retain the tie to the internalized object, to keep open the perceptual, psychological avenue which leads back to the parental figures (Chapter 2). Because we answer the separation crises of infancy by internalizing the people we have to give up, and because the capacity for language, for symbolic thought, is the culmination of the internalizing process, a developmental feature that is actually goaded into operation by the anxiety surrounding separation, we cling to the symbolified mode of perception which arises from the early time and which provides us with the familiar, "ordinary" world.

But the translation of the "thing" into the symbol can only occur in time. Internalization, in other words, can only occur in time. In a sense, it *is* time. Hence, time as duration is voluntarily maintained by the individual because time as duration permits the "translation" (or "predication" in Chomsky's terms) upon which his ordinary emotional security rests. Needless to say, the accompanying spatial parameters which "house" the conceptualizations of everyday "reality" develop inwardly in close association to the symbols that keep appearing as the ordinary universe takes shape. Our "space," in short, "contains" our time-bound words. We keep on making our temporal, spatial, symbolical world over and over again because just beneath it, we believe, lies the void, separation, isolation, oblivion. What Roheim calls "dual-unity," the ability to be separate from the object of infancy and yet, at the same time, to maintain contact, is grounded in the ability and the will to keep time going, for as long as time is kept going internalization and the ordinary world of space, cause, and symbol which is its product can also be kept going.

What one "knows," deep down, in a break is that his well-being does not necessarily reside in his tie to the internalized object. The perceptual world that serves as a "transitional phenomenon" can be given up and one can still be all right. To be without one's linear time, one's ordinary space, one's habitual symbolic associations, one's obsessional predication of the object through language, does *not* mean disaster. On the contrary, it means that one has a "self" which is not derived entirely from the "mirror relationship" and from the conflictual stages of separation that follow it. The love of the self, or the delight in the self, as we ordinarily experience it and conceive of it, is derived primarily from the caregiver's ministrations and affection. It is her love for us which we transfer to ourselves through internalization (and her frustration and anxiety too!). What we ordinarily take to be love of the self is actually love of the made self, the symbolical self, the self we can analyze and think about, the self that leads to the self-image, the reflection of the mirror, the ego.

To merge with the good object, then, is merely the regressive answer to the problems of being a person, a regressive answer sometimes revealed with striking clarity during the course of a "local" religious conversion as witnessed, for example, on television. There is a crucial psychological difference between that kind of experience and the kind described in *Through an Eastern Window,* where the author, a psychiatrist from New York named Jack Huber (1967), sits for weeks in a Japanese monastery attempting to "empty his mind" only to do so at last amidst a burst of powerful sobs. While the mourning that often accompanies a break may come from refinding the "good object" once again, it may also come from bidding farewell to the good object, from "breaking" the old, dependent tie, from refinding *oneself* again. The mourning of the latter experience arises from the deepest conscience, the conscience that lies beneath the "superego," beneath the influence of the parents, beneath the culturally induced "sense of right and wrong." Such mourning arises from the "sudden" knowledge that although one's self was betrayed during the early period, and after, it is still there, awaiting "rebirth." Love for our good objects can bind us and hold us back as much as hate for our bad ones.

It is also important to note in this connection that the moment of "illumination" is sometimes described in the mystical literature as the moment of the "great death" (Shibayama 1974, p. 32). What one "dies to" as one "breaks free," or finds oneself "breaking free," is the self of everyday consciousness, the self that is life-lined into the ordinary world of time, space and symbol. *Linear* time, in fact, may be figuratively thought of as a kind of "line" or "cord" on which one's vital, sustaining internalizations are strung. The "line" is "hooked" to the absent caregiver through the psychic "magic" of "dual-unity," the "illusion" of "transitional space." Now, as we saw in Chapter 2, the actual fear of death in human beings is a catastrophic one connected inextricably to the anxiety over loss, separation, and rejection which one experiences through the primary interaction with the caregiver. Thus the link between the break and the "great death" is more than merely metaphorical. It reveals the affective, psychodynamic *meaning* of *giving the object up.*

Perceptive Mind-Rest

Here I am interested in *practice,* practice designed to diminish the stress accumulated during the primary years and to foster a non-projective perception of "objects," an epistemic alteration of the manner in which one apprehends not only the external environment but the "world" within oneself. Although spontaneous breaks with ordinary consciousness may have beneficial effects upon the individual and may offer us valuable insight into the phenomenological nature of "mystic" experience, they cannot, obviously, provide us with a foundation on which to build a program for genuine, lasting change. The perceptive mind-rest explored in the next few pages may be best achieved — and by "best" I mean most conveniently and safely — through a number of techniques, all of which fall under the heading of "concentrative meditation," a "complex, non-linear phenomenon involving somatic, affective, perceptual, and cognitive" alterations (Kornfield 1979, p. 41). Let us look briefly at several major "schools" to acquaint ourselves with both historical traditions and actual methods.

(1) Hindu Bhakti. Here the "devotee," having removed himself to a

quiet location and adopted a comfortable, sitting position, keeps the thought of his "ishta," or meditational object, "foremost in his mind at all times." He may also repeat, mentally or aloud, the name of his "ishta" in a rhythmic, concentrative way. By "bringing his mind to one-pointedness" through the "constant remembrance of the ishta," the practitioner reaches the "first level" of "meditative consciousness." Subsequently he experiences a lessening of the need to "cling to the external form of his devotional object." The "states" that it once "evoked" become the "fixtures" of his own awareness. Concentrating upon "pure being" as it begins to manifest itself "internally," the meditator proceeds along the "path" of "spiritual evolution" (Goleman 1977, pp. 42–46).

(2) Jewish Kabbalah. Here, the "training of the will" and the development of the capacity "for unwavering attention" are facilitated by concentration upon selected single subjects including, most notably, the sacred items of the Kabbalist "Tree," a "map" of the "hierarchies and attributes of the many planes that interplay in the world and within man." By focusing upon these "names" and directing his attention away from "the forms of this world," the meditator achieves an "ecstatic state" called *Daat,* or knowledge (Goleman 1977, pp. 52–53). "Where attention is," writes Halevi (1976, p. 126), "there is power."

(3) Christian Hesychasm. In this tradition, the "constant remembrance of God" is the "mainstay." The practitioner meditates "with verbal or silent repetition of a single phrase from the Scriptures," a phrase which may be regarded as the Christian "equivalent" of the "ishta" or "mantra." Once again, a peaceful location, an upright posture, silence, and practice are essential to "stilling the mind." With the banishment of all "images, thoughts, and sense perceptions," what is called "introversion," or the "concentration of the mind on its own deepest part," can begin. Eventually, such "introversion" will lead the "soul" to "God" (Goleman 1977, pp. 55–57).

(4) Sufism. The chief meditational practice of this "school" is called *zikr,* which means "remembrance." The seeker attempts to "overcome the mind's natural state of carelessness and inattention" through an oral repetition which later becomes silent. The most eminent and influential *zikr* is, translated, "there is no god but God." According to the Sufis, ordinary human consciousness comprises a kind of "sleep" in a "nightmare of unfulfilled desires." With "transcendence," which is brought about by "not letting [one's] attention wander for the duration of a single breath" (Goleman 1977, p. 64), this nightmarish condition gives

way to what is termed by Indries Shah (1971, p. 62) "objective consciousness," an "extra dimension of being" that operates concomitantly with "normal" or everyday cognition.

(5) Transcendental Meditation. The best known meditational technique in the west, TM asks its practitioners to follow "the classic Hindu mantra meditation," that is, to meditate upon a brief word or phrase derived from Sanskrit sources. Examples might be "Shyam," a name of Lord Krishna, or "Aing," a sound sacred to the "Divine Mother" (Goleman 1977, pp. 69–70). Instructed to avoid "effortful concentration" by "bringing his mind back gently to the mantra as it wanders," the student "narrows his attention," eventually reaching more and more "subtle" levels of thought until his mind "transcends the experience of the subtlest state of thought and arrives at the source of thought" (Maharishi 1969, p. 470). With steady, long-term practice, one enhances his ability to "experience objects through the senses" while at the same time "maintaining his essential nature—Being" (Maharishi 1966, p. 53).

(6) Ashtanga Yoga. In the view of this "school," the mind is replete with "thought waves" which create the very "gulf" the practitioner seeks to "bridge." By "calming" these "waves" the yogi will find "union." When the individual's mind becomes "clear and still" he can "know himself as he really is." And as a "liberated man," he will be able "to don his ego or discard it like a suit of clothes." First, however, the student must subject himself to a rigorous mental and bodily discipline that begins with "concentration" or "bringing the mind to one-pointedness" (Goleman 1977, p. 75). In the end, as the anonymous biographer of Sri Ramakrishna puts it (M. 1928, p. 27), the successful devotee is "devoid of ideas of 'I' and 'mine'." Dwelling neither on the past nor the future, he lives his life in the "eternal present." Continuous, deep meditation not only affords one "bliss" but, through "divine detachment," removes one's fears and anxieties in a lasting, even permanent way (Goleman 1977, p. 78). No longer "touched by the infinite variety of phenomena," one "surveys the world with an eye of equality" (M. 1928, p. 27).

(7) Zen. Here one's training commences with a "firm grounding in concentration." Sitting quietly in an effort to achieve a state of "oneness" in which "the differences between things dissolve," the seeker concentrates upon his *koan* (a mental puzzle without a rational solution) or upon his breathing. The principal "fruit" of successful practice

is *satori,* a profound "awakening" during the course of which one "sees into his true nature" (Goleman 1977, p. 93). Paradoxically, it is the "empty mind" one achieves through meditation that provides the "power" to gain this special "sight." We must remember here, following Blofeld (1962, p. 111), that *satori* does not signify "trance-like dullness," but a "brilliantly clear state of mind in which the details of every phenomenon are perceived, yet without evaluation or attachment." In the ultimate Zen condition of "no mind" the intuitive clearness of *satori* infuses itself into all of one's actions. "Means and ends," as Goleman (1977, p. 95) expresses it, "coalesce."

Distilling this material for a general understanding of that perceptive mind-rest in which I am interested here, I would suggest that it *commences* in the choice of a quiet location, the adoption of a relaxed yet straight-backed posture, and the focusing of attention with the accompanying renunciation of stimuli, and *consists* in a regularized training of awareness "aimed at modifying mental processes so as to elicit enhanced states of consciousness and well-being" (Walsh 1982, p. 77). As for the explicitly "religious" aspect of the ancient technique, I would set it aside in keeping with my stated conviction that traditional "practice" comprises, in part, the human species' intuitive, inchoate attempt to reduce the psychobiological tension of the infantile period, specifically the mirror and separation phases. We are now in a position to employ such "practice" in a conscious, secular, therapeutic manner, or, if I may put the matter baldly once again, to get from it what we will. In precisely this spirit, let us begin to examine at length the physiological, phenomenological, and psychoanalytic implications of this methodology.

The Human Mind and the First Relationship

We must recognize from the outset that we are dealing with the human *mind,* not simply with the human *brain,* and that the distinction is fundamental. True, our behavior is composed to a considerable extent of automatic responses to sensory inputs. However, to understand the motivations that underlie our actions we must know something of the "genetic determinants, cultural elements, and intercerebral mechanisms" that are involved in "various kinds of behavioral performance" (Delgado 1971, p. 9). More specifically, because all mental functions are related to inner or outer stimuli, because mind can manifest itself only in behavior, and because the mind cannot exist without a functioning brain, we can conclude that the mind is linked, necessarily, "to stimuli, to behavior, and to the brain." Without stimuli, the "mind cannot exist," and without behavior, it cannot "be recognized." In this way, "mind" may be defined as "the intercerebral elaboration of extracerebral information," and the focus is on the "origins, reception, dynamics, storage, retrieval, and consequences of this information. The basis of the mind is cultural, not individual" (Delgado, 1971, p. 27). In what we may regard as a key utterance in our discussion, "mind is born... early in life [as] an infant is attracted to sources of comfort and repelled by sources of distress." Such experiences "lead to the intelligent recognition of objects and persons associated with positive and negative reinforcement," and they will (i.e., the experiences) "determine selective patterns of behavioral response" (Delgado 1971, p. 46). The origin of mind, then, is pinpointed at precisely the time in which the infant begins to interact with the objects (both "good" and "bad") that will enter integrally into his mental structure. It must be stressed that such structure cannot be understood, developmentally or motivationally, apart from these objects. There is no mind, there can be no mind in any genuine, human sense, without the fundamental internalizing activities of the early period. Hence, if "perceptive mind-rest" has something to do with "the mind" in a hard, explicit, physiological way, and if "the mind" is crucially determined by the internalizations I have been describing, then "perceptive mind-rest" *also has to do with these internalizations.*

While all of this implies that the mental cannot be grasped apart from the physical, it does not imply that the mental can be reduced to the physical in a crude, simplistic fashion. "From the formal logic of Gödel, from Heisenberg's uncertainty principle, and from probability theory," writes Pelletier (1978, pp. 52–53), "comes the consistent conclusion that there is a fundamental... limit upon the classical mode of inquiring into certain aspects of reality... aspects [which] concern individual events at an infinitesimal level of analysis." More particularly with regard to mental processes, "infinitesimal size is by no means a limitation" upon the consideration of consciousnesss "as interacting consequentially with matter" at the quantum level. Indeed, quantum physics supports this idea in that infinite energy can be a feature of an infinitely short wave length; an "infinitely small radius" is capable of storing "infinite energy " (Pelletier 1978, pp. 59–60). The most recent investigations into the "reticular activation system" have given rise to a model of continuous informational exchange between the "subcortical sectors of the brain" that is "supplanting the dualistic model." Neurological data indicate a "dialogue" between autonomic and cortical processes that contrasts with "an incessant, all-or-nothing struggle between these processes vying for dominance."

While this model "does not include an equation of unconscious psychological processes with autonomic neurological" ones (the former are "symbolic" and the latter "electrical"), it does suggest, because the functioning of psychological and neurological systems is intertwined, that "insights" derived from one system "illuminate" the "problems" of the other (Pelletier 1978, pp. 79–80). Thus "consciousness" is tied to the brain "by means of quantum mechanical wave function." The brain is a "logical instrument that employs a certain physical process" for "some of its data management," and this process can only be accurately suggested by quantum physics. Most important of all, "events in the brain are governed by a higher order," or what is called a "hidden variable" in physics, and it is precisely this "hidden variable" that is "synonymous with consciousness." By exerting "spatio-temporal fields of influence" that "become effective through [the]... function of the cerebral cortex," the human "will" alters the "spatio-temporal activity of the neuronal network... Unobservable psychological factors could have profound effects" (Pelletier 1978, pp. 137–38). Can anyone fail to grasp the role of the "unobservable" internalized object in this advanced theoretical picture? (1) Mental structure is determined by energic, informational processes which transpire at the quantum level, at the interface between the organism and the stimulus field. (2) The mind is born in the infant's interaction with the object of the early period. (3) The process of internalization is an integral aspect of human mental development, of the characteristically human manner in which our brains grow and function in the characteristically human, mental world. In this way, (4) internalizing processes — specifically, internalization of the psychological object — may have actual structural, physiological effects on the human mind-brain.

Writing of the "complex and reciprocal interaction between object-relations and internalizations," Meissner (1980, pp. 237–38) reminds us that the "mind" is "built up out of internalized relationships and their associated affects which are then integrated into structures." With the idea of quantum energic processes in view we may now recognize that

65

these "structures" are far more rooted in our bodily functioning than a purely "psychological" or "informational" approach would suggest. "In learning something," writes Leonard Stevens in *Neurons* (1966, p. 4), "a brain actually experiences physical changes." Because the related problems of projective perception and neurotic discontent are linked inextricably to this mind-brain through the "stimuli" of the primary years an answer to those problems may be hidden here, at the structural level where the split object of the early period shapes the developing human *will,* guides the developing human personality in a way that has its consequences in the symbolic, cultural universe which, in turn, lends *its* "stimulation" to the creature, offers *its* "information" to the "processing" activities of the "system." With the accent of current research on the relational fields that harbor the mental events of our existence ("mind is the ongoing comparison relations within an organization of neural nets" writes Edgar Wilson [1979, p. 78]), we must not fail to emphasize the relations between people, between the baby and its internalized caretaker, which impinge in a determining way upon the growth of a mental instrument with an enormous potential for engendering stress as well as feelings of exhilaration and bliss. It will help to recall in this connection the nature of human memory, particularly the very close tie between retrieval and sheer stimulation.

Memory functions as essentially a "two-step process." A stimulus "such as a smell, or sound, or image" arouses a person's "short-term memory" which then "resonates through the infinite complexity of the [brain] . . . until an association is triggered in long-term memory." The "correspondence between an immediate sensory stimulus and a fragment of a stored memory initiates the retrieval of the entire stored memory" (Pelletier 1978, p. 118). This is because the brain is ultimately a "holographic" structure (Pribram 1982, p. 32), that is to say, a structure with the property of "storing the whole in each part, each part being capable of generating the whole" (Pelletier 1978, p. 118). Experiments involving laboratory rats, for example, have "indicated that memory is retained intact if just one small segment of the brain remains intact" (Pelletier 1978, p. 120). Additional striking support for this view has come from the work of Pietsch (1972, p. 66), who established that the brain function of salamanders remained sound in spite of wholesale alteration, and even obliteration, of their brain tissues. "Specific memories," writes Pribram (1982, p. 31), "are incredibly resistant to brain damage."

For our purposes, however, the most compelling evidence derives from the work of Wilder Penfield (1950, pp. 164–67). Operating upon a girl of fourteen for epilepsy, whose attacks were invariably preceded by a traumatic, hallucinatory recollection from her seventh year in which a strange "man" asks her to crawl into a bag filled with snakes, Penfield discovered that electrical stimulation of the cortex of the temporal lobe reproduced the hallucination. Furthermore, when the electrode was held in place, the memory disclosed itself sequentially, as in a film. The cause of the young woman's seizures was discovered to be a portion of brain that had been damaged during infancy. The scarring that had developed with the passage of time was precipitating the fits. As to why those fits were invariably preceded by a recollection of the fright she underwent in her seventh year, Penfield maintains that the injured area was "triggering" the memory that had been formed with the occurrence of the psychological trauma, and it was this area that he was able to arouse with the electrode. Anthony Campbell (1975, p. 102) writes of this material that it offers us "direct experimental evidence of a severe stress having been recorded in the cortex" and reminds us of psychoanalysis's tenet that "it is not necessary for a conflict to be present in awareness if it is to produce effects." True, our estimation of this particular case is "complicated by the epilepsy caused by the earlier brain damage," but "even if there had been no brain damage the experience would still have been recorded and might well have given rise to nightmares and other behavioral disturbances" (Campbell 1975, p. 102). Penfield's subsequent explorations, of course, dramatically confirm this conclusion.

Through the employment of electrical implantations in a wide variety of individuals, Penfield disclosed not only the regions of the cortex that "have a particular relationship to the *record of experience*[,] and [to] the reactivation of that record," but the amazing fact that *all* experiences undergone by human beings form "ganglionic patterns" which remain "intact and available to the stimulating electrode" in later years (Penfield 1959, pp. 48, 51). From the "cries of other children," to the "honking of horns," to the "barking of dogs," the stimuli with which we are touched as we merely live our lives remain embedded and *resonating* in the folds of our mind-brains. "Every individual," concludes Penfield (1959, p. 54), "forms a neuronal record of his own stream of consciousness . . . from childhood to the grave." Let us bring to mind, now, not only the second chapter of this book in a general way, but the specific, related points that the child's perception of the environment and of himself is tied inextricably to his relationship with the caretaker ("the child's perception is the mother's perception") and that "unconscious fantasy activity provides the mental set in which sensory stimuli are perceived and integrated.... Because specific sensory stimuli become tied to objects and evoke in condensed form the history of... object relationships" we are obliged to recognize that "internal reactions to sensory stimuli do not follow exclusively physiological laws." The "regulation of bodily functions" in which "sensory organs are used" is determined by the degree to which and the way in which the object and the senses have come to be associated (Mushatt 1975, pp. 86–88, 102).

At the deepest level of "mind," *all stimuli are received in the context of the first relationship,* including the mirror and separation phases with their anxiety, terror, expectation, and bliss. The "good" and "bad" experiences of the initial, "split" stage of life become the foundational, "ganglionic" a priori of all that subsequently happens to us simply because mind is in large measure "stimuli" and all stimuli are able to "recall," or to "reactivate," the object of the primary years with which they were originally "fused." In the links between the stimulus, internalized object, mind, and memory we reach the very bone level of the stress in our bones. Merely being sentient, merely receiving stimulation, can be anxiety-provoking to the anxious animal that we are.

We grasp from this perspective both the analytic and epistemic significance of that *renunciation of stimuli* and *focusing of attention* which reside at the heart of the meditative tradition, from which perceptive mind-rest may be gained. Ornstein (1972, p.169) writes that "continuous repetition of the same stimulus [the "ishta" or "mantra" for example] may be considered the equivalent of no stimulation at all. ... Concentrative meditation is a practical technique which uses an experimental knowledge of the structure of our nervous system to 'turn off' awareness of the external world." Thus, the "techniques" of concentrative meditation are not "deliberately mysterious or exotic but are simply a matter of practical applied psychology." Similarly, Deikman (1973, p. 225) contends that the "deautomatization of response" upon which the "alteration of awareness" depends may be straightforwardly induced by "renunciation," specifically the renunciation of sensorial input or stimuli. We may now add that concentrative meditation is a practical technique which uses *psychoanalytic* knowledge of the structure of the *psyche* to moderate the tie to the internalized object upon which one's ordinary perception of the world is automatically and conflictually based.

We also grasp from this angle the analytic significance of that "empty mind" which stands as the highest philosophical and spiritual achievement of the meditative tradition. Writes Shunryu Suzuki (1973, pp. 128–29), "when you have something in your consciousness you do not have perfect composure. The best way toward perfect composure is to forget everything. Then your mind is calm, and it is wide and clear enough to see and feel things as they are without any effort. . . . Actually, emptiness of mind is not even a state of mind, but the original essence of mind which Buddha and the Sixth Patriarch experienced." To the degree that one lessens his tie to the internalized object he empties his mind. As we have seen, the world of ordinary awareness, of ordinary time and space, of ordinary symbolified thinking, was achieved in the effort to retain that tie. The very running on of our thoughts became our habitual way of preserving our security. That is why it is so difficult to stop the running on.

When Freud writes (cf. Bonaparte 1940, p. 467) that we project our sense of duration onto an external universe which we create out of that very sense, he accurately describes the inception of everyday consciousness which is the filling of our minds with our own projections. When the tie to the object is eased we are able to see the variety and freshness of the world because we are able to be "objective" in the double sense we are developing, because we no longer need to see that, or primarily that, which re-establishes and reconfirms our bond to the object within. No wonder that "innocent" individual subjects who are deprived of sensory stimuli during the course of psychological experiments become irritable, childish, depressed, hallucinatory, and "eager for stimulation" (Heron 1972, p. 62). They feel bad in their bodies because they have been deprived of their psychophysical nourishment, the stimulation that hooks them up with the inner realm, that permits ordinary awareness to transpire, and that re-establishes thereby the old, habitual security. There is an incalculable difference between this kind of brutal sensory deprivation and the gradual, rational achievement of the perceptual alteration I am describing here.

Flexibility and the Empty Mind

A variety of studies indicate the human organism's capacity to respond in a positive, concrete way to what I have chosen to call "practice." The "brain," writes Roger Walsh (1979, p. 178), "is a plastic organ whose structure and function mirror its ecology. Moreover, this structure and function are largely dynamic, continuously adapting to changing functional demands." Our "neural components" show "complex interconnections and interdependence; changes in any one part of the brain are likely to affect many if not all other parts." More specifically on this score, experiments with radioactive tracers have established that every emotion and every thought creates a "radical redistribution of blood in the brain." If one persistently brings blood to a certain pattern, one begins to "grow more cells there" and "less cells" elsewhere. With "very strong thoughts," synapses tend to get "fixed." In this way, "thought" produces a "brain structure" which is both "set" and "changeable" (Bohm and Welwood 1980, p. 30). The results of recent psychological investigations permit us to apply such conclusions to the very organs of the human body.

Take, for example, the work of Kohler (1972, p. 108), who concentrates his efforts on the functioning of the eye. Having "saddled" his human subjects with a certain kind of goggle that "distorted" what we may term their "normal" vision, Kohler discovered the extent to which the "organ" of sight is able to "abandon" its "established habits" and "to respond" in a manner that is genuinely "new." He writes, "when we make the system break down and learn a new way of functioning, we do not believe we are forcing the system to function artificially or abnormally. We assume, rather, that a single mechanism is at work at all times." The mechanism "that removes or minimizes" a "created disturbance" is the "one that brings about a normal functioning." And he goes on to say, "organs are not rigid machines but living and variable systems, the functioning of which is itself subject to variation." When a "sensory system" is "exposed to a new and prolonged stimulus" that "departs from the one normally experienced," the system "can be expected to undergo a fundamental change in its normal mode of operation." Or take Dicara's work in the area of "autonomic" response. Guarding against the "contamination" of results, Dicara (1972, pp. 74–76) administered curare to each of his experimental animals (rats). While the drug "paralyzes" the "subject's skeletal muscles" it "does not interfere with consciousness or with the transmitters that mediate autonomic responses." Dicara's experiment "showed that the instrumental learning of two visceral responses can occur independently of each other and that what is learned is specifically the rewarded response."

Such findings "have profound significance for theories of learning." They "should lead to better understanding of the cause and cure of psychosomatic disorders and of the mechanisms whereby the body maintains homeostasis, or a stable internal environment." The autonomic nervous system, then, is not so "autonomic" after all. "Visceral responses" can be "modified" by "learning." These and similar experiments[2] have led investigators to recognize generally what a recent issue of *Brain-Mind Bulletin* (3 October 1983, p. 1) calls the "startling human capacity" for "spontaneous internal reorganization."

Bertalanffy (1952, p. 134) raises this notion to the level of biological principle when he states that the "separation between the preestablished structure and processes occurring in this structure does not apply to the living organism," which is the "expression of an everlasting orderly process... sustained by underlying structures and organized forms." What is "described in morphology as organic forms and structures is in reality a momentary cross-section through a spatio-temporal pattern. What are called structures are slow processes of long duration; functions are quick processes of short duration." When we maintain that a "function, such as the contraction of a muscle, is performed by a structure," we mean that "a quick and short process wave is superimposed on a long-lasting and slowly running wave." The psychoanalytic and philosophic implications are striking. On the one hand, what the infant experiences during the mirror and separation phases will be "learned" in his body, in his organs, in his chemistry, in his "visceral brain," as pointed out in Chapter 2. Because function is structure and structure function, because we cannot separate the two, what we do is what we are. To internalize the caretaker in response to specific early traumata is to internalize her into the body-ego, where she will continue to lodge, and to dictate our perceptual style, until a change occurs. On the other hand, what we take to be our "normal" perception is a conflicted mind-body system of *belief* that can be modified significantly through practice that reaches down to the foundational, "organic" levels with their accumulated tension and stress.

The question arises, *is* there any evidence of the change I am describing? *Does* this so-called perceptive mind-rest have tangible psychologic and epistemic effects? The answer is, assuredly. And much of the evidence surrounds a facet of "practice," as well as of "transport," that is frequently recorded in the literature.

Let us recall that in virtually every instance the "mystical interludes" which James reports in his *Varieties of Religious Experience*[3] are accompanied by a degree of mental and muscular relaxation. "Suddenly," writes Symonds, "at church, or in company, or when I was reading, and always, I think, when my muscles were at rest, I felt the approach of the mood." Dr. Burke's "enlightenment" transpires as he sits calmly in his hansom driving home after a strenuous evening of philosophical discussion. Mr. Trine's "mystical policeman" invariably undergoes his alteration when he has just gone "off duty" and is "on the way home in the evening." The "loveliness of the morning" comes over Mr. Trevor when he is no longer experiencing the unpleasant obligation to attend a church service in the company of his "wife and boys." To "go down there to the chapel, would be for the time an act of spiritual suicide." Kingsley's "mystical consciousness" is awakened as he "walks in the fields" without purpose or aim. Nor can we fail to recall that Horton's (1974) patient whose "mystical experiences" I touched upon earlier is sitting quietly in church when her "change" occurs.

Everywhere in the religious and meditative literature one discovers similar clues. "There is a state of mind, known to religious men, but to no others," writes James ([1902] 1958, p. 53), "in which the will to assert ourselves... has been displaced by a willingness to close our mouths and be as nothing in the floods and waterspouts of God." In such a state of mind, "what we most dreaded has become the habitation of our safety.... The time for tension in our soul is over and that of happy relaxation, of calm, deep breathing, of an eternal present, with no discordant future to be anxious about, has arrived." According to the Chinese text, *The Awakening of Faith* (cf. Huxley 1970, p. 290), the individual who proposes to "stop" his ordinary thoughts and to achieve thereby another kind of awareness must "retire to some quiet place and there, sitting erect, earnestly seek to tranquillize and concentrate the mind." "All our actions must be devoted, in the last analysis," writes Huxley (1970, p. 165), "to making ourselves passive in relation to the activity and the being of divine Reality." "Zazen practice for the student," writes Kapleau (1973, p. 238), "begins with his counting the inhalations and exhalations of his breath while he is in the motionless zazen posture. This is the first step in the process of stilling the bodily functions."

According to the Lama Govinda (cf. Kapleau 1973, p. 238), "from this state of perfect mental and physical equilibrium and its resulting inner harmony grows that serenity and happiness which fills the whole body with a feeling of supreme bliss." "Good and bad is not the point," writes the Zen master, Shunryu Suzuki (1973, p. 128), "whether or not you make yourself peaceful is the point, and whether or not you persist to do so." And indeed, as Goleman points out (1977, p. xxiv), the majority of meditative "schools" strive to induce in the "seeker" a "happy" or "positive" change of awareness by helping him to achieve a state of "relaxation," of "composure" and "peace." Nor is the psychiatric literature without significance on this score: Stanley Dean's *Psychiatry and Mysticism* (1975), a book which strives to position "practice" squarely within the purview of the scientific, psychological community as a salubrious aspect of human behavior, devotes many of its pages to the central importance of the "relaxation response" in the attainment of therapeutic progress. It would appear, in fact, that an altered state of consciousness can arise quite naturally from a relaxed condition. Why should this be so? Because the process of infantile "conversion" is a *bodily* process. The infant and young child who takes in the object experiences that object in his body, in his anxious respiration, in his posture of avoidance, in his stiff, contracted frustration and rage. The splitting and divisiveness of the early time transpire within the cells of the organism, only later to be "elevated" to the level of symbolical representation. But even when anxiety, tension, and divisiveness are "raised" to the symbolic level, they still retain their hold upon the body; they still exist, as persistently and as powerfully as ever, in the individual's "length of blood and bone."

To "empty" or to "tranquillize" the mind is to empty or to "tranquillize" the body precisely because the symbol, with its time and space, is rooted in the body, grows out of the body, is but a "higher" development of bodily awareness. We grasp from this perspective the psychodynamic significance of recent experiments with individuals in the midst of meditative trances, experiments which establish not only a significant rise in "skin resistance," a sign of diminishing anxiety, but also a significant drop in lactate production and consequently in the blood-lactate level. Wallace and Benson (1972, p. 131) suggest in the face of these results that meditation "generates an integrated response, or reflex, that is mediated by the central nervous system. A well-known reflex of such a nature was described many years ago by the noted Harvard physiologist Walter B. Cannon; it is called the "'fight or flight' or 'defense alarm' reaction." The excited sympathetic nervous system "mobilizes a set of physiological responses marked by increases in the blood pressure, heart rate, blood flow to the muscles and oxygen consumption. The hypometabolic state produced by meditation is of course opposite to this in almost all respects." And then, "during man's early history the defense-alarm reaction may well have had high survival value."

What these authors miss is that each man's "early history" begins with his birth and infancy. The defence-alarm in question is triggered not only when the baby undergoes expulsion; it is triggered, to one degree or another, throughout the primary years, throughout the time in which the terrors of separation beset the child, throughout the time in which frustration and rage are upon him, in which he defensively internalizes the object, in which the entire "conversion" process transpires. In this way, the peaceful body one attains during meditation is the somatic equivalent of the empty mind. To relax is to stop one's "bodily thoughts," to sever the connection with the early period at the unconscious, bodily level, the level of physiological processes. That such relaxation should go hand in hand with an epistemic, or mental, alteration is perfectly natural when we recall that ordinary consciousness, in time and space and symbol, is the outgrowth of physical processes and the means of retaining the tie to the object within.

With regard more specifically to the rhythmic aspects of meditation which are manifested in the repetition of the "mantra" or in the concentration upon breathing, note that "rhythm has been universally recognized as a natural tranquillizer, with regularly repeated sounds or rhythmic movements spontaneously used . . . to quiet agitated infants." If "contacting deep biological rhythms in oneself is a prominent component of meditation, then regular meditation might be expected to have a deeply soothing effect" (Carrington 1982, p. 69). Such an effect has been measured in a wide variety of well-known studies, recounted by Walsh (1979, p. 166), in which the EEG patterns of meditators have displayed a considerably higher frequency of alpha waves than those of non-meditators. It is significant to observe in this connection that such frequency *increases* with practice (Walsh 1979, p. 166). Further studies also employing EEG measurements have suggested that meditative concentration promotes a synchronized or integrated functioning of the brain's right and left hemispheric lobes (Earle, 1981, p. 162). Summarizing the empirical research, Walsh (1982, p. 81) maintains that the benefits of practice may include "relaxation and global desensitization, deconditioning, behavioral reactivity, heightened awareness, behavioral self-control skills, and facilitation of psychological development and maturation," as well as "reduced arousal and hemispheric lateralization, and electroencephalographic resonance and coherence."

As for epistemic changes, they are obviously more difficult to measure, but there is a fascinating paper contributed by Brown and Engler (1980, p. 166) in which it is specified that advanced meditators responding to the Rorschach cards "actually witness energy/space in the moment-by-moment process of arising and organizing into forms and images; and conversely, witness the forms and images becoming absorbed back into energy/space." By contrast, meditators in the beginning stages respond with the customary projective versions of persons and objects, the "normal" situation. In my view, such a result not only supports Carrington's contention that meditation gives rise generally to a "withdrawal of projections" (Carrington 1982, p. 68), but deepens the meaning of Garfield's discovery that "long-term meditation" is an "effective tool" for the "reduction of the individual's level of death-fear" (Garfield 1975, p. 165). As already noted, the fear of death is inextricably tied to the traumata of the separation phase and in particular to the "bad object" that we internalize during that phase. At their deepest pathological ground, our projections are born here. Hence, to encourage an epistemic condition in which projections tend to be "withdrawn" is to encourage a state in which the fear of death will perforce be lessened. Can anyone fail to discern the importance of such a development for the human species, whose endless appetite for destruction and violence may well be rooted in its furious wish to deny the "reality" of a "death" that is unconsciously equated with the catastrophes of the infantile period?

A Systems Approach: The Primary and Secondary Process

My purpose in this section is to sharpen the theoretical picture presented thus far by focusing upon it the classical psychoanalytic distinction between the primary and secondary process, or the modes of mentation associated with those terms. I will avoid the endless controversy that swirls about this aspect of psychoanalytic thought[4] and simply render the distinction as it emerges from the work of Rogers (1978, p. 18). "The primary process," he writes, "operates mainly in the service of the id as a mode of discharging free, mobile psychic energy. It employs a crude, analogical, associative form of symbolism in a magical, wishful fashion without regard for ordinary reality, time, space, and logical consistency. While the mentation itself may be conscious, its sources are apt to be dynamically repressed." Primary process thinking is frequently associated with the symbols, or the "language" of dreams. "The secondary process," Rogers goes on, "operates mainly in the service of the ego. The psychic energy at its disposal is bound, or neutralized, or sublimated energy. As a mode of expression it is rational, conceptual, analytical. It utilizes higher, more abstract forms of discourse such as conventional lexical language and standardized mathematical signs." The work of art or literature stands somewhere in between the primary and secondary process, incorporating the intuitive and symbolic features of the unconscious, fantasy, and the dream into an ordered, structured framework that "makes sense" at the "higher" perceptual levels of reason and morality.

Rogers, in a subsequent discussion (1980, pp. 5, 14–15), takes the emphasis off the energic model and writes that "Freud's insights into the bimodal nature of mentation need to be incorporated into a computer model involving hierarchical structures of routines and subroutines with storage and retrieval systems consonant with contemporary perspectives on the complexity of brain functioning," and further, that "redefining the primary and secondary processes as information processes by replacing Freud's energy matrix with an informational one strips away the problematics of Freud's dynamic perspective with its crude, closed-system hydraulics, and in one bold stroke eliminates endless possibilities for confusion inherent in such Procrustean dichotomies as Thing versus Word and Reality versus Pleasure." Now, when we recall the manner in which the object of the early period is taken into "the ego," when we recall, in short, the extent to which the ego harbors the unconscious (the so-called id of the "primary process") we begin to see the direction from which "perceptive mind-rest" derives its therapeutic and philosophic significance.

In the achievement of this condition as defined in previous sections (moderation of the tie to the internalized object) the secondary process is quieted, even stilled. Hence, its insidious infusion of conflicted unconscious contents into the waking state—primarily through language—is curtailed. The loaded ego is allowed release from the "normal" perceptual activities which reactivate internalized materials precisely because such materials were internalized into a "perceptual apparatus" that is synonymous with the ego itself. In addition, while the discursive proclivity is diminished, and while the proximity to the primary process is correspondingly increased, one remains psychologically removed from that actual process. One enjoys the advantages of increased intuitiveness, increased freedom from the stress of ordinary time and space, increased access to the perceptive realm of the body, and to the fluid sources of fantasy and wishing. Yet one maintains his existence in a high state of mind in which the primary and secondary processes fuse but without the words and signs of the secondary process linking the individual to the transitional preoccupations of the early period and the "crude symbols" of the primary process drifting in from deeper levels with raw, reactivated "associations."

The customary, forced separation of these "realms" is relaxed, and from this derives the relaxation of "practice," of the "empty mind." It is as if the traditional "schools" have contrived to give the individual who successfully negotiates the methodology the psychic and physiological advantages of both the primary and secondary realms without the disadvantages that derive from each as each is experienced in isolation, or relative isolation, from the other—the "normal" state of affairs. Surely one can see here new potentialities for the meaning of "integration." That is, the isolation of the primary and secondary realms is the isolation of the individual from aspects of his existence which do not "go together" in the normative, acculturated world, the world of ordinary, everyday awareness—not to mention the world of what Lewis Mumford (1967) might call "the mechanized modern order." As for the apparent similarity of the altered state to the state of artistic creation and/or response, it is destroyed by an over-riding consideration crucial to the discussion as a whole. While both states do exist somewhere between the primary and secondary processes, the altered one exists there without the identification, the devotion to symbols, that permits the universe of art to function and that keeps the beholder of the artistic object tied to the objects of his inner world: identification and symbolism are rooted in internalization.

All of this bears crucially upon the recent shift in psychological and philosophical circles toward an informational or "systems" approach to human behavior. "There is an elaborate and subtle information network and feedback relationship between the outer world and the programs whose activity corresponds to the world of personal psychological experience," writes Peterfreund (1971, pp. 159–60). "Evolutionists have recently become increasingly aware of the complex feedback relationship between organism and environment." The point is, the achievement of perceptive mind-rest alters the manner in which we receive and process the sensorial "data." *It alters the feedback system at its ground.* The "perceptual apparatus" is opened because the internalized presences through which it established and maintained its power are without their implacable, customary rigor, their drive to maintain identity, or ego-identity, by governing the channels and modes of perception. Peterfreund (1971, pp. 121 360) reminds us in another place that the "information" which "impinges" upon people from the "outer world" is "paralleled" in the organism by specific "psychological experiences." Moreover, "in all biological systems every stimulus can be initially processed only by existing programs." The "learning of the past is always 'displaced' onto the stimuli of the present . . . information from the stimulus is classified by these old programs." And then, "almost every human relationship seems to reveal something akin to psychoanalytic transference phenomena."

Accordingly, detachment in the hard, perceptual sense diminishes the tendency to see the world through an unconscious filter loaded with the narcissistic injuries, vengeful hostilities, and schizoid inclinations of the early period precisely because the ambivalent object is taken into the perceptual system "automatically" by the organism's drive to internalize its surroundings and, hence, to forge its symbolical world. Here, of course, psychological and epistemological meanings come firmly together. Suzanne Langer (1942, Chapter 10) has written that in the understanding of symbols emotion and knowledge unite in a way that is characteristic of human perception. Shall we say *ordinary* human perception? For in the altered state of mind, emotion and knowledge unite in the putting off of the symbolical mode. Ties to the inner world are loosened. What is there in the universe is permitted to be there—just there.

This model, of course, is a verbal one, but as Bertalanffy (1968, p. 24) points out, "models in ordinary language have their place in systems theory." A "verbal model is better than no model at all, or a model which, because it can be formulated mathematically, is forcibly imposed upon and falsifies reality. Theories of enormous influence such as psychoanalysis were unmathematical or, like the theory of selection, their impact far exceeded mathematical constructions which came only later and cover only . . . a small fraction of empirical data." Whether or not "mathematical constructions" will ever characterize the psychodynamics of perceptive mind-rest is entirely a matter of speculation at this stage. If it does come to pass, however, and if it serves some useful purpose, the distinction between transitional and non-transitional states will be as crucial to the presentation as the distinction between positive and negative integers is to the theory of numbers.

Once again Bertalanffy (1968, pp. 55–56) helps underscore a fundamental point. "A system can be defined," he writes, "as a set of elements standing in interrelations. Interrelation means that elements, P, stand in relations, R, so that the behaviour of an element P in R is different from its behaviour in another relation, R^1. If the behaviours in R and R^1 are not different, there is no interaction, and the elements behave independently with respect to the relations R and R^1." Explicitly with reference to the interrelation of elements, the "change" achieved through transitional (or regressive) religious experience, which can be called R, must be distinguished from the condition of altered awareness achieved through non-transitional (or rational) practice, which can be called R^1. *The former leaves the object in the percept while the latter gets it out,* and because the latter gets it out, the "perceptual apparatus" as a whole is modally transformed. The generality of this approach must not deter us; on the contrary, as Bertalanffy (1968, pp. 99–100) says, it is the "changes in the general frame of reference that matter." A new definition of "objectivity" constructed along these lines may help us to survive our current technological age, which devotes itself to the pursuit of a scientific "objectivity" that is totally purblind to the psychological object which lurks within its projective, pathogenic activities.

Old Play, New Play

It was suggested during the discussion of Ashtanga Yoga ("Perceptive Mind-Rest," pp. 60–63) that rigorous practice may culminate in the ability to "don the ego and to put it off, like a suit of clothes." Let us conclude this chapter by focusing on this notion from a fresh psychoanalytic perspective.

As we have seen, separation from the caregiver sparks anxiety in the child, anxiety that is offset by substitute objects. In Winnicott's words, the "good-enough mother" begins by adapting almost completely to the "infant's needs" (1971, pp. 12–14). As time goes on, "she adapts less and less completely . . . according to the infant's growing ability to deal with her failure" through his own "experience." If "all goes well," the infant can actually "gain" from his "frustration" by developing his own idiosyncratic style of relative independence. What is essential is that the mother give the baby, through her "good-enough" care, the *"illusion* that there is an external reality that corresponds to the infant's own capacity to create." It is precisely within this area of "creativity" that the infant will begin to make his "transition" away from the maternal figure by choosing "transitional objects" — blankets, teddy bears, story-books — which afford him the "magical" or "illusory" belief that he is moving *toward,* or staying *with,* the caretaker *at the same time that he is moving away from her or giving her up.* Such "magic," such "illusion," such "creativity," provides the child with his primary link to the *cultural* realm, to the religious, artistic, and scientific symbols that comprise the shared, "illusory reality" of grown-ups in general. The "matter" of "illusion," writes Winnicott (1971, p. 15), "is one that belongs inherently to human beings and that no individual finally solves for himself or herself." The "task of reality-acceptance is never completed. . . . No human being is free from the strain of relating inner and outer reality." It is the "intermediate area of experience" including "arts, religion, etc." that provides "relief from this strain" and that is "in direct continuity with the play area of the small child who is 'lost' in play." In this way, there is a "direct development from transitional phenomena to playing, and from playing to shared playing, and from this to cultural experience" (p. 60). I come now to the nub of the issue.

In order to "get the idea of playing," it is "helpful to think of the preoccupation that characterizes the playing of a young child. The content does not matter. What matters is the *near-withdrawal state,* akin to the *concentration* of older children and adults" (ibid.; emphasis added). Playing "involves the body," is "inherently exciting and precarious," and transpires amid the "experience" of a "non-purposive state" which is characterized, above all, by "relaxation" (pp. 60–61, 64). It is "only in playing," Winnicott concludes, that the "child or adult" is "free to be creative" and that the "world" he inhabits becomes "invested" with a "first-time-ever quality." Can anyone fail to note the striking analytic connection between these materials and the techniques involved in achieving the perceptive mind-rest with which we have been concerned?

The concentrative meditator returns in his body, mind, and *method* to the origin of that illusory, egotic "world," that illusory, egotic *dwelling place,* which inherited the anxiety and stress of the early period and served as a "magical" substitute for the lost object. His aim is not "regression." It is *deconstruction.* He retraverses the actual steps he took in fashioning his substitutive universe, his perceptual realm of "away from" and "toward," in order to shed the mind-body tension, or the "strain" to use Winnicott's word, that perforce accompanied the formation of that universe, that realm. Anxious, egotic "gripping," as well as illusory "creations," is consciously, knowingly, intentionally replaced with deep relaxation, deep letting go, and an "empty" or clear, non-projective perception of the external, "separate" environment. In a nutshell, the concentrative meditator *plays with the play that magically and stressfully filled the gap left by the absent object.* He plays with the play that culminated in our ordinary consciousness, and in doing this he not only fulfils, finally, his highest, grown-up "capacity to create" but "invests" his world with a "first-time-ever quality."

This, ultimately, is what it means in psychoanalytic terms to attain the ability to "don the ego and to put it off, like a suit of clothes." We go back not to deny, or hide, or cling, but to *master,* to place the realm of "magic," symbols, projections, more squarely in the sphere of our will, to break the deadly spell of that *serious play* which forged the ordinary cultural world and ourselves as part of it. And that, after all, is the irony. For all of its "magic," for all its "illusion," for all its "creativity," our ordinary, normative play *is* terribly serious, at least in large measure *if only because it was goaded into life by the serious problem of separation.* Thus it underlies our *serious* religion, our *serious* music and literature, our *serious* devotion to the symbols of the market-place, to money and influence and corporate power, our *serious* technology, our dangerous "game" of weapons, and nations, and territories. Because the normative play described by Winnicott is "directly linked" to the "bad" as well as to the "good" object, because it is the outgrowth of an *ambivalent* early experience loaded with anxiety, frustration, and hatred as well as with security and bliss, it is as much a source of our "discontent" as of our pleasure. We are never free of the "strain" because we are always somewhere in between, seeking on the one hand to *have* the object and on the other to retaliate and destroy it. This is our present perceptive, emotive, evolutional condition. This is "man."

Virtually every aspect of playing presented in Huizinga's classic *Homo Ludens* (1950) has its serious, indeed its grievous side, from the combatants in battle to the contestants in court. As Huizinga (1950, p. 95) puts it, "blood can flow." It is not a happy picture. Yet there are hints in Huizinga (pp. 12, 22) of the kind of play I am recommending here, the kind that brings "ordinary life" to a "standstill," that "abolishes the world." To grasp such "abolition" fully we must keep in mind the crucial philosophical difference that exists between simply meditating and *thinking about* the meditating that one is doing and has done (Gimello 1978, p. 189). In its complete, epistemic development the perceptive mind-rest I am depicting does not merely allow one to "play" with "ordinary play" but to detach oneself *perceptively* from an entire mode of perception, to *see* the way in which one *sees*—in a word, to reach what Gregory Bateson (1980, p. 210) calls a new "level of logical typing" from which to discern the "realities" of everyday behavior and consciousness.

It is both encouraging and fascinating to note in this regard the enormous, unactualized potential of people to do this. A recent study of 1,500 "normal" or "representative" American adults, for example, revealed that nearly 600 persons, or two-fifths of the sample, replied positively when asked whether or not they had "ever had the feeling of being very close to a powerful spiritual force that seemed to lift [them] out of [themselves]?" (Greeley and McCready 1979, p. 179). About 300 persons said "they had had it several times," and about seventy-five said "they had had it often." Obviously the reply to such a query does not permit me to say "for sure" whether or not an individual has undergone a "mystical experience" in the classical sense of the term. Further research is required. It does permit me to suggest in a preliminary way, however, that "ordinary people" have the capacity, and perhaps the proclivity, to put off their "ordinary consciousness" in a rewarding, beneficial, *developable* manner.

Nor would I imply by this that "therapy" in the usual sense has become, or should become, superfluous. On the contrary, it will always be vital for people to analyze rigorously and at length the feelings, thoughts, and *words* which are connected integrally to their "neurotic" side, which reach back to the first, conflicted years of life, and which must be "abreacted" or "worked through" for release and change to occur. Frequently in reading the literature of altered awareness one comes upon the notion that "neurosis" is "unreal," a kind of "number" that one does on oneself. "Going into the turbulence of [our] emotions," declares Welwood (1979, p. 36), "is like entering the eye of a hurricane... if you really go into it there is nothing there." Because we are "complete and perfect from the beginning" (Kapleau 1965, p. 47), because the "self" does not "really" exist (Wilber 1977, p. 305), because "pure subjectivity" (Shannon 1981, p. 82) and "clear perception of the object" (Goleman 1981, p. 130) are simply "waiting there" for us to take them up, we have only to get on with the "atom-smashing" (Wilber 1982, p. 39) of ordinary consciousness to arrive at the desired goal.

The problem with such heady rhetoric, of course, is that something *is* "really there." The *internalized object* is there, as well as the "self" and the mind-body awareness that are grounded in that object "from the beginning." Far from being "complete and perfect," from possessing the capacity to simply adopt at will a "clear perception of the object," we are *loaded* with anxiety and stress from the start, and our "clear perception" will only come *after* we have acknowledged and honestly explored the unconscious *realities* of our "ordinary" lives. As Carrington (1982, p. 71) says, "meditation . . . can leave intact specific inner conflicts and their psychopathological solutions, even as it fosters positive personality traits on a more general level." Rather than comprising a panacea, then, or a magical epistemic formula for the attainment of "the truth," perceptive mind-rest constitutes one essential prong in a two-pronged assault on the distortions and discontentments that inhere in our normative manner of perceiving and being-in the world. Analysis alone will not foster the relaxation and detachment required in the mind *and the body*. Detachment and relaxation alone will not foster the analysis required in the emotions *and the mind*. Kipling once wrote that "east was east" and "west was west" and "never the twain shall meet." One can hope that, at some point in the not-too-distant future of our planet, they shall meet, knowledgeably, and bear lasting fruit.

4
FREUD, THE STRUCTURAL THEORY, AND PERCEPTION

I want in this chapter to explore those works of Freud which are generally considered to represent his final position, the position that shifted the emphasis of psychoanalysis away from instinct and repression and toward the problems of anxiety and ego development. My purpose in doing this is to demonstrate that Freud stood upon the verge of a truly perceptual psychology within the framework of the structural theory itself, that he was close, very close, to the view generated here, and that we can in a theoretical, or perhaps hypothetical way, complete certain tendencies in his work by adding to it insights recently gained and thus permit a new psychoanalysis of perception to emerge from its developmental ground.

Freud's early and overwhelming interest in perceptual matters has been scrutinized by such psychoanalytic writers as Rapoport (1960), Strachey (1966), Pribram and Gill (1976), Sulloway (1983), and Ricoeur (1970). What emerges from their work is the widely accepted notion that Freud's early efforts to create a neuronic, physiological psychology of perception along energic lines gave way gradually (and incompletely) to his tendency to create a structural model of psychological behavior along predominantly motivational lines. The marked disagreements among the authors cited relate, on the one hand, to the extent to which Freud's early physiological writings contain purely psychological problems and solutions, and on the other hand, to the degree to which his physiological bent persists into the productions of his later years. I will not detail these disagreements here. I will stress, however, that all the writers mentioned obscure the most remarkable aspect of the structural theory itself, namely its persistent, implicit suggestion that matters of motivation (unconscious and otherwise) are tied to perceptual elements which cannot be distinguished from psychological structures as we know them. To put the entire business differently, not only are Freud's theories of anxiety and ego development — the heart of his final position — quite as perceptual in their ultimate significance as the explicit, physiological, perceptual theories of his *Project* of 1895, but this notable, revealing fact has been hidden by the accepted opinion that Freud moved away from perceptual matters as his ideas underwent their growth. The argument to follow will highlight the issues presented in the first three chapters in this book. It will italicize further the dangers and weaknesses of our current "ego psychology" which, I repeat, distorts the spirit and nature of Freud's endeavors. And it will anticipate the subsequent chapters of the discussion by focusing explicitly upon epistemological problems as they turn up in Freud's writings.

The Unconscious Ego

Freud wrote *The Ego and the Id* ([1923] 1974, p. 7)[1] with a growing realization that it was not merely the id, or the instincts, which "held" the unconscious, irrational side of man, but that the ego itself was in part an unconscious, irrational entity: "We have come upon something in the ego itself which is also unconscious, which behaves exactly like the repressed — that is, which produces powerful effects without itself being conscious and which requires special work before it can be made conscious. From the point of view of analytic practice, the consequence of this discovery is that we land in endless obscurities and difficulties if we keep to our habitual forms of expression and try, for instance, to derive neuroses from a conflict between the conscious and the unconscious. We shall have to substitute for this antithesis another, taken from our insight into the structural conditions of the mind — the antithesis between the coherent ego and the repressed which is split off from it" (p. 7). And again, in an even more dramatic utterance: "We recognize that the unconscious does not coincide with the repressed; it is still true that all that is repressed is unconscious, but not all that is unconscious is repressed. A part of the ego, too — and Heaven knows how important a part — may be unconscious, undoubtedly is unconscious" (p. 8).

Thus the "characteristic of being unconscious begins to lose significance for us" (p. 8). The ego, then, is not partly and insignificantly unconscious; it is partly and significantly so. Indeed, so fraught with unconscious materials are our ego processes, our so-called conscious states, that the crucial distinction between conscious and unconscious begins to lose its meaning. Yet there is far more to be digested here. Not only does "the act of perception tell us nothing of the reason why a thing is or is not perceived" (p. 5), but "perception" itself "plays the part for the ego which in the id falls to instinct" (p. 15). Clearly, Freud is extraordinarily close to realizing that the very "perceptual apparatus" we rely on is, in its *perceptual workings,* a vehicle for *dynamic, unconscious processes.* Because we perceive the world loaded with unconscious materials our instrument of "rationality" is not so "rational" after all—unless one means to correlate the rational with what is derived from the realm of the unconscious, which would be the final absurdity of those who will save reason at all costs.

The significance of the point that perceptual processes are linked to the ego in the same way that instinctual processes are linked to the id simply cannot be overemphasized. If Freud is shifting to an ego psychology he is also shifting, or perhaps in some sense returning, to a perceptual psychology, for the ego and the percept are as integrally bound together as are the id and the instinct. Moreover, when we realize, by recalling the opening sections of this book which deal with the recent discoveries of psychoanalysis, that internalization is occurring from the inception of human life and that the object of the early period is taken into the perceptual system and hence into the ego, which becomes tied forever to that very system, we realize that the unconscious part of the ego of which Freud says, "Heaven knows how important it is," consists precisely of the primary object. In other words, the object that enters the infant's "dawning psyche," that comes to be inextricably associated with the infant's reception of stimuli, to be fused with all his sensorial modalities, forges not only the tie between the percept and the ego, but the tie between the percept, the unconscious, and the ego.

What prevented Freud from taking the matter all the way, from identifying the relationship of perception to neurosis? "Whatever the character's later capacity for resisting the influences of abandoned object-cathexes may turn out to be," he writes in one place, "the effects of the first identifications made in earliest childhood will be general and lasting. This leads us back to the origin of the ego ideal; for behind it there lies hidden an individual's first and most important identification, his identification with his father in his own personal history" (p. 21). He then goes on: "At a very early age the little boy develops an object-cathexis for his mother, which originally related to the mother's breast and is the prototype of an object-choice on the anaclitic model; the boy deals with his father by identifying with him" (ibid.). The point is, Freud will *not* accord the mother a *structural* place in his developmental scheme. What the infant human organism experiences in its first relationship with the maternal figure is described as an "object-cathexis." Only later, in the relationship with the father, does internalization occur. Thus perception is left neutral at the start. And as perception cannot be divorced from the ego any more than instinct can be divorced from the id, the ego too is left neutral at the start. Manifesting his persistent, well-known tendency to place the father at the centre of things and to back away from a close, detailed exploration of the mother's interaction with the infant, Freud quite simply misses the decisive structural events of the early period, including, of course, the "conversion" (cf. Chapter 2) which impinges decisively upon our ordinary perception of the world.

Precisely the same difficulty stands behind Freud's persistent, lifelong preoccupation with the problem of anxiety. He talks in this book of the ego's "dependent relationships" (p. 47) and designates the ego as anxiety's "actual seat" (p. 47). He then discovers the source of anxiety in the ego's fear of doing that which will alienate the superego, which will cause the ego to lose the "love" of the "conscience" (pp. 46–47). Behind the fear of the superego, however, there lies another, deeper dread, namely that of castration; it is "the nucleus around which the subsequent fear of conscience has gathered" (p. 47). Yet this is not the end. For when the dependent human ego feels unloved by the superego, when it feels a lack of protection and approval provided during the early period by "the father" [!] (p. 48), it is experiencing an anxiety that recalls not only "the first great anxiety-state of birth" but the "anxiety due to separation from the protecting mother" (ibid.). Thus for the ego "living means the same as being loved" (ibid.).

One feels that Freud, at this point, would be *obliged* to recognize the decisive structural role of the maternal object in the perceiving ego's development. Surely if the fear of separation from the mother resides etiologically at anxiety's very ground the mother's relation to the "dependent ego" is a genuine, structural one, is more than an "object-cathexis." Yet in the very next sentence, the one which follows his declaration that anxiety's ground is separation from the mother, Freud asserts that "the fear of conscience," like "the fear of death," must be regarded as "a development of the fear of castration" (ibid.), and we are back to the fundamental importance of the paternal figure who does the castrating. Freud simply cannot, or will not, break through. He simply cannot, or will not, make the structrual connection between the profound observation that "to the ego living means being loved" and the equally profound observation that "separation from the mother" is anxiety's source, for such a connection would oblige him to root the ego structurally in the first great tie of life, the tie to the mothering figure. It would oblige him to see in the infant's first relationship to his primary object considerably more than the postulated "object-cathexis." In a word, it would oblige him to see internalization transpiring *before* the "identification with the father."

Which brings us to a central observation: if perception is to the ego what instinct is to the id, and if the ego is structurally grounded in the primary relationship to the mother, then it is not merely "living" that means "being loved" to the ego, *perceiving itself means being loved.* That is what Freud could not see, and that is why he failed to make explicit the perceptual implications of his "ego" psychology. Ordinary consciousness is the human animal's principal method of maintaining his libidinal tie to the maternal presence and has, accordingly, transitional implications. It is not the love of the superego which our perceiving egos crave at the deepest level. It is the love of that structural unit which was internalized into the perceptual system at the very beginning. It is the love of that structural unit out of which our love for the superego arose. "The later, oedipal conflict," writes Swan (1974, p. 33), "appears to be the development of a conflict already shaped in an earlier mother-infant relationship." Freud's re-emphasis upon "castration" as the crucial element in "anxiety" and "conscience" (pp. 48–49) witnesses his need to ground our being in phallic objects, not in the vagina and the womb. It may be noted parenthetically that in *The New Introductory Lectures on Psychoanalysis* ([1932] 1953, pp. 86–87) Freud again stresses the fear of castration as the source of anxiety. Here, however, he goes further and suggests that even the desire to return to the womb is ultimately a phallic wish in disguise, that is, a wish for copulation with the mother.

The Link to Ordinary Consciousness

To leave perception neutral at the start, to locate the beginnings of internalization in the Oedipal stage of development, expresses not only Freud's struggle to stay with the father, to avoid too close a contact with the maternal realm, it also expresses his struggle to stay with a guiding rationalism that he is perilously close to relinquishing here. Even to admit that the ego, the very instrument of perception, contained at some level, at some stage, unconscious, irrational elements must have been troublesome, perhaps terrible, for one who relied entirely on science and reason, who rejected the occult, who rejected religion, who made the goal of his psychology the replacement of the id with the ego ("Where id was, there ego shall be" [Freud (1932) 1953, p. 80]). To discover internalization at the start, internalization of a maternal object into a kind of proto-ego which cannot be divorced from the "perceptual apparatus," would mean to relinquish reason as a trustworthy guide altogether. To leave the ego and the "perceptual apparatus" intact until later, until the period in which internalization brings the superego into the picture and hence the distortion of perception through guilt, is to preserve a last little bit of rationality for the system because the guilt might possibly be gotten out through psychotherapy.

Freud's analysis of words, of memory, and of hallucination illustrates the matter perfectly. While he concentrates upon words in *The Ego and the Id,* and while he sees in words "mnemic residues" (p. 10) of previous developmental stages (thus does the ego "carry" the unconscious), he is simply in no position to grasp the crucial affective connection between the development of language and the problem of internalization, for language begins early and is structural, whereas internalization begins late, in the identification with the father. In this way, Freud is unable to recognize in the very employment of language a method of preserving the tie to the significant other. He writes: "We think of the mnemic residues as being contained in systems which are directly adjacent to the system *Perception-Consciousness,* so that the cathexis of those residues can readily extend from within on to the elements of the latter system. We immediately think here of hallucinations, and of the fact that the most vivid memory is always distinguishable both from a hallucination and from an external perception; but it will also occur to us at once that when a memory is revived the cathexis remains in the mnemic system, whereas a hallucination, *which is not distinguishable from a percep-*

tion, can arise when the cathexis does not merely spread over the memory trace on to the *perceptual* element, but passes over to it *entirely"* (p. 10, my emphasis).

When we recall that ordinary perceptual consciousness, including the employment of language therein, is ultimately forged in and through the internalizations of the early period, and particularly in and through the internalization of the infant's primary, imperfect object, we recognize that ordinary perceptual consciousness is itself fated to contain "hallucinatory" features. Because it "automatically" reactivates the object through its very use of words which contain "mnemic residues" at the elemental, structural level, such consciousness will reside somewhere between "objectivity," that is, perception which is not influenced by the dynamic presence of the object in the "apparatus," and "hallucination," that is, perception in which the "mnemic trace" (of the object) *entirely* controls the perceptual event. This is, of course, merely a way of underscoring Freud's own point that all perception (in ordinary reality) is significantly projective in nature (cf. Ornston 1978).

The Persistence of Infantile Anxiety

With *Inhibitions, Symptoms, and Anxiety* ([1926] 1959, p. 18)[2] Freud's gradual shift toward a perceptual perspective within the structural theory takes a further turn. Not only is perception to the ego what instinct is to the id, but the ego's "intimate connections with the perceptual system" actually "constitute its essence." In this way, we grasp the manner in which Freud's developing thought impels us toward the realization that anxiety, which makes the ego its "actual seat," *makes the perceptual system its actual seat.* The "love" the ego equates with "life" is inextricably connected to the mode of perception in which the ego is "constituted," a symbolic, internalizing mode that, because it preserves the tie to the object within, also preserves the anxiety associated with the negative, "bad" aspects of that tie. What is of particular interest here is the manner in which Freud adumbrates what I have chosen to call (following Winnicott) the transitional side of the issue.

He writes, "with what tenacity the ego clings to its relations to reality and to consciousness, employing all its intellectual faculties to that end—and indeed how the very process of thinking becomes hypercathected and eroticized" (p. 45). When we rid this passage of its dualism, when we remember that "reality" and "consciousness" are inseparable from the ego and from the object of the early time, when we recall that "reality" is not simply given but made, made defensively along specific psychobiological lines that characterize the human organism's method of coping with separation, we are in a position to appreciate what Freud is sensing here, namely the way the ego "clings" to its manner of perceiving the world. For once again, we cannot split the ego off from its perceptions. The ego "clings" not to "reality," but to an aspect of itself, an aspect that cannot be differentiated modally from the internalized object of the primary years.

Nor are transitional implications lacking in Freud's explicit treatment of the maternal figure's etiological role. "In man and the higher animals," he states, "the act of birth, as the individual's first experience of anxiety, has given the affect of anxiety certain characteristic forms of expression" (p. 19). Having acknowledged the connection of anxiety to the womb, however, Freud immediately warns us not to place "undue stress" on it. "Biological necessity demands that a situation of danger should have an affective symbol" (p. 20). Yet the word "symbol" alerts us at once to the structural possibility. In another place he declares: "I have no intention of asserting that every later determinant of anxiety completely invalidates the preceding one. It is true that, as the development of the ego goes on, the earlier danger-situations tend to lose their force and to be set aside, so that we might say that each period of the individual's life has its appropriate determinant of anxiety. . . . Nevertheless, all these danger-situations and determinants of anxiety can persist side by side and cause the ego to react to them with anxiety at a period later than the appropriate one; or, again, several of them can come into operation at the same time" (pp. 67–68). While the emphasis upon castration, so conspicuous in *The Ego and the Id* (and in the later *New Introductory Lectures*) is diminished considerably with this passage, Freud must still offer *some* qualification of the matter. Not surprisingly, yet ever so erroneously, it is women who are singled out as most vulnerable to the transitional dilemma. It is women, not men, in whom "the danger-situation of loss of object seems to have remained the most effective" (p. 69). Recent clinical analyses, such as those of Robert Stoller (1974), appear to suggest the very opposite.

What We Call Normalcy

I can indicate now the full significance, for me, of Freud's declaration that "anxiety" is "the fundamental phenomenon" and "the main problem of neurosis" (p. 70). Because the ego is anxiety's "actual seat" and because perception "constitutes" the ego's very "essence," the "funda-mental phenomenon" and "the main problem of neurosis" is as much our perception as it is our anxiety. Indeed, our anxiety is our perception to a degree hitherto unrecognized by the psycholanalytic community. What this implies, of course, is that our ordinary consciousness—our ordinary, clinging, egotic consciousness, structurally developed during the period in which "loss of object" predominated as anxiety's source—comprises in itself a psychological disturbance of quantita-tively and qualitatively critical importance. Can such an implication be supported with Freud's own words? It certainly can. "Even a normal person," Freud maintains, strives "to keep away not only what is irrele-vant and unimportant, but, above all, what is unsuitable because it is contradictory. He is most disturbed by those elements which once belonged together but which have been torn apart in the course of his development.... Thus, in the normal course of things, the ego [our perceptual mode] has a great deal of isolating work to do" (p. 47). As for the neurotic, his ego is merely "more watchful" than that of the "normal" subject. The ego of the neurotic, Freud says, using a term which calls to mind the central role of the relaxation response in the development of perceptive mind-rest, "must not relax," but is "con-stantly prepared for a struggle" (p. 47). Yet there is more.

All people, writes Freud, are not merely "disturbed" in their perceiv-ing, anxious egos, they are actually psychologically defective in their composition, and their defect cannot be disassociated from the manner in which their egos, their perceptual modes of behavior, come about. A "causation of neuroses," Freud asserts, "resides in a defect of our men-tal apparatus which had to do with precisely its differentiation into an id and an ego, and which is therefore also attributable ultimately to the influence of the external world." And then, "in view of the dangers of external reality, the ego is obliged to guard against certain instinctual impulses in the id and to treat them as dangers. But it cannot protect itself from internal instinctual dangers as effectively as it can from some piece of reality that is not part of itself. Intimately bound up with the id as it is, it can only fend off an instinctual danger by restricting its own organization and by acquiescing in the formation of symptoms" (pp. 81–82). Can anyone fail to realize, after this, not only the theoretical weakness but the actual danger of our current "ego psychology" with its emphasis upon "adaptation" and the "conflict-free sphere of the ego"? How can there be a "conflict-free sphere" for an animal that is defective and disturbed? How can one successfully "adapt" such an animal to a "reality" the anxiety of which it actually fosters through the employment of its "perceptual apparatus," an apparatus, moreover, which cannot be differentiated from the "ego" upon which the analyst relies for his therapeutic progress? Why do the ego psychologists ignore this aspect of Freud's work? Why do they claim to have their foundations in Freud when they fail to confront his position on a matter vital to the overall theoretical picture? According to Freud himself, who takes a radical, uncompromising view of the issue, we are constitutionally unfit for a fully satisfying existence, and it is our mental apparatus (the ego) that stands behind the unfitness.

As it turns out, Freud's radical and essentially accurate rendering of the *condition humaine* is qualified decisively by two considerations; first, "reality" is in large measure made rather than given, and second, the ego, in its perceptual functions, is an open, not a closed, system. The "instinctual dangers" which, in Freud's view, oblige the ego to "restrict its organization" are not merely "instinctual" but egotic in nature as well. They are forged in and through the internalizations of the early period, which cannot be differentiated accurately from "instinct" and to which the ego "clings" perceptually in an effort to retain its security, its dependent, transitional bond. In this way, to alter one's perception in the restful, positive manner earlier described is to lessen those dangers, for it is ultimately one's mode of perception (or the "organization" of one's "ego") that keeps them, ironically and somewhat paradoxically, alive. Freud is virtually telling us here that our common or "normal" neurosis is a tragical dwarfing of our sensorial capacity: the ego which is "restricted" in its "organization" is, by Freud's own definition, precisely our "perceptual apparatus." Yet the "ego psychologists" are at no point in their writings concerned with the alteration of perception. The very source of the human animal's disturbance is simply ignored in spite of the fact that Freud makes anxiety the chief problem of neurosis, the ego the "seat" of anxiety, and the "perceptual apparatus" the "essence" of the ego! Everything is sacrificed to the passion for adjustment. Does the potential for sensorial liberation threaten a profession that has become closely bound up with the material successes of the establishment? Are "restricted" but "adjusted" egos in keeping with the order of the day? Perhaps. But what is certain in all of this is the impossibility of altering the ego in a happy human way without altering the mode of perception in a hard physical and

93

epistemological way. To do less is to return a disturbed animal *still disturbed* to a world that is already too full of disturbance.

Just after having depicted his "defect" in the "mental apparatus," Freud wrote, "further than this... our knowledge of the nature and causes of neurosis has not as yet been able to go" (p. 82). In another place he declared, "affective states have been incorporated in the mind as precipitates of primaeval traumatic experiences, and when a similar situation occurs they are revived like mnemic symbols" (p. 19). Thinking about the object of the early period and, above all, about its incorporation into the perceptual system, we realize that we are currently in a position to "go" a little "further" than Freud was "able to." We are capable of recognizing that ordinary, symbolic consciousness itself, our everyday mode of perceiving the world, is the "similar situation" that reactivates continuously those "primaeval traumatic experiences" which load our anxious egos.

There are, of course, epistemological implications in Freud's developing psychology of perception. How do they relate to those passages in his work which touch upon philosophical matters explicitly?

Philosophical Applications

When we take Freud's writings in their entirety, his views upon and his attitudes toward philosophical issues are far from consistent, indeed, may even be said to present themselves in a somewhat contradictory fashion. Ultimately, however, what he has to say on this score is of enormous interest and value. In spite of his schooltime ambition to become a philosopher himself, Freud often expresses a certain contempt for philosophy, as well as a certain haughty disinterest in its chief epistemological preoccupations. For example, in his *General Introduction to Psychoanalysis* ([1917] 1968, pp. 91, 102) he dubs those who cannot make head or tail of dreams because dreams do not "make sense," that is to say, those who refuse to try to interpret difficult mental operations, "philosophers." When it comes to the interpretation of dreams, Freud writes acidly, "of philosophy we have nothing to expect, unless it be a lofty repetition of the reproach that our object is intellectually contemptible." To the end of his life Freud was scornful of philosophy for its unwillingness to deal with any but conscious mental processes, as if they held the whole of mental life. But more of that later.

Freud addresses himself in *The Future of an Illusion* ([1927] 1953,

p. 102), written a decade after the material just cited, to the Kantian problem of the thing-in-itself—one epistemological preoccupation of modern philosophy—and has this to say: "The problem of the nature of the world irrespective of our perceptive mental apparatus is an empty abstraction without practical interest." So much for the thing-in-itself. Shortly before this, however, Freud does take time to indicate something of his view of perceptual matters, and his remarks are worth underscoring. He maintains, first, that "our organization, *i.e.* our mental apparatus, has been developed actually in the attempt to explore the outer world, and therefore it must have realized in its structure a certain measure of appropriateness." Of course this only leaves tantalizingly open the entire problem of perception and conversion, or that "defect in our mental apparatus" of which Freud spoke in *Inhibitions, Symptoms, and Anxiety,* one year before the publication of *The Future of an Illusion.* What is the "measure of appropriateness" in this "certain measure"? And if the "measure" is only a "certain" one, might there not be a portion of the "mental apparatus" that is inappropriate? The view of man which emerges from *The Future of an Illusion,* and from its companion piece, *Civilization and Its Discontents,* written a year or so later, a view which highlights dramatically the repressed, obsessive, superstitious, exploitative, narcissistic, and generally miserable condition of the species, hardly jibes with the notion of perceptive "appropriateness" expressed here. Indeed, had Freud concluded the opposite, as he does in *Inhibitions, Symptoms, and Anxiety,* that we appear to be somehow troubled in our "perceptual apparatus," he would have reached a conclusion considerably more in keeping with the picture of man that adorns *The Future of an Illusion.*

Having addressed himself to the problem of perceptual "appropriateness," Freud ([1927] 1953, pp. 101–2) makes a further point. Our "mental organization," he declares, is itself "a constituent part of that world which we are to investigate, and readily admits of such investigation." But this is only to italicize the issue, for it is the mind itself that is doing the investigating of the mind. Simply pushing the problem of self-reflection aside, Freud leaves us sitting squarely on the horns of the dilemma. Perhaps that is why he makes his next observation, namely that "the task of science is fully circumscribed if we confine it to showing how the world must appear to us in consequence of the particular character of our organization." But surely if a mind that has already been shaped by the nature of its experiences in the world—and what mind has not been thus shaped? — is employed "scientifically" to explore the nature of the mind's "particular organization," the results of "science," to put it as mildly as possible, are going to be suspect with regard to their "objectivity." Freud, apparently, is conscious of all this when he makes his final declaration that the "findings of science, just because of the way they are attained, are conditioned not only by our organization but by that which has affected this organization." However, this only makes the muddle worse. Freud takes up the problem of the thing-in-itself with considerably more success in other writings, to which I will turn momentarily.

New Objects, New Objectivity

In his ground-breaking essay, *On Narcissism* ([1914] 1971, pp. 53–54) Freud maintains that the early narcissistic wounds which attend the frustration of one's wish to possess the mother are assuaged partially through internalization of the paternal figure: by identifying with the father, by setting up an "ego-ideal" within, by striving to fulfil the goals of that ideal, in short, by becoming the hero of one's inner eye, one regains a measure of the narcissistic supplies lost in the defeats of childhood. Such an insight is astonishing; as well, it is an insight that has guided later investigators to the modern theory of narcissism, which also focuses upon internalization but which pushes the issue back to the very early periods of development and to the schizoid and aggressive inclinations that reside there. Of special importance to my present purpose is Freud's suggestion that as one begins to derive narcissistic gratification from fulfilment of mental goals, goals tied inextricably to the "ego-ideal," one begins not simply to eroticize mental functions but to feel ambivalent toward the demand for satisfactory performance which inheres in the relationship to the key internalization. He writes, "the revolt against this *censorial institution* springs from the person's desire . . . to liberate himself from all these influences, beginning with that of his parents. . . . His conscience then encounters him in a regressive form as a hostile influence from without."

This development, Freud asserts, helps us to grasp not only the psychodynamics of paranoia but the self-observation that comprises philosophy itself, and in particular the tendency to make philosophical systems: "The lament of the paranoiac shows also that at bottom the self-criticism of conscience is identical with, and based upon, self-observation. That activity of the mind which took over the function of the conscience has also enlisted itself in the service of introspection, which furnishes philosophy with the material for its intellectual operations. This must have something to do with the characteristic tendency of paranoiacs to form speculative systems." Freud's inclination to find something vaguely pathological in the philosopher's proclivity to construct world views may be simply a further expression of his own ambivalence toward philosophy as a whole. However, his recognition that the world of philosophy is integrally connected to internalization, that philosophizing and internalizing are somehow related, helps us to grasp the epistemological implications not merely of Freud's tendency, already explored, to make the internalizing ego the seat of our perceptions, but his explicit postulation of an inner world of objects with which philosophy must deal if it is to fulfil its ancient purpose of increasing our awareness: "Just as Kant warned us not to overlook the fact that our perception is subjectively conditioned and must not be regarded as identical with the phenomena perceived but never really discerned," he writes, "so psychoanalysis bids us not to set conscious perception in the place of the unconscious mental process which is its object."

And then, "the mental, like the physical, is not necessarily in reality just what it appears to us to be. It is, however, satisfactory to find that the correction of inner perception does not present difficulties so great as that of outer perception—that the inner object is less hard to discern truly than is the outside world" (Freud [1915] 1971, p. 104). As pointed out in the opening chapter of this book, Freud gives us in this passage (for the first time in western intellectual history) not merely two kinds of philosophical objects, those of the inner and those of the outer world, but an inner object with an unconscious, dynamic, perceptual dimension. Thus he points the way toward the epistemological synthesis, toward the unified philosophic and psychoanalytic understanding of our characteristic mode of "discerning" the universe, that I seek to fashion here.

The Impressionable Wax of Infancy

On one or two occasions Freud's philosophical bent, working harmoniously with his psychological interests, prompted him to offer theoretical descriptions of our perceptual mechanism in operation, descriptions which recall specific features of the *Project* of 1895. Presenting us with a "simple model" of a physical organism into which "stimuli" are received through a "shield" that is partially "protective" and partially "receptive," and building toward the crucial problem of inward contents which also "stimulate" the "perceptual apparatus," Freud writes in *Beyond the Pleasure Principle* ([1920] 1959, pp. 54–55), "we are today in a position to embark on a discussion of the Kantian theorem that time and space are 'necessary forms of thought.' We have learnt that unconscious mental processes are in themselves 'timeless.' This means . . . that they are not ordered temporally, that time does not change them in any way, and that the idea of time cannot be applied to them. . . . On the other hand, our abstract idea of time seems to be wholly derived from the method of working of the perceptual system and to correspond to a perception on its own part of that method of working." He then continues, in a vital utterance, "this sensitive cortex . . . which is later to become the system, Consciousness, also receives excitations from within. The situation of the system between the outside and the inside and the difference between the conditions governing the reception of excitations in the two cases have a decisive effect on the functioning of the system and of the whole mental apparatus. Towards the outside it is shielded against stimuli. . . . Towards the inside there can be no such shield; the excitations in the deeper layers extend into the system directly." A similar model is featured in Freud's short essay, *On the Mystic Writing-Pad,* published a few years after the remarks just examined.

Here Freud ([1925] 1959, pp. 179–80) has in mind the child's toy with which one writes upon a sheet of celluloid that is covered with waxed paper and that rests against a slab of wax. As one raises the paper the writing vanishes, although an impression of it is retained in the wax below. "I do not think it is too far-fetched," Freud maintains, "to compare the celluloid and waxed paper cover with the perceptual system and its protective shield, the wax slab with the unconscious behind them, and the appearance and disappearance of the writing with the flickering up and passing-away of consciousness in the process of perception." Freud goes on, "the cathectic innervations are sent out and withdrawn in rapid periodic impulses from within into the completely pervious system, Perception-Consciousness. So long as that system is cathected in this manner, it receives perceptions (which are accompanied by consciousness) and passes the excitation on to the unconscious mnemic systems; but as soon as the cathexis is withdrawn, consciousness is extinguished and the functioning of the system comes to a standstill." And finally, "it is as though the unconscious stretches out feelers, through the medium of the system Perception-Consciousness, toward the external world and hastily withdraws them as soon as they have sampled the excitations coming from it. . . . I further had a suspicion that this discontinuous method of functioning. . . lies at the bottom of the origin of the conception of time." Bearing in mind the theoretical simplicity of these models, a simplicity acknowledged by Freud himself, and recalling the crucial importance of the mother-infant symbiosis in the growth of the perceiving organism, we are in a position to make certain modifications to Freud's scheme which underscore from still another angle the central contentions of this chapter as a whole.

It is not a generalized "unconscious" that puts out "mental feelers" at the inception of the human organism's perceptual development. It is, rather, the vulnerable human infant that puts them out, that "cathects" the environment, most notably the mother, and that receives the object of the early time into its soft, "waxy," impressionable brain. In a very real sense, the "wax" on the "pad" is the brain's internalizing tendency, its inclination to retain the sensorial impression at levels which correspond to particular stages of growth, all the way from the neonate's "visceral brain" to the grown-up's "creative intellect." Forever tied to the perceptual system, forever a part of the perceiving ego, the infantile unconscious is imprinted from the beginning with the "excitations" that occur in the first, ambivalent relationship. It is these that "stimulate" the "perceptual apparatus" from "within," that link ego, perception, and inner object together. And it is these that fuse with our developing sense of time. As we have seen, "the infant's postponement of gratification from its mother's supplies is a trauma, and . . . residues of infantile reactions to this trauma can be found in the psychology of later years. . . . Time is subjectively experienced in terms of man's separation from the nourishing object, a traumatic event that dictates his defensive projections" (Schiffer 1978, pp. 11–12). By the time the individual has reached "maturity" the unconscious "feelers" he extends "toward the external world" and then "hastily withdraws" are loaded with transitional motivations derived directly from the early period and embedded in the "perceptual apparatus," the very "essence" of the anxious "ego." Those "feelers" emanate from a perceptive potentiality that has been egotically narrowed by the person's defensive reply to the traumas of infancy and childhood. The manner in which the "perceptual apparatus" works cannot be divorced from the manner in which "man" has responded to the disappointments — indeed the woes — of his experience. Just as all thought is not comprised in consciousness (one of Freud's favorite observations), all perception is not comprised in ordinary awareness.

Neural Nets and Internalized Objects

Freud's contempt for the "mystical," his tendency to reduce "oceanic feelings" of oneness with the world to regressive, "infantile" events, his inclination to create a father-centred, patriarchal psychology — these have of late been vigorously addressed in the literature. Deriving his inspiration from Freud's famous anxiety attack on the Acropolis, Irving Harrison (1979, pp. 411–18) points out that "even in the 1930's [Freud] had not taken the infant's early experiencings of its mother into account," but "stubbornly adhered to the assumption of an archaic heritage." In fact, Freud "ousted from the foreground . . . the role of the mother as experienced by the infant in relation to . . . 'limitless narcissism'." The "record suggests," Harrison writes in explanation of this, "that the mother-goddess of Freud's unconscious fantasy was closer to Ayesha of Haggard's novel (mentioned in Freud's associations to his dessicated pelvis dream) — all-giving, but possessive, mysterious and, ultimately, devouring and terrifying," than to the "all-good" mother-goddess of various myths and legends. Harrison concluded by noting "how tempting to any man harboring such latent potential for terrors and rages must be the mystical vision of regaining total bliss — of the ocean as womb! And psychoanalysis, for all its selective inattention to that theme, may have been born of Freud's resolute determination to resist just that temptation."

The point is, Freud's resistance to "religion," to the "mystical," to the "ocean" of life that resided within him, did not influence psychoanalysis as a discipline in a general way. With such key works as The Ego and the Id, Inhibitions, Symptoms, and Anxiety, Beyond the Pleasure Principle, and The Mystic Writing-Pad before us, we recognize that that "resistance" influenced psycholanalysis in such a way as to bring its founder struggling ambivalently toward a perceptual, structural psychology, toward a view in which the "chief problem of neurosis" is an

100

"anxiety" that is rooted in an "ego" which cannot be disassociated from the "perceptual apparatus," and concluding sadly that the entire problem must be attributed, deterministically and presumably unchangeably, to a "defect" in our psychological constitution. Had Freud been willing to enter the "oceanic" realm, to "take the infant's early experiencings of its mother into account," to accord the maternal figure a structural as opposed to a "cathectic" role in the development of mankind's general neurosis, he might have identified not only the connection between anxiety and perception, but the various psychological directions from which "spiritual" phenomena derive. He might have identified in "mystical exercise" not a regressive, transitional attempt to regain "the womb," but a sophisticated, concrete methodology designed to enable the individual to leave the womb—of which his ordinary (egotic) consciousness is an extension—by enabling him to moderate the perceptual tie that binds him to the internalized object, the source of both the ego and the ego's persistent anxiety. In short, he might have seen that "practice" was, potentially at least, an emancipating, not an infantalizing activity, and that emancipation meant precisely detachment from the ego, the seat of our ordinary, anxious perception.

Freud's postulation of an unconscious object to which philosophy must ultimately address itself is somewhere in his thoughts toward the very close of his career. Returning to his old charge that philosophy's great shortcoming stems from its refusal to deal with the whole mind, from its callow assumption that all thought is conscious thought, he writes in an unfinished essay wryly titled, *Some Elementary Lessons in Psycho-Analysis* ([1983] 1959, p. 379), "the equation of what is mental with what is conscious had the unwelcome result of divorcing mental processes from the general context of events in the universe and of setting them in complete contrast to all others. But this would not do, since the fact could not long be overlooked that mental phenomena are to a large extent dependent upon somatic influences." Freud continues: "If ever human thought found itself in an impasse it was here. To find a way out, the philosophers at least were obliged to assume that there were organic processes parallel to the conscious mental ones . . . which acted as intermediaries in the reciprocal relations between 'body and mind,' and which served to re-insert the mental into the texture of life. But this solution remained unsatisfactory. Psycho-analysis escaped such difficulties as these by energetically denying the equation between

101

what is mental and what is conscious. No; being conscious cannot be the essence, of what is mental. It is only a *quality* of what is mental, and an unstable quality at that."

Psychoanalysis may have "escaped" that difficulty by "denying" that "equation." However, by also denying the maternal figure's structural role in the human organism's developing mentation, by relying upon an "unconscious" that had been forged entirely in "repression" rather than in repression and internalization, it only created other "difficulties," difficulties candidly acknowledged by Freud, who wrote in *Inhibitions, Symptoms and Anxiety* ([1926] 1959, p. 75) that "after tens of years of psychoanalytic labour" he was still unable to answer the question, "whence does neurosis come?" When we recall the manner in which the materials of the primary years are taken into the "perceptual apparatus" and hence into the individual's "ego," we discover not only the reply to Freud's question, we discover, too, those "organic processes," which are also psychological and unconscious in nature, that "act as intermediaries" in the "reciprocal," mind-body relations of which Freud speaks. We discover, in a word, the human, social, and physical solution to that "impasse" of "human thought," that epistemological problem with which we have been dealing. I want to be very specific here, and to underscore the thesis from an angle that not only recalls Chapters 2 and 3 but that focuses philosophical issues through the severity of the empirical language used.

"While mind is not a substantial something," writes Edgar Wilson (1979, pp. 77–79), "neither is it a nothing; it has to do with the organization of the behaving system." Wilson goes on: "The basis of 'mind' is taken to lie in the covert microprocesses in the neural nets comprising the decision elements of the central nervous system. . . . The dynamic relationships between the states of the physical organisation of neural nets embodying memory in the brain and the changes in state brought about by internal and external processes are not additional to the discrete neural elements. . . they are the non-physical basis of mind. . . . Mind is the ongoing comparison relations within an organization of neural nets." And finally, "consciousness has to do with the functional integration of the brain's neuronic sub-systems into functionally superordinate systems. . . . It is the *relation* between the various multiple activities that is of importance." The point is, the neural relations which give rise to "mind" (both conscious and unconscious) cannot be disassociated from the internalizations of early experience, that is, the object relations, which lend human development its characteristic shape. The taking-in of the parental object always accompanies the attainment of "reality," "objectivity"—what we are pleased to call normal or ordinary awareness. To distinguish between "the world" and "the ego" is, in the beginning, to distinguish between what is loved and hated, "good" and "bad."

As Margaret Mahler (1968, pp. 44–45) expresses it, "the infant's first orientation in his extrauterine life is according to 'good-pleasurable' vs. 'bad-painful' stimuli. Since hunger is the infant's most imperative biological need, these qualities of 'good' and 'bad' become equated with 'edible' and 'inedible' substances. Through the inborn and autonomous perceptive faculty of the primitive ego, deposits of memory traces of the two primordial qualities of stimuli occur." It is to the internalized object, to "the mother," writes Mahler, that these "traces" become firmly "anchored." Here is the first, and the most fundamental, of the "comparisons" to which Wilson refers: those "superordinate systems" which permit the "integrated" perception of objects exist in inextricable association to the "objects" that "enter" the organism at the dawn of perceptual life. Hence, it is not merely the "dynamic relationships between the states of the physical organization of neural nets" that comprise the "non-physical basis" of "mind." As far as the human mind is concerned, the "dynamic relationships" (in the psychoanalytic as well as the physiological sense) between the perceptual apparatus and its internalized, non-physical "inhabitants" are as much a "basis" of mentation as the "nets" which embody "memory" in the superficial, non-dynamic signification of that term.

Freud's developing perceptual psychology brought him to the verge of a "Copernican revolution" in human understanding greater than that which he had already effected in his analyses of dreams and the dynamic unconscious. David Regan (1979, p. 137) has reminded us that "it is easy to overlook that fact that much of [our] neural output . . . does not reach conscious awareness at all. For example, many visual signals are concerned with 'housekeeping' activities of the body, such as adjusting the size of the pupil of the eye in response to changing light intensities." Psychoanalysis fulfils its revolutionary potential, on the one hand, by informing us that our anxious, transitional mode of perception itself "does not reach conscious awareness," that our ordinary, everyday manner of perceiving the world is itself fraught with irrational, unconscious assumptions, and on the other hand, by rediscovering in the hated "mystical realm" the very methods of diminishing that anxiety and irrationality through perceptive mind-rest, through detachment from the internalized object that contorts the perceptual system from the beginning of our dependent, egotic life. In all of this, psychoanalysis, whose aim is to make us wise about ourselves, meets philosophy, whose name means love of wisdom. Indeed, with an expanded definition of "the object" as the focal point, these disciplines become capable of uniting to a degree Freud could not have imagined, or dreamed.

5
EPISTEMOLOGY AND THE QUESTION OF PURE EGO

PART ONE
THE TRADITION: DESCARTES, HUME, KANT, AND HEGEL

I mean to concentrate here on those thinkers who stand directly, or perhaps most directly, behind the modern philosophical development in which I am ultimately interested, namely the phenomenology of Husserl and Merleau-Ponty. For it is the phenomenological perspective that can be most fruitfully combined with a new psychoanalysis of perception, and with the practice of relaxation and detachment, to produce the unification of knowledge mentioned at the outset of this book. Phenomenology is grounded, ultimately, in what is known as the "reduction," a perceptual behavior designed to stimulate a fresh awareness of the world, a kind of spontaneous awakening to ordinarily obscured aspects of mentation and feeling. I plan to approach the reduction in terms which reflect the psychodynamics of developing perception as we have explored them to this point. Let me hasten to add, however, that my exclusion of Locke, Berkeley, and Leibniz is not meant to suggest their unimportance. With considerations of length and of scope in mind, I simply had to draw the line somewhere, and this seemed an acceptable place, particularly as Husserl, in his *Ideas* ([1931] 1969, p. 166), singles out Descartes, Hume, and Kant as the most crucial influences upon his thought, and as Hegel commences the phenomenological "school" explicitly with his *Phenomenology of Mind*.

In my analyses of earlier thinkers I strive to be sensitive to original meanings while, at the same time, I regard all productions from the past as open to analytic investigation. Just as the blood circulated through the body before Harvey proposed his theory, so did people internalize objects and apprehend "reality" in a way that reflected the influence of the unconscious before Freud and his followers came on the scene. By attempting to locate the "place" in which the object "resides" in previous philosophical systems, I hope to enable the reader to understand, in what might be termed a novel manner, a covert or hidden dimension of western thought. We can better grasp where we are as perceivers by grasping where we have come from. Recent breakthroughs oblige us not only to discover the unconscious side of our perceptual habits but to re-evaluate the assumptions of those individuals whose works shaped our ideational environment. My psychohistorical efforts may, of course, offend the "experts," and I am likely to face the old, shopworn charge of holding authors such as Descartes and Kant responsible for views with which they could not have been acquainted. What can I say in reply to this but that I have endeavored not to make this error? It is always risky to go back and try to see things freshly. There may be an even greater risk, however, in failing to apply the findings of psychoanalysis to major facets of our intellectual history.

Descartes' Method

Descartes ([1627] 1969, p. 37)[1] tells us that our attention should be concentrated upon "only those objects . . . to the sure and indubitable knowledge of which our mental powers seem to be adequate." Indeed, "it were better not to study at all" than to come away with less than clear and certain information (p. 37). As for the fields which "alone are free from any taint of falsity or uncertainty," they are "Arithmetic and Geometry" (p. 39). Hence, these disciplines provide us with a major source of the exactitude we are seeking. Yet it is not merely that "Arithmetic and Geometry" can be used in our actual investigations of specific problems; they afford us a model by which we may be guided generally; they urge us to declare "that in our search for the direct road towards truth we should busy ourselves with no object about which we cannot attain a certitude equal to that of the demonstrations of Arithmetic and Geometry" (p. 40). The ultimate tool Descartes recommends to us as a prober or discoverer of "the truth," however, is not applied mathematics or mensuration, but something he calls "intuition."

We must be careful not to regard this term in the light of our present usage, where it comprises a kind of "mystical" faculty rooted in an extrasensorial talent. On the contrary, "by intuition," says Descartes, "I understand not the fluctuating testimony of the senses, or the misleading judgment that proceeds from the blundering constructions of imagination, but the conception which an unclouded and attentive mind gives us so readily and distinctly that we are wholly freed from doubt about that which we understand. . . . *Intuition* is the undoubting conception of an unclouded and attentive mind, and springs from the light of reason alone" (p. 42). Descartes goes on, "this evidence and certitude, however, which belongs to intuition, is required not only in the enunciation of propositions, but also in discursive reasoning of whatever sort. For example, consider this sequence: 2 and 2 amount to the same as 3 and 1. . . . We need to see intuitively not only that 2 and 2 make 4, and that likewise 3 and 1 make 4, but further that the third of the above statements is a necessary conclusion for these two" (pp. 42–43). Intuition, then, or what Descartes in another place calls revealingly the "natural light" (p. 312), gives us our "principles," while "remote conclusions are furnished . . . by deduction" (p. 43). There can be "no falsity in the intuition of things," in the "simple and naked intuition of single and independent objects" (pp. 88, 95). And what we cannot reach in the manner suggested we must "reject" out of hand as unworthy and "dangerous" (p. 43).

Now, to ensure the proper working of this "method," to make certain nothing "hampers" it—and here we reach a critical stage in the discussion as a whole—the "senses must be banished" from "examinations" altogether (p. 77). Everywhere in his writings Descartes repeats and underscores this: only those who are able to "detach their minds from affairs of sense" will find themselves in a position to discover the truth of things (p. 166). As he gravitates closer and closer toward that truth, Descartes becomes more and more "accustomed," as he puts it, "to detaching his mind from his senses" (p. 194). In what can only be regarded as one of the most significant statements in the history of western thought, Descartes declares, "it is the mind alone and not the mind and body in conjunction, that is requisite to a knowledge of the truth" (p. 217).

The implication, of course, is that Descartes actually believes the mind and the body to be separate entities, a notion which he announces everywhere in his work. While the mind is *in* the body it is merely "lodged" there, as a "pilot" might be "lodged" in a "vessel." As for the "sensations of hunger, thirst, pain, etc.," they are "in truth none other than certain confused modes of thought which are produced by the . . . apparent intermingling of mind and body" (p. 216). Because "the mind of man is really distinct from the body" (p. 164), and because knowledge gained through the employment of the senses can deceive, all that Descartes knows with genuine assurance is that he is "a thinking thing," indeed, "a substance whose whole essence or nature is to think" (p. 214). Such material is not only fascinating in itself, it is crucial to an understanding of those empirical sciences which developed after Descartes' demise and which adopted his assumptions and methods as their chief theoretical and practical guides. However, such material is, in my estimation, eclipsed by certain other passages of Descartes which indicate not simply an epistemological or perceptual difficulty in his system but a reluctant awareness of it on his part. While the overriding emphasis in Descartes is clear, the package he offers us is not as neat, not as perfect, as the sciences would have it.

Descartes' Intuition

Note, first, Descartes' remark that we must strive with our "intuition" to discover the world's "pure" essences because, in truth, there are very "few" of them (p. 52). Additionally, the "light" through which we discover those "pure" essences is itself a somewhat mysterious entity. What Descartes in other places confidently calls "reason" and "intuition," a kind of clear or "natural" beholding of objects, is in the sixth section of his *Rules for the Direction of the Mind* regarded problematically, as if he cannot make up his mind about precisely what it is, as if the passion for certitude (and the hatred of doubt) cannot be entirely satisfied. It is "either our experiences" or, as he says, "some sort of innate light" — what sort? — that takes us to the essences we seek (p. 52). Subsequent utterances highlight this uncertainty. Indeed, there is one series so remarkable for its awareness of the problem, and for its curious solution to the problem, that it must be presented fully.

Descartes writes that "no direct experience can ever deceive the understanding if it restrict its attention accurately to the object presented to it, just as it is given to either at firsthand or by means of an image; and if it moreover refrain from judging that the imagination faithfully reports the objects of the senses, or that the senses take on the true form of things, or in fine that external things always are as they appear to be;

for in all these judgments we are exposed to error" (p. 82). In other words, says Descartes, *accept* the data of "intuition" without question. Do not ask if we get what we get *accurately*. Avoid the problem of what our "experience," or "some sort of innate light," is giving us. Cease to enquire into the difference between "direct" experience—whatever that means—and other experience of "objects." For such questions can be dangerous, can lead us into "error," can destroy the feeling of certitude and the progress of our "examinations."

In fact, says Descartes, a "wise man" will never assert that the "object passes complete and without any alteration from the external world to his senses" (p. 82). Wise men know that what gets into the senses does not get there purely. "We ourselves," he states, "are responsible for the composition of the things present to our understanding when we believe that there is something in them which our mind perceives immediately without any experience" (p. 82). Here, then, is the nub of the issue. Because objects do not enter the sensual creature unalloyed but are "touched" by the creature himself, only that which is not sensual, only that which is the product of "intuition," or "direct" experience, or "some sort of innate light," can be relied on with assurance when it comes to ascertaining "the truth." Is not all of this rather too "mystical," too obviously "mystical," to be trusted methodologically, not to say philosophically, by "science"?

I will not dwell here on the schizoid implications of this material: Daniel Stern (1965) has done that well enough. Descartes *wants* to contemplate the "truth" with some sort of reliable faculty because, as he puts it, "in the contemplation of truth" is "practically the only joy in life that is complete and untroubled with any pain" (p. 36). Like many individuals who suffer wounds and losses, Descartes longs to escape the body, the senses, longs to discover surety and peace in the cool review of intellectual abstractions. And just as the early direction of psychoanalysis may have been overwhelmingly influenced by Freud's dread of the maternal realm, so the shape of modern science may have been overwhelmingly influenced by the sickly, melancholy Descartes' agonizing loss of both mother and daughter (Stern 1965, p. 91). The truth which emerges from his work, his references to "some sort" of "innate light," his recognition that "objects" do not enter the "understanding" unmodified, and his insistence that we must not "judge" the accuracy or inaccuracy of our "direct experiences," is that he does not know what "intuition" is, that he simply assumes its existence because such an assumption, the product of a lengthly meditation on the matter, allows him a measure of certainty.

There is nothing special about Descartes' "intuition." It is merely a heightened perception, a restrictive, concentrative aspect of observational tendencies rooted in ordinary consciousness. Moreover, when we recall the manner in which the internalized object invariably participates in the apprehension of objects "out there," we reach a pivotal conclusion, namely that in the philosophy of Descartes it is precisely "intuition"—that mysterious, "innate" faculty—that "harbors" the object of the inner world. The "purities" of "deduction" themselves are not exempted, for it is not only the use of words that recalls the mother's interaction with the infant, that keeps alive "automatically" the entire course of one's mental and physical development, the use of numbers too "echoes" the early period. The capacity for ordinal arrangement, closely tied to the maternal figure through its tight association with space and time, precedes and shapes the capacity for cardinal succession (Brainerd 1979, pp. 203–5). Descartes' "search for a universal symbolism" (Mahoney 1980, p. 150) has its psychoanalytic as well as its historical significance.

Descartes' God

Note the manner in which Descartes' use of "God" strikingly underscores the thesis, for Descartes employs the notion of a deity—a notion we now recognize as grounded in the infantile longing for security and protection—to justify his claim that it is possible to be certain about the nature of "reality," that we do not have to doubt everything, that we are not condemned to live among chimeras and phantoms. He writes, "our ideas and notions must have some foundation of truth. For otherwise it could not be possible that God, who is all perfection and truth, should have placed them within us" (p. 132). Because in Descartes the "truth" is derived from "intuition," an "innate light" which "springs" from "reason alone" (p. 41), and because God in Descartes is both man's creator and a figure of perfect rationality, the source from which all that is "in us," including reason, "issues" (p. 131), it becomes clear that a *transitional* significance resides in Descartes' postulation of "intuition" as the root of our intellectual security, our certainty. "Intuition" comprises Descartes' attempt to cope with his own dynamic insecurity, with his deep, intuitive sense of the projective nature of all "experience," or, to put it in terms appropriate to seventeenth-century Europe, with his deep, intuitive sense of the illusions of the mind (cf. Weitz 1983, pp. 99–100).

When Descartes strives to explain why, in spite of our derivation from a perfect God of reason, we are prone to be so frequently in error, he offers us a revealing, unforgettable solution by ascribing the dilemma to what he calls "the prejudices of childhood." Here are his words: "In the first years of life the mind was so closely allied to body that it applied itself to nothing but those thoughts alone by which it was aware of the things which affected the body; nor were these as yet referred to anything existing outside itself, but the fact was merely that pain was felt when the body was hurt, or pleasure experienced when the body received some good." Descartes goes on, "moreover because it did not as yet remark that the earth turned on its own axis, and that the superficies was curved like a sphere, it was more ready to apprehend that it was immovable and that the surface was flat. And we have in this way been imbued with a thousand other such prejudices from infancy, which in later youth we quite forgot we had accepted without sufficient examination, admitting them as though they were of perfect truth and certainty, and as if they had been known by means of our senses or implanted in us by nature" (pp. 332–33). What Descartes cannot see, of course, is that this intimate relationship between body and mind is most powerfully affected by the internalizing process, by the rooting of the object in our perceptual system, and that the consequences of this process, this rooting, do not cease, even "later" when we commence to "reason" on events. Hence, when Descartes maintains that in developing a reliable method for ascertaining the truth we must "forget" these childhood prejudices, indeed when he declares that such a "forgetting" is absolutely essential to the avoidance of epistemological "errors" (p. 334), he provides us, curiously and somewhat paradoxically, with both an answer to and a deepening of the dilemma.

I mean, because there is no way, no "method," simply to "forget" the internalizations of "childhood" which "prejudice" our "examinations" of the world, because the "light" of "intuition" is not innate but internalized, fraught with projections and "innate" in that sense, a genuine method for ascertaining "the truth" resides not in "forgetting" but in recontacting the influences of the early time and, through specific transformational practices, diminishing their power at the bodily level,

111

where they live. Ironically, it is only when we realize that the body and the mind are not separate and that perception (including "intuition") entails a fusion of the body and the mind, that we discover ourselves in a position "to get the object out of the object" and to achieve, thereby, a version of the "objectivity" Descartes so passionately sought. Methodologies that are ultimately mentational in nature only leave the object presiding in what we are accustomed to call the ego, for the ego never "forgets" its transitional, bodily origins.

Hume's Experience

Hume's final judgement on epistemological issues emerges early in his treatise: "We cannot go beyond experience; and any hypothesis, that pretends to discover the ultimate original qualities of human nature, ought . . . to be rejected as presumptuous and chimerical" (Hume [1739] 1975, p. xvii).[2] No one, he declares a moment later, "whether [he] be such as are cultivated in the schools of the philosophers, or practised in the shops of the meanest artisans . . . can go beyond experience, or establish any principles which are not founded on that authority" (p. xviii). From the beginning, note, "experience" is employed by Hume in the singular, in a manner that entirely ignores the modal issue. Hence there is in Hume an implicit postulation of "reality" which cannot genuinely entertain the problem of various and changing perceptual relations to the world (open systems).

Developing his central contention, Hume writes in a key utterance that "all our simple ideas in their first appearance are derived from simple impressions, which are correspondent to them, and which they exactly represent. . . . Our impressions are the causes of our ideas, not our ideas of our impressions" (pp. 4–5). A moment's reflection on the closeness of the words impression and imprinting calls to mind a basic similarity between Hume's position and Freud's, as set forth in the *Mystic Writing-Pad* (Freud [1925] 1959). The stimulus which "enters" the organism from the external world comprises for both men the chief source of what is registered in the "mental apparatus." However, whereas Freud regards that which is registered within as the projective ground of ensuing experience—the unconscious dimension of the "wax" which "colors" subsequent "impressions" as they "enter"— Hume concentrates upon "experience" entirely in conscious terms as comprising in the main images and ideas, including sensual "impressions" such as sweet and bitter, hot and cold. To express the matter in terms commonly attached to discussions of Hume, we merely "associate" one item with another and perceive the world around us accordingly. Our ideas are equal to their impressionistic sources. Consciousness is not yet, as it becomes in Kant, the condition of our "associations" (Merleau-Ponty 1963, p. 1973). In a passage which highlights this pivotal issue, Hume maintains "that the memory preserves the original form, in which its objects were presented, and that wherever we depart from it in recollecting any thing, it proceeds from some defect or imperfection in that faculty" (p. 9). "When we have found a resemblance among several objects," Hume continues, "we apply the same name to all of them. . . . After we have acquired a custom of this kind, the hearing of that name revives the idea of one of these objects, and makes the imagination conceive it with all its particular circumstances and proportions" (p. 20). We are now in a position, I believe, to appreciate Hume's attitude toward the critical postulations of Descartes.

Hume's Perception

Here is the heart of the matter: "Nothing is ever present to the mind but perceptions, and since all ideas are derived from something antecedently present to the mind, it follows that it is impossible for us so much as to conceive or form an idea of any thing specifically different from ideas and impressions." And then, "let us fix our attention out of ourselves as much as possible: Let us chase our imagination to the heavens, or to the utmost limits of the universe; we never really advance a step beyond ourselves, nor can conceive any kind of existence, but those perceptions, which have appeared in that narrow compass" (pp. 67–68). For Hume, then, the "intuition" of Descartes is neither more nor less than *another perception* in a world of perceptions. What Descartes calls "direct" experience is a specious "idea" which would grant something special to what is ultimately a mere impression. "The *Cartesians,*" Hume writes explicitly, are wrong to suggest "that we are perfectly acquainted with the essence of matter." The "principle of innate ideas," quite simply, is "false" (pp. 159–60). As for the ultimate cause of human perception, the notion that "God" is not merely involved but instrumental in assisting us to make use of our "reason," Hume has this to say: "If every idea be derived from an impression, the idea of a deity proceeds from the same origin." Hence, "the supposition of a deity can serve us in no stead" (p. 160). When we recall the manner in which the object of the inner world becomes linked inextricably to all our "impressions," including those which "suppose" the existence of "God," we recognize that whereas in Descartes it is "intuition" that "carries" the internalized object, in Hume that object "resides" in the term "impression." To maintain we can never "go beyond experience" is, *for us,* to maintain we can never go beyond the object that impinges from within on our reception of stimuli—our "impressions."

The point is buttressed by Hume's depiction of the manner in which individuals go about setting up their view of "reality." Note, in particular, the transitional implications: "Of [the] impressions or ideas of the memory we form a kind of system, comprehending whatever we remember to have been present, either to our internal perceptions or senses; and every particular of that system joined, to the present impressions, we are pleased to call a *reality"* (p. 108). Although "there is nothing in any *object,* considered in itself, which can afford us a reason for drawing a conclusion beyond it," we *"transfer* our experience in past instances to *objects* which are resembling, but are not exactly the same with those concerning which we have had experience" (pp. 139, 147, my emphasis). This "multiplicity of resembling instances... constitutes the very essence of... connection, and is the source from which the idea of it arises" (p. 163). In contrast with other animals, declares Hume, only "man" is pleased to fabricate such a "reality," to transform "custom" and "habit" into epistemological "truth" (pp. 178, 183). Nor can "man" really help himself here: "Nature, by an absolute and uncontrollable necessity has determined us to judge as well as to breathe and feel; nor can we any more forbear viewing certain *objects* in a stronger and fuller light, upon account of their customary connection with a present impression, than we can hinder ourselves from thinking as long as we are awake, or seeing the surrounding bodies, when we turn our eyes toward them in broad sunshine" (p. 183, my emphasis). In a crucial utterance which begins to disclose the defensive aspect of ordinary perception in earnest, Hume writes, "objects have a certain coherence even as they appear to our senses; but this coherence is much greater and more uniform, if we suppose the objects to have a continued existence; and as the mind is once in the train of observing a uniformity among objects, it naturally continues, till it renders the uniformity as complete as possible" (p. 198).

Needless to say, such "coherence" among "objects" is rooted in psychodynamic as well as in psychobiological requirements, in the need to establish a perceptively stable world as a counterpoise to the "objective" instability within. And indeed, observes Hume, even to reflect on all this makes us uncomfortable: "Nothing is more certain from experience than that any contradiction... to [these] sentiments... gives a sensible uneasiness" (p. 205). At all costs we must fend off the recognition, expressed rather disconcertingly in Hume, "that what we call a *mind,* is nothing but a heap or collection of different perceptions" (p. 207).

However, it is not only our awareness of external objects that is grounded in our peculiar, defensive perception; our very identity, says Hume, derives from a similar psychological direction. He writes: "For my part, when I enter most intimately into what I call *myself,* I always stumble on some particular perception or other, of heat or cold, light or shade, love or hatred, pain or pleasure. I never can catch myself at any time without a perception, and never can observe any thing but the perception. When my perceptions are removed for any time, as by sound sleep, so long am I insensible to *myself,* and may truly be said not to exist" (p. 252). Hume "ventures to affirm" on this basis that "mankind" itself is "nothing but a bundle of perceptions," and that "personal identity... cannot have a different origin, but must proceed from a like operation of the imagination upon like objects" (pp. 252, 259). Hence the desire for a "coherent" world is inseparable from the desire for a coherent self. To express the matter psychoanalytically, the ordinary "reality" which springs from the early period, from the mind's *internalizing* tendencies (Hume's "imagination"), includes within it the "personal identity" to which we habitually turn in an effort to preserve our precarious, egotic selfhood. It is in precisely this perceptual manner, "innocent" as it is, that we perpetuate the stressful relationship which we have taken up with the objects of the inner world, the objects we have incorporated into our perceptual structure, the objects which fuel the epistemological doubt in the first place. These are the "objects" we "associate" with our conscious, ongoing "impressions."

Hume's Melancholy

Toward the close of his book Hume confesses that his philosophical considerations have brought him to a rather melancholy conclusion: if we are willing to face the truth of our condition as human beings, if we

115

refuse to be ruled by "fancy," our choice becomes one between "a false reason and none at all." That is, we either accede to the illusions bred of our perception and hence accede to being without reason, to "going mad," or we persist in according sense to what is actually "nonsense," a mere "heap" of perceptions. "For my part," writes Hume in a candid, powerful moment, "I know not what ought to be done. . . . I can only observe what is commonly done; which is, that this difficulty is seldom or never thought of; and even where it has once been present to the mind, is quickly forgot and leaves but a small impression behind it. Very refined reflections have little or no influence upon us; and yet we do not, and cannot establish it for a rule, that they ought not to have any influence; which implies a manifest contradiction."

Moreover, Hume declares, "the intense view of these manifold contradictions and imperfections in human reason has so wrought upon me, and heated my brain, that I am ready to reject all belief and reasoning, and can look upon no opinion even as more probable or likely than another. Where am I, or what?" (pp. 268–69). Here, unforgettably, is the same doubt, the same philosophical despair, which characterized the ruminations of Descartes, who also came to disbelieve in the sensual world in which he existed, to experience the illusory nature of his perceptual life and the anxiety and dread that accompany such an experience. Both men "fear and tremble" in their ability and inclination to *reduce* "reality," its thick, habitual substance, right down to the chimerical, "subjective" screen of their own perceptual tendencies.

Descartes, as we have seen, resolves the dilemma by offering us a "method" for attaining certainty, a method rooted in our "innate light of reason," in a sort of "intuition" that ostensibly provides us with a world of "essences" which can be rendered exactly in pure, mathematical terms. There *must* be such a method and such a world, claimed Descartes, for God is not a trickster. To *some* degree, at least, he will allow us to participate in his perfection. Hume, on the other hand, flies not to mathematics and God to regain his security: he flies to his club, to his friends, to the smoky, chatty world of the senses. There, he tells us, he may be able to "obliterate" the products of his thinking. "I dine, I play a game of back-gammon, I converse, and am merry with my friends; and when after three or four hours' amusement, I would return to these speculations, they appear so cold, so strained, and ridiculous, that I cannot find it in my heart to enter into them any farther. Here then I find myself absolutely and necessarily determined to live, and

talk, and act like other people in the common affairs of life" (p. 269).
Clearly, from one angle, both Descartes and Hume manifest what psychoanalysis would call "schizoid tendencies," tendencies to "dissociation," to loss of contact with "reality," to states of anxiety in which the boundaries and firmness of the self and the world slip away (cf. Dussinger 1980). Clearly too, both men strive in a defensive fashion to regain contact with the infirm object through, in the one instance, a reliance on intellectual procedures, observational methods, reasonings about "God," and in the other, a pursuit of social activities, company, cards, conversation. An obvious transitional significance resides in both the thought, and the resolution of the thought, of these philosophical figures. But this is only one side of the issue.

From another angle, one that is sensitive to the struggle of the evolving individual to moderate the tie to the internalized object, to detach himself from the everyday "reality" which preserves his old, stress-filled relationships, his precarious "security," his commonplace world of ordinary consciousness — from this angle, both men stand upon the verge of a breakthrough, upon the verge of a relaxed, fresh sensorial existence in which the object ceases to govern the channels and modes of perception. Note that Descartes is *meditating* as he reaches his transitional crises and the transitional resolutions to them. That meditation might have gone either way. Certainly the fact that Descartes' "meditation" was not an habitual, bodily practice grounded in a specific bodily method crucially determined the nature of his conclusions about "the way" to "the truth."

Note too that Hume is always alone and *relaxing* as he begins to gravitate toward his philosophizing. "At the time... that I am tired with amusement and company, and have indulged in a reverie in my chamber or in a solitary walk by a river-side, I feel my mind all collected within itself, and am naturally inclined to carry my view into all those [philosophical] subjects" (p. 270). Yet, in another place, Hume writes, "I am affrighted and confounded with that forlorn solitude, in which I am placed by my philosophy, and fancy myself some strange uncouth monster, who not being able to mingle and unite in society, has been expelled from all human commerce, and left utterly abandoned and disconsolate; fain would I run into the crowd for shelter and warmth, but cannot prevail with myself to mix with such deformity" (p. 264). Such language calls to mind, of course, the literature of altered awareness itself, literature in which one's "night journey," one's "despair," frequently leads to a substantive discipline capable of working a modal shift in one's perceptual orientation toward "the real."

Which is precisely the point. Neither Descartes nor Hume provides a genuine method for changing one's perception of the world, a method that includes in a hard, physical way the perceiving body in which the object has come to be rooted. Neither man offers a method that relaxes the organism and thus soothes the anxiety of detachment at the same time that it works a structural shift in the "perceptual apparatus" by disrupting the tie between the internalization and the senses. As we have seen, Descartes' "intuition" is merely a restricted and heightened ordinary perception. Not only is the body nowhere about, it is eschewed. And Hume, in his melancholy belief that "experience" comprises a perceptual dead end, holds out no true method at all but simply goes to his club to make the best of it. While I may never, as Hume puts it, "go beyond myself," I have no reason to regard that self, modally, as a closed perceptual system. As we shall see, it is not only Descartes and Hume who cannot get past "doubt" to an actual altered perception which dispels the issue; all of western philosophy shares in the dilemma because all of western philosophy leaves the body out of its methodological schemes.

Kant's Breakthrough

Kant's reasoning is essentially as follows. Yes, the nature of our mentation does determine significantly our "impressions" of the world. However, that does not mean we are fated to "experience" a jumble of perceptions onto which we clap a false "coherence" through our tendency to "associate" one thing with another. For our mentation works upon the data not through its adherence to a series of original impressions, the source of its ensuing "associations," but through the shaping influence of its intrinsic constitution. Because our consciousness is the condition of all that we "associate," our ideas cannot equal our "impressions." Hence, our perception transpires in a manner that affords us, through the synthetic activities of our "mental apparatus," an integrated, ordered, experiential outlook. Within the limits of our cerebral interaction with the universe we can achieve an exact, indeed a scientific knowledge of the objects which surround us (cf. Chessick 1980, p. 458). But Kant goes much further than this.

While we are fated through our given, "a priori" mental qualities, our sense of space and time, our sense of cause and effect, to "knead" the data available to us, we are able to achieve a "pure" or "rational" understanding *of* that aspect of our mentational "experience." Time and space may hum receptively in our heads awaiting information from the "outside world," but we can know that. And such knowledge is as absolute, as reliable, as "pure," as the logical forms it assumes when it is operationally expressed. The picture of man that emerges here is far different from that which emerges from Hume. We behold a creature who, in spite of its determined perceptual nature, possesses a genuine synthetic power to establish empirical connections and thus to grasp the way the world actually behaves in relation to it. Additionally, we behold a creature which, in its capacity for rational thought, is able to attain a knowledge of its own condition apart from mere perception, a knowledge which affords it an accurate recognition of its intellectual life. In this way, the "empirical" dilemma is resolved. We cannot see what is there, the thing-in-itself, because of the nature of our "data processing instrument," and that's that. But the problem of "scepticism" is also resolved, and that is the "miracle" of Kant's position: we can know something accurately through our reasoning about that which is not reasonable but sensational; and that which is sensational can also be comprehended perceptively within the limits of our synthesizing minds.

Kant's Objects

"The principal thing" to which "we must attend" in developing a "critique of pure reason," writes Kant ([1787] 1950, p. 39),[3] is that "no conceptions must enter it which contain aught empirical." In other words, our "knowledge" must be "completely pure" (pp. 39–40). For "transcendental philosophy," as Kant dubs the substance of his *Critique,* "is a philosophy of the pure and merely speculative reason." On several occasions Kant underscores this central idea: "In transcendental logic we isolate the understanding... and select from our cognition merely that part of thought which has its origin in the understanding alone" (p. 69). And then, employing the word "object" in a manner that adumbrates *for us* the limitations of his position, Kant declares that this "pure cognition" in which "transcendental logic" is grounded "depends" upon "intuition" supplying it with "*objects*" to which it can be "applied"; for "without intuition the whole of our cognition is without

119

objects, and is therefore quite void" (p. 69, my emphasis). Thus, while our conceptions are related to the "objects" with which "intuition" provides us, they are not directly related to them.

Indeed, it is precisely because they are not that we are able to achieve the kind of "knowledge" to which the *Critique* is devoted. In a sentence that does not merely adumbrate limitations but pins them down, Kant writes: "A conception *never* relates immediately to an *object,* but only to some other representation thereof, be that an intuition or itself a conception" (p. 73, my emphasis). In this way, to dissect the whole of our "a priori" experience is to gain an "understanding" that "distinguishes itself not merely from everything empirical, but also completely from all sensibility.... [Such] conceptions spring pure and unmixed out of the understanding" (pp. 70–71). Kant then asserts that he will "follow up the pure conceptions even to their germs and beginnings in the human understanding" (p. 71). But that would mean, of course, to follow them into the early stages of human life, the stages in which the "significant other" enters not only "perception" but the sources of "cognition" generally.

As Hume ([1739] 1975, p. 108) quite correctly declared, "reasoning itself" is a "species of sensation." Even as Kant stands "purely" contemplating the "abstract" propositions in his head, perhaps with his eyes shut tight and his nose and ears plugged firmly, he is still in his body. He is still perceiving those "objects" which, as Freud so rightly said, stimulate from within, those "objects" which cannot—and this is the crux—be divorced from our contemplative activity. Because the psychological object comprises the "germ" to which Kant refers, there is nothing in his method capable of bringing us to a direct apprehension of anything. The projective mechanism is left operant, indeed vigorous, in the mind.

The A Priori

"Space," Kant tells us, "is not a conception which has been derived from outward experiences"; it is "a necessary representation *a priori,* which serves for the foundation of all external intuitions." We "never can imagine or make a representation to ourselves of the non-existence of space." Thus "space" is the mere "form" of "all the phenomena of the external sense" (pp. 43–45). "Now," Kant goes on, "because the receptivity or capacity of the subject to be affected by *objects* necessarily antedates all intuitions of these objects, it is easily understood how the *form* of all phenomena can be given in the mind previous to all actual perceptions, [and] therefore *a priori*" (p. 54, my emphasis). Kant then turns to "time" and writes that "it is a *pure form* of the sensuous intuition," that it is "nothing else than the *form* of the internal sense," that it is "only of *objective* validity in regard to phenomena" (pp. 48–50, my emphasis). The problem, *for us,* is that space and time cannot be comprehended apart from the internalizing, interpersonal events which contribute integrally to our mental development. Kant is *in* space and time as he is thinking his thoughts *about* space and time. And we are in space and time as we read them. Hence, Kant's thoughts can only remind us that *all* thought, of whatever kind, is "phenomenal," including all thought about thought. The entire issue is given striking expression when Kant writes, first, that it is only when we "depart from the subjective condition" and adopt a "transcendental conception of phenomena" that we are able to gain a "pure" understanding of "form," and then goes on to declare, unforgettably, that it is "only from the human point of view that we can speak of space, extended objects, etc." (pp. 46–47). The point is, "the human point of view" is the only one available to Kant, or to anyone else.

The implications are clear: while the concept of "intuition" "holds" the internalized object in Descartes, and while the notion of "impression" "holds" that object in Hume, "form" or "pure form" "contains" the internalized object in Kant. The following utterance perfectly expresses the matter: "If I take away from an empirical intuition all thought. . . . there remains no cognition of any object. . . . But if I take away all intuition, there still remains the form of thought, that is, the mode of determining an *object*" (pp. 187–88, my emphasis). Which calls to mind the entire problem of the *Ding an sich,* or thing-in-itself.

Because Kant cannot get out of his body, the purest of his "forms of thought," namely the thing-in-itself, is ultimately an aspect of his perception. The symbolic proclivity, tied inextricably to the psychological object, affords Kant, finally, this "transcendent" representation of "the world." We are able to conceive as "apart" the "universe apart" which it postulates precisely because our big, internalizing brains are able to conceive all things as "apart." To express the matter somewhat differently, "thing-in-itself" is a linguistic expression for a perceived (and emotively loaded) abstraction. It comprises a kind of trick the mind plays on itself in ordinary consciousness as a result of its tendency to internalize objects and thus to behold, as in a mirror, "another realm."

121

Not only does Kant stand there looking at that realm, he believes it "exists" apart from his looking. What Lacan (1966) would call "the Imaginary" becomes, in Kant, "the Real."

Interestingly enough, but not surprisingly, there is a schizoid dimension to this business. Kant's philosophy upon its publication engendered despair in some people because it postulated this thing-in-itself, this complete, "objective" world "apart," this truth in other words, and then declared we can never know it.[4] Now the longing to know such a "place," "thing," realm of certainty and truth, is, as we saw with Descartes, frequently related to the transitional goal of reunion with the lost or relinquished "other" of infancy and childhood. Turning once again to Lacan, as his ideas are employed in the work of Anthony Wilden — and we must observe how these quotations carry us explicitly toward the Kantian notion of "pure form" — we have the following: "The Imaginary is the region of relationship that generates... reason and logic by creating the principles of identity and negation.... The emergence of the Imaginary is first expressed in the child's playing with the relation between presence and absence, as... described by Freud. The development of the Imaginary is also revealed in the child's fascination with his mirror image, the *stade du miroir* in Lacan."

The child's experience "is that of looking 'through the glass' and seeing himself on the other side where he knows he is not." Because "the Imaginary" becomes "the Real," it "has effects in the real world.... [It] projects 'final causes' toward which the individual is drawn within the overdetermined possibilities of his situation." The Imaginary may even be held in "higher esteem" than material symbols, "because 'pure' reason is thought to be supreme." The thing-in-itself, then, comprises a kind of "object-exchange" between specific, dynamic facets of the object-seeking self. "It is the lack of object which circulates in [such] exchange." Indeed, the exchange *is* "the exchange of this lack" for an Imaginary, "pure" substitute. As for the primary source of the "object" mediated in such acts of exchange, it is, of course, "the breast" (Wilden 1972, pp. 275–86). Thus Kant, in the end, returns us not merely to Hume's notion that we cannot go "beyond ourselves," but also to the modal implications of Hume's thought. It is when the tie to the internalized object is moderated through "practice" that we are able to "go beyond" the selves of "imaginary exchange," of ordinary consciousness, and to experience directly our fundamental (and certain) relationship with the world, a relationship which dispels our epistemological loyalty to, or longing for, a *Ding an sich*.

Limitations of Pure Reason

"Pure reason" holds for Kant the solution to more than epistemological dilemmas. The social sphere, the moral sphere, is also profoundly affected by the manner in which we apply our minds to the objects around us. "Pure reason," he writes, "contains... in its practical, or, more strictly, its moral use, principles of the *possibility* of *experience,* of such actions, namely, as, in accordance with ethical precepts, *might* be met with in the *history* of man. For since reason commands that such actions should take place, it must be possible for them to take place" (p. 458). And then: "I call the world a *moral world* in so far as it may be in accordance with all the ethical laws—which, by virtue of the freedom of reasonable beings, it *can* be, and according to the necessary laws of *morality* it *ought to be*" (p. 458). And finally, in a passage which returns us to the psychological problem we have been exploring all along, Kant declares, "the idea of a moral world has, therefore, *objective* reality, not as referring to an *object* of intelligible intuition... but to the world of sense, conceived... as an *object* of pure reason in its practical use" (p. 459, my emphasis).

While there can be no question about the accuracy of linking the epistemological and moral worlds, about the degree to which our treatment of one another is fundamentally influenced by our view of "reality," there can also be no question about the hopelessness of "pure reason" as a "practical" guide to the social domain, the "world of sense." The only "objective reality" which "the idea of a moral world has" is, at the present time at least, the "reality" of the unconscious, transitional object which dictates our grievous, irrational behavior, our persistent exploitation of one another. What vitiates the notion of "pure reason" in the speculative realm, vitiates that notion in the moral realm as well. No wonder the Age of Reason, epitomized in Kant's work, faded into our Age of Unreason, epitomized in Freud's notion of the unconscious object. The worm was left, unnoticed, in the bud.

Hegel: The Elusive Absolute

Apart from its intrinsic fascination, Hegel's attempt to resolve the dilemma of subjectivity initially addressed by Descartes harbors particular significance for us on three counts. First, it develops Kant's assertion that epistemological and moral problems are vitally connected. Indeed, after Kant and Hegel that connection will have become an integral aspect of philosophic speculation. Second, the writings of

123

Hegel exert an enormous influence on Marx, and through Marx on the direction of recent social and economic thought which is everywhere bound up with views of both "reality" and "the nature of man." Third, Hegel's work anticipates in a curious, paradoxical way the notion of "mental" or "psychic" objects which informs the world of modern psychology. Accordingly, what Hegel has to say will be with us, in one form or another, for the remainder of this book.

"In my view," writes Hegel in his monumental *Phenomenology of Mind* ([1806] 1967, p. 80),[5] "everything depends upon grasping and expressing the ultimate truth not as Substance but as Subject as well." And he goes on, "true reality is merely this process of reinstating self-identity, of reflecting into its own self in and from its other, and is not an original and primal, immediate, unity as such. It is the process of its own becoming, the circle which presupposes its end as its purpose, and has its end for its beginning" (pp. 80–81). Accordingly, "reflection" or "mediation" has to be included as an *actual part* of the "ultimate truth," as an actual "moment of the Absolute" (pp. 82–83). Indeed, declares Hegel, it is "reflection" that not only "constitutes truth" but "does away with the contrast between result and the process of arriving at it" (p. 83). Such considerations prompt Hegel's announcement that "ultimate reality" or "ultimate truth" is inseparable from the spirit which moves the universe and about which we can obtain, through philosophy, an "objective" *idea:* "That the truth is only realized in the form of a system, that substance is essentially subject, is expressed in the idea which represents the Absolute as Spirit (*Geist*—the grandest conception of all, and one which is due to modern times and its religion. Spirit is alone reality. It is the inner being of the world, that which essentially is and is *per se;* it assumes objective, determinate form, and enters into relations with itself—it is externality (otherness), and exists for self; yet, in this determination, and in its otherness, it is still one with itself—it is self-contained and self-complete, in itself and for itself at once" (pp. 85–86). Thus Kant's resolution to the epistemological dilemma—and Hegel has Kant explicitly in mind—is merely *one* resolution in a *series* of resolutions which lead the individual, finally, to a felt appreciation of Spirit. "A so-called fundamental proposition or first principle of philosophy, even if it is true, is yet none the less false just because and in so far as it is merely a fundamental proposition, merely a first principle, merely . . . the beginning" (p. 85). For once we *get* an idea, says Hegel, we can *also* get an idea of that idea, and *that* idea is closer to the Idea, or

124

Spirit, than the one originally gotten (p. 86). Much of Hegel's philosophy resides in these notions. However, it is when he begins to employ the terms "object" and "objective" in earnest that he reveals the uniqueness, perhaps the peculiarity, of his position.

Hegel's Objects

When an original concept is "presented to itself as an object," writes Hegel, it may *as an object* "annul and transcend" this "objective form" and "find itself reflected" in "its own object" (p. 86). When "thought pure and simple" knows "its object to be itself" it attains its highest condition and manifests the Absolute, the essence of the world (p. 97). For the "object" *corresponds* to the "notion" and the "notion" to the "object" (p. 138). And since "consciousness is to itself its own notion" it "immediately transcends what is limited," namely "its own self." In other words, "consciousness" becomes, *actually becomes,* what *was* the "object" because, as we have been told explicitly, "reality" is "spirit alone" (p. 86) and the "activity of knowledge" is the "immanent self of the content" (p. 113). The point can hardly be overstressed. In the alteration of the knowledge [that the object is merely a way to the idea of the object]," the "object itself . . . is altered," altered "in point of fact" (p. 142). It becomes a "new object," a new *real object,* which "contains the nothingness of the first," the first which has not been negated *finally* but negated only to become that which is created *out* of its negation. Thus "consciousness is, on the one hand, consciousness of the object, on the other, consciousness of itself; consciousness of what to it is true, and consciousness of its knowledge of that truth." The "new object" is precisely "the *experience* concerning that first object" (pp. 141–43).

The use of Hume's word "experience" in this last declaration opens the way to analytic understanding of Hegel's thought. If it is our "experience" of the "new object" which *is* the "new object," then such experience will have lurking within it, I suspect, the object of the early time, the object which is tied perceptively to our mentation, including the mentation that becomes "conscious of itself." What is fresh and memorable here, and what takes us a step beyond Kant where the object also lurks "below" Pure Reason, is that Hegel himself postulates the objective reality of the "mental" object and thus invites us explicitly to see the object of the unconscious, the internalized object of infancy and childhood, "residing" in the body-world "below" the "Absolute Spirit."

At the same time, by transforming self-reflection into an object, an object that ostensibly answers the dilemma of "subjectivity," and by making *that* object, in turn and by fiat, correspond to the "absolute truth," Hegel skirts the epistemological issue from a conscious, logical standpoint. He simply leaves the problem of self-reflection hanging in the metaphysical air. While the Absolute resolves the problem for Hegel, it does not resolve it for other philosophers (cf. Habermas 1971, pp. 7–22). Indeed, it is precisely this sort of "religious," or perhaps "dogmatic," quelling of logical objections that has contributed to Hegel's decline as an epistemologist in recent years. The entire matter emerges most strikingly from Hegel's methodological schemes.

Hegel's Method: The Logic of the Narcissistic Dilemma

Hegel commences his "observations" on the "method" by which one may carry out the "absolute" metaphysical enterprise by reminding us that "consciousness," when it "relates" itself to something, also "distinguishes" itself from that to which it is related. He then asserts in a rather remarkable utterance that "what really lies in these determinations does not further concern us here; for since the object of our inquiry is phenomenal knowledge, its determinations are also taken up, in the first instance, as they are immediately offered to us. And they are offered to us very much in the way we have just stated" (pp. 139–40). Hence, in coming *methodologically* to pure knowledge of the "absolute truth" all one has to do is "reflect" on the "object" of one's "reflection." As "consciousness tests and examines itself, all we are left to do is simply and solely to look on," for the "origination of the new object which offers itself to consciousness" occurs "without consciousness knowing how it comes by it" (pp. 141, 144). We are dealing here, Hegel informs us, with a "new mode" of "consciousness," one that functions somehow by virtue of an inexplicable "necessity" (pp. 141–44).

Of particular interest is Hegel's total unconcern with the relations between the "new object" of the mind and the body which harbors "mental" operations that carry out the modal shift. He simply ignores—I mean intentionally—the perceptual implications of the business, the we who are looking on at the transformational events. "Being in itself" is "being for itself," says Hegel, and that is the end of the matter. Here is the curious, authoritarian passage in which he tells us to drop it: "We do not require to bring standards with us, nor to apply *our* fancies and thoughts in the inquiry" (p. 141). Hegel's position is closely bound up with his peculiar manner of regarding what he calls "the ego": it is not "merely the self," he maintains, it is the "identity" of the "self" with "itself" (pp. 802–3). "If we call the movement of knowledge 'conception,' and knowledge, [as] simple unity or Ego, 'the object,' we see that not only for us tracing the process, but likewise for knowledge itself, the object corresponds to the conception. . . . Ego is the content of the relation, and itself the process of relating. . . . With self-consciousness . . . we have . . . passed into the native land of truth" (pp. 218–19). In one place Hegel actually expresses the idea in mathematical terms, writing "Ego = Ego" (p. 802). The point is, by denying explicitly the ego's role as differentiated observer Hegel removes the perceiving body from the discussion. The living, breathing organism disappears into "higher functions." Thus Hegel, in the end, merely plays with the words "object" and "objective." Objects are no longer objects when we "self-reflect." Objects metamorphose into "ideas" when we think of them "reflectively." It is a word game. Yet we know better: because "objects" exist in the body, in which exists the "mind," there can be no modal shift without a method that includes the body in a concrete, physical way. It is not enough "simply to look on." Allow me to present the entire issue in another, more crucial light.

As we have seen, the "moment of truth" to which Hegel refers is a "moment" of intensive "reflection upon reflection," a moment in which the "objects" of the world ostensibly change their nature and bring one to a "knowledge" of the "Absolute." Logically, however, that "moment" comprises an experience of infinite regression in both the numerical and sensational sense, an experience that calls to mind the image of opposing mirrors and the mirror stage of human infancy in which self-reflection begins. When Hegel writes of the spirit "entering into relations with itself" (p. 86) he expresses the problem exactly, not merely with regard to the development of narcissism, the self-reflection which reflects the parent's love onto the self, but also with regard to the epistemological question which cannot be divorced from the psychological one. For if one "reflects" upon an "object" and alters it through that reflection into a "higher object" which is also a real object, as real as the "first," one confronts the necessity of further alteration of the new object so that it too might offer a "knowledge" that is "absolute." *Every* "Idea" of the "truth" is only a "beginning." One can reflect on his

127

reflection of his reflection, for all reflection actually contains as object the "object" of the previous "reflection." When Hegel squelches this problem in his philosophy by asking us not to think about it, when he refers us forcefully to an Absolute that obtains upon the initial self-reflection, he disrupts arbitrarily the very infinite regression he himself has set up through the terms of his argument. Why does he do this?

Hegel's disruption in psychoanalytic terms comprises the cathexis of an intellectual scheme which allows him to feel united with a projective version of the "good" parental object (The Absolute), an object that was forged in the early, defensive splitting of the caregiver. He halts at the initial attainment of the Absolute, and insists that we also halt there, because to follow the infinite regression all the way would mean to experience not merely an intellectual absurdity or "danger," but an emotive absurdity or "danger" as well, a kind of "spin" toward the very irrationality with which "the system" copes at the level of conscious defence. In this way, Hegel's "dialectic," his transformation of "objects" at the "top" of the philosophy, has its unconscious counterpart "below" where the "bad" object is suppressed and transmuted into "good." The disruption of an infinite regression which would lead to a narcissistic dilemma, a dilemma of the mirror stage or the stage of inchoate reflection, is a symptom of the tension that resides deep within the internalizing mechanisms of this "mind." The unreasonable stopping of the logical issue is the passionate, illogical act that argues the problem of objects in the other, dynamic sense. Needless to say, the rigorous avoidance of the body in all of this is essential to the chief protective strategy. Unlike poor Narcissus, Professor Hegel will not fall into the mirror pool of his own reflection.

We come, then, to a somewhat arresting conclusion. While "intuition" in Descartes "contains" the internalized object, while "impression" "contains" it in Hume, and "form" or "pure form" in Kant, the term "object" itself "harbors" the internalized object in Hegel. It is precisely in his employment of the term, in his effort to make "object" commensurate with a "reality" that is both determinate and immaterial, that he points us toward an epistemological acknowledgement of the degree to which the internalized object impinges on our "knowledge" of ourselves and the world we inhabit.

The full consequence of Hegel's denial of the body emerges later of course in his *Philosophy of Right* ([1821] 1967, pp. 127–38, 155–219) with its callous indifference to the sufferings of war and its purblind idealization of the patriarchal monarch. It is by no means absent, however, from *The Phenomenology of Mind*. I do not refer merely to Hegel's angry swipes at those passionate, poetical philosophers who incline toward the worship of "nature" and who presume to speculate publicly on the meaning of existence (pp. 124–27); I refer as well to his numerous presentations of various aspects of social life. The "family," for example, is not in Hegel's view an "institution" of emotional give-and-take, or ordinary living as we usually conceive of it; rather, it is a "natural ethical community" whose most "immediate existence" is its "ethical existence" (p. 468). Not "love" or "sentiment" but "ethical relations" is the universal "element" of a "family." Among its members "divine law holds sway" (p. 474). Remarking on the political realm, Hegel tells us that "government" is "the spirit . . . pure and simple," the "ethical substance" of the entire social world (p. 472). He put forth this view during an historical period of incredible chaos, brutality, and corruption.

As for children and their parents, it is "reverent devotion" that they characteristically manifest toward one another (p. 475). Listen to the following on the female as wife and mother: "In a household of the ethical kind, a woman's relationships are not based on a reference to this particular husband, this particular child, but to *a* husband, to children *in general*, – not to feeling [my emphasis here], but to the universal. The distinction between her ethical life . . . and that of her husband consists just in this, that it has always a directly universal significance for her, and is quite alien to the impulsive condition of mere particular desire" (p. 476). "In the husband," however, "these two aspects get separated; and since he possesses, as a citizen, the self-conscious power belonging to the universal life, the life of the social whole, he acquires thereby the rights of desire, and keeps himself at the same time in detachment from it" (p. 477).

Brothers and sisters? Note this passage, written during an age in which Goethe and von Kleist were exploring the turbulence of familial bonds: "The brother . . . is in the eyes of the sister a being whose nature is unperturbed by desire and is ethically like her own; her recognition in him is pure and un-mixed with any sexual relation. . . . Her duty toward him is the highest. . . . The brother is the member of the family in whom its spirit becomes individualized. . . . The brother leaves . . . this . . . ethical life of the family, in order to acquire, and produce the concrete ethical order" (p. 477). These striking idealizations, these wondrous expectations of human beings, attest to a total, uncompromising denial of the body, an adamant refusal to accept the creatureliness of the earth's children, women, and men.

This denial calls to mind the final pages of Hegel's treatise in which his philosophical notions are aligned with a religion that has also manifested a reluctance to accept the fleshy aspects of our experience, that is, Christianity. "Essential Being, Divine Being, Absolute Knowledge, and Spirit" are all not merely one, maintains Hegel, they find their unified expression in the "divine man," or the "historical Christ" (pp. 780–84). Hence the "goal" is the "spiritual kingdom." Indeed, "science and history... form at once the recollection and the Golgotha of Absolute Spirit.... The chalice of this realm of spirits foams forth to God His own Infinitude" (p. 808). Hegel's philosophy is a defence of the old, religious idea that matter is spirit and spirit reality. Traditional Christian dogma is transmuted, rather thickly, into "metaphysics." Hegel strives to gut "objects" of their materiality in a transitional attempt to expunge what he perceives to be the *bad object* from his, and mankind's, existence. The enemy, at all costs, must be kept at bay. Perhaps this is why war came to be so attractive to Hegel ([1821] 1977, pp. 209–11); it provided an opportunity to rationalize passion through the state.

A final word. Hegel's philosophy, perhaps more than any of the others we have examined, with the exception of Descartes', reminds us in its religious dimension that the deep, unconscious purpose of western epistemological speculation generally is not merely to discover a "transcendence" which provides the individual with an "objective" method of determining the "truth," but also to discover a resolution to the problem of "objectivity" as it emerges from that other realm of "objects," that realm in which resides the legacy of internalization, the psychodynamic tensions of infancy and childhood. With its dialectical approach to objects, Hegel's philosophy calls to *our* minds the precarious "security" of ordinary consciousness, the doubt that arises from an inner world the "inhabitants" of which are continually changing and shifting their relations to one another. Hegel's emphasis on "Spirit" attests to the "allure" of those erotic, aggressive aims that are linked to the "Ego" in its unconscious aspect and that keep the individual in a state of bodily tension from which he seeks relief and relaxation. We have here, of course, an important link with materials developed in previous sections.

Hegel's "moment" of "transcendence" in which we quietly "look on" while "truth" obligingly unfolds itself for us recalls not only the quiet moments of Descartes' "meditations," Hume's peaceful walks along the river during which the "mind" becomes "collected," and Kant's serene contemplation of "pure reason," it recalls as well those traditional texts in which descriptions of perceptive mind-rest, of the relaxed, non-transitional detachment from objects, offer themselves to the reader. Such texts were available at the time Hegel lived and wrote. Indeed, they began increasingly to influence the quality of western metaphysical thought, most notably and explicitly, perhaps, through Schopenhauer. Yet, as indicated, Hegel's inadequate method, rooted in his negation of the body, prevents his scheme, in which psychic "objects" are said to contain active, energic "contents," from "transcending" its own transitional, regressive predilections and arriving at an integrated, balanced position, one which might offer the adherent an actual way to alter his perception of the world. To a considerable extent, Hegel's metaphysics call to mind Freud's provocative notion that philosophers share with paranoiacs the inclination to make "systems."

PART TWO
PHENOMENOLOGICAL
PERSPECTIVES:
HUSSERL AND MERLEAU-PONTY

In current epistemological discussion Descartes' "problem" is still with us. Indeed, an overwhelming issue of modern philosophy is precisely that of "objectivity," of "mind" working on the "data" it perceives and thereby altering them. I say "data" to make plain that scientific thought, which discovers it most radical support in Machism, has left the philosophic question unresolved, and even unaddressed in many quarters. For "scientific" observation simply takes the "data" of the senses, or of instruments which are extensions of the senses, and then declares, either explicitly or by implication, that such "data" provide us with a "true" representation of the world. From an epistemological standpoint, there is really no more to it than that. "Scientific observation" is simply a species of empiricism, rooted in a naïve acceptance of Descartes' "intuition." Even when the scientist perfects his "experiment" and invites us to view matters accordingly, he only offers us, within the confines of ordinary perception, alternative "data" as "truth." What he takes for granted and leaves entirely unexamined is the whole universe of mentation already developed, the perceptual and behavioral "context" in which he lives and does his work. The very terms he employs—fast, slow, round, square—his very use of language and number, are items of philosophic concern. Let me put it another way. There is nothing wrong with offering someone perceptual "data" and then asking him to register and record them. But to claim they are "true," philosophically "true," or "true" to the extent that they cannot be "falsified," is a huge step, one that must not be taken without rigorous epistemological analysis. After all, do we *want* to be fools? It is just this dilemma Husserl ([1911] 1965, pp. 85–95) had in mind when he characterized phenomenology as an attempt to restore reason to the modern, scientific world.

Phenomenology begins by accepting Hume's dictum that we cannot go beyond ourselves. While it also accepts Kant's attempt to discover the limitations of human perception, his concentration on time, space, and causality, it rejects his "transcendent" position, his belief that "reason" can be exercised "purely," apart from all "sensuous" input. It then proceeds to describe meticulously, basing its descriptions upon actual observations, the manifold ways in which "consciousness" behaves in its perceptual dealings with "reality." The purpose of these descriptions suggests itself: to express the nature, the essential structure, of our perceptive conduct, here in the world we inhabit. Where Hume and Kant desist, phenomenology persists. In its own special sense, it becomes psychological. To reject the transcendent perspective, to attend to all aspects of human perception as they transpire at the human level means of course a huge descriptive catalogue, one that might conceivably go on forever. Thus the aim of phenomenology as a continuation of the epistemological tradition and as a response to the rise of the modern empirical sciences is not to disclose the "truths" of the universe around us, but to disclose the "truths" of our perceptions of that universe. It is the perceptual foundations of "objective" investigations that will be, in this manner, revealed. Which calls to mind another, vital point.

Phenomenology strives to escape what looks like its subjective position by discovering through its meticulous examination of consciousness a method that will enable us, as perceivers, to stand in a true, accurate relation to the world of our perceptions, our objects. Calling this method "the reduction," it follows Descartes' lead, not into "the world," but into the perceptual sphere. It suggests we can modify our outlook in a manner that affords us "objective" insight into the perceptual essences of our concrete mental activity. For our purposes, this matter of the reduction is of enormous consequence. It resides, as a matter of fact, very close to the theoretical place at which the psychoanalysis of objects and the phenomenology of objects can meet in a genuine synthesis of understanding. With all of this in mind, let us turn to the work of Husserl, an individual who is to the development of phenomenology what Freud is to the development of psychoanalysis.

Husserl's Method

Husserl strives in the early sections of *Ideas* ([1913] 1969, p. 5)[6] to make plain the purpose of his phenomenological studies, the direction his philosophy will take. There is a realm of "direct experience," he tells us, which has "so far remained inaccessible" to systematic investigation. This realm is not only "universal," a realm of "essences," of "truths," it is one that can be contacted, or "intuited," through specific methodological procedures. What are they? "Turning inwards in pure reflection, following exclusively 'inner experience' and 'empathy'. . . and setting aside all the psychophysical questions which relate to man as a corporeal being, I obtain an original and pure descriptive knowledge of the psychical life as it is in itself, the most original information being obtained from myself, because here alone is perception the medium" (p. 7). Husserl is quick to realize, of course, that "it must be felt at first as a most unreasonable demand that such a 'nuance' springing from a mere change of standpoint should possess such great, and indeed, for all genuine philosophy, such decisive significance" (p. 9). Yet we are asked to believe that it does.

The problem with Husserl's "method" already begins to emerge, for the question arises, to what extent will this "turning inwards" comprise a "countertransference," a defensive distortion of the "psychical life" predicated by the deep structures of the unconscious as they "rise to meet the challenge" of the introversion, the attempt to observe or "perceive" one's behavior, and to be analytic about the observation? Is there not an unconscious mind, and will not what we have chosen to call its "objects" influence one's phenomenological self-perception, one's attempt to be "objective" about the "essences" of his mental activity? Why, when one turns "inwards," is his "reflection" apt to be more "pure" than it is when he turns "outwards"? Until one confronts the influence on the "perceptual apparatus" of what Freud called the "inner stimulus," the "psychophysical" side of the "corporeal being" which Husserl chooses to ignore, his "transcendental subjectivity" (p. 5) will leave entirely unresolved the actual nature of his perceptual conduct, precisely what Husserl wants to capture. This is, however, only the most preliminary statement of the difficulty.

After telling us that Hume's *Treatise* constitutes "the first systematic sketch of a pure phenomenology," Husserl calls our attention to the fundamental importance of Franz Brentano's notion that objects perceived are not simply there but "intentionally" there. Always as human beings we "read" some human "intention" or "purpose" into the items upon which we focus attention. Accordingly, phenomenology sets out to explore not merely "consciousness" but "intentional consciousness," consciousness as people actually experience it, rather than as a Kantian critique might reason on it. Further, and this is crucial to the entire business, because "the objects" of "intentional experience" belong "inseparably" to the "description" of "the object as such" they have what Husserl calls an "objective meaning," an existence which cannot be divorced from any presentation of "objects" without suppressing a genuine aspect of human mentation (pp. 17–18). Hence, what phenomenology can be "objective" about are its "descriptions" of "intentional consciousness," or "consciousness-of." It can "clear up the modes in which knowledge and object stand to each other in the conscious life itself" (p. 19). A moment's reflection, however, reveals that Husserl's "intentionality" merely offers a superficial description of "projection," projection gutted of the unconscious intention, the internalization of the early period which has come to be projectively tied to our "observation" of both the inner and outer world. "Intentional objects" are always intentioned by the whole mind. In a very real sense, adumbrated by Freud's growing recognition of the degree to which "the ego" is rooted in "the unconscious," there is no such thing as "consciousness" at all, "consciousness" in the way we are used to thinking of it. As for Husserl's "pure consciousness," or "transcendental subjectivity," or "pure eidetic description" (p. 6), it only brings us to one of the central contentions of this section: while "intuition" "holds" the object in Descartes, while "impression" "holds" it in Hume, "form" in Kant, and "object" in Hegel, the concept of intentionality "contains" the internalized object in Husserl (and in phenomenology generally) and prevents his philosophy from guiding us to an accurate understanding of the way we "mean" or "intend" the world.

Like Hegel, Husserl aids us greatly through his insistence that an "intangible" — in this case the "intention" — comprises a facet of the object, that objects have in human perception a real human dimension which is always there; at the same time, he goes no further than Hegel in recognizing the unconscious side of the issue. Husserl cannot "clear up," as he puts it, the "modes in which knowledge and object stand to each other in the conscious life" because, during an age in which psychoanalysis is on the rise, there for him to see, he will not deal with the "modes" in which "knowledge" and inner object "stand to each other" in the unconscious life. There is genuine irony in Husserl's contention that "phenomenology" is "very relevant to psychology" (p. 18). For while that is true enough, the obverse is also true: psychology — and in particular the psychology of internalization — is "very relevant" to phenomenology. Until phenomenology faces up to that it will be unable to offer us a genuinely "new way of looking at things" (p. 39).

Even Husserl's famous notion of "bracketing" perceptions, which resides at the heart of his methodological scheme, cannot survive what we may call his "intentional" omission. Husserl suggests that one gets past ordinary consciousness, or the "natural attitude" in which what is "there" is naïvely and automatically accepted as "real," by doubting radically the genuineness of everything one encounters, either directly through one's perceptions or indirectly through one's stored information. The entire given world is suspended, bracketed, so as to open the mind to the essences or forms that lie behind the thick, customary "impressions" we are used to. In order to get at "the form of Being itself," or the "indubitable sphere of Being," writes Husserl, we "suspend" the entire "fact-world," we "disconnect" it, we "bracket" it, and precisely through this "method" we attain the phenomenological "epoche" or "reduction" which alters the "ground of knowledge" (pp. 95–99).

But when Husserl goes on to declare that his "method" applies "exclusively to that zone of consciousness which belongs to the model essence of a perception as 'being turned towards an object'," when he states that "we are aware of things not only in perception, but also consciously in recollections... and in the free play of fancy" (p. 106), all the old problems re-emerge. For the internalized object impinges directly upon the "essence" of the methodological suggestion. It lurks within the brackets. It accompanies and vitiates the attempt to change the mode of awareness. There can be no "disconnection" of ordinary consciousness while the object in which that consciousness is rooted is left connected at the bodily level and hence governing the perceptual life. There can be no "suspension" of the ordinary world, and hence no "sight," without a bodily practice, a bodily method, which gets at the internalization in a hard, physical manner. If one removes the tip of the plant while leaving the roots intact he is not really entitled to call a new tip "new" in the way Husserl "intends" the word. We grasp from this perspective why Merleau-Ponty (1964, p. 72) once remarked that Husserl's "intuition" was really no different than Descartes' and that in matters of methodology Husserl quite simply failed to break new ground. From our perspective, Husserl appears to have been the "philosopher" Freud had in mind—although I feel certain he actually was not—when Freud ([1938] 1959, p. 378) wrote that philosophy's chief problem resided in the philosopher's inclination to deal only with the phenomena of consciousness.

Husserl's Doubts

Remarkably, Husserl himself came to realize the inadequacy of his entire project and to struggle against that realization. He knew he was going nowhere, he knew he was unable to "present" in a theoretically acceptable, "scientific" fashion (p. 19) the methodological pathway to the "structures" of "the mind" (p. 6). The passages in which this struggle occurs are not only striking and unforgettable in themselves, they bring home again the urgent need for a synthesis of phenomenological and psychoanalytic insight, particularly with regard to object relations. It is hardly a coincidence, as we recall Freud's gradual appreciation of the degree to which the ego contains unconscious materials (Chapter 4), that Husserl's agonized attempts to salvage his philosophical edifice transpire as he wrestles with the notion of "pure ego," that is, the "ego" which permits us to "experience" the "Pure intuition" of perceptual life, of "Being."

Husserl's dilemma emerges in earnest during the course of his chapter on "Consciousness and Natural Reality" when he writes: "Even an experience is not, and never is, perceived in its completeness; it cannot be grasped adequately in its full unity. It is essentially something that flows, and starting from the present moment we can swim after it, our gaze reflectively turned towards it, whilst the stretches we leave in our wake are lost to our perception. Only in the form of retention or in the form of retrospective remembrance have we any consciousness of what has immediately flowed past us. And in the last resort the whole stream of my experience is a unity of experience, of which it is in principle impossible... to obtain a complete grasp. But *this* incompleteness... which belongs to the essence of our perception of experience is fundamentally other than that which is of the essence of 'transcendent' perception [?]" (p. 127). Shortly thereafter, as he develops his methodological recommendations of "bracketing" and "suspension," and as if he is bothered by the same logical problem of "pure experience" (p. 151) or "pure consciousness" (p. 151) or "transcendent perception" (p. 127) which he touched on in the long passage just cited, Husserl asks: "How fares it then with the *pure Ego*? Is even the phenomenological Ego which finds things presented to it brought through the phenomenological reduction to transcendental nothingness? Let us reduce till we reach the stream of pure consciousness. In reflection every *cogitatio* on being carried out takes the explicit form *cogito*. Does it lose this form when we make use of a transcendental reduction?" (p. 156).

What is the answer? "We shall never stumble across the pure Ego as an experience among others within the flux of manifold experiences which survives as transcendental residuum; nor shall we meet it as a constitutive bit of experience appearing with the experience of which it is an integral part.... The Ego appears to be permanently, even necessarily, there.... It belongs to every experience that comes and streams past, its 'glance' goes through every actual *cogito,* and towards the object" (p. 156). And then, in a candid moment that reveals the logical trap in which he has placed himself, Husserl remarks, "the pure Ego appears to be *necessary* in principle." While "it can *in no sense* be reckoned *as a real part or phase* of the experiences themselves," it "lives out its life in a special sense.... In the words of Kant, 'the I think must be able to accompany all my presentations'" (p. 156). Necessary "in principle" perhaps, but Husserl fails to pin down for us what that "special sense" is in which the "pure Ego... lives out its life." By returning us (in desperation?) to the authority of Kant, he merely returns us to the very dilemma of a transcendent position out of which he wants, ultimately, to get.

137

Not only does the dilemma refuse to go away, it has been around a long time: "In the *Logical Studies* I took up on the question of the pure Ego a skeptical position which I have not been able to maintain as my studies progressed" (p. 157). Husserl could not maintain that sceptical position because the concept of "pure Ego" is the bedrock of his entire system, "*necessary* in principle" but *inexplicable in experience*. A few pages later Husserl tells us that phenomenology, "if it figures as a science within the limits of . . . immediate intuition," as a "science of Essential Being," has given to it "in advance" the "nature of its procedure" as "something that needs no further explanation" (p. 174). In other words we are now simply to assume the possibility of the existence of the "pure Ego" because phenomenology deals in "essences." The nature of the discussion guarantees the validity of its methodological tools. Clearly, this pathetic circular argument is rooted in the same nagging problem which informs all those earlier passages. "It must be possible through fresh reflections to convince oneself . . . that statements in the methodological propositions can be given with complete clearness," Husserl fairly cries out in the ensuing paragraph. It must be possible to achieve a practical understanding of the elusive "pure Ego," otherwise the whole phenomenological initiative is tainted by the problem of reflection reflecting on itself, a perceptive experience.

The nadir of Husserl's attempt to defend the "pure Ego" comes as he maintains that "it would be going too far to say that all self-evident apprehension of the essence demands that the subsumed particulars in their concrete fullness should be fully clear. It is quite sufficient when grasping essential differences of the most general kind, as those between colour and sound, perception and will, that the exemplifying instances should show a lower grade of clearness" (p. 181). This is, obviously, nothing more than a backing off, a compromise, an assertion that leaves the whole question open. What is Husserl to do? He finally bursts out with, "Let the reader figure the situation for himself in vivid intuition." And then, doubting the very nature of his quest, throwing his hands up in despair, he asks: "Is it right to set phenomenology the aims of pure description? A descriptive eidetic: is that not something altogether perverse?" (pp. 181, 184). There is far more here than a mere descriptive difficulty. Indeed, as Eugen Fink made clear as early as 1939 (Fink [1939] 1981, p. 6), the descriptive problem is rooted in the conceptual dilemma: "No philosophy can be in complete possession of all its concepts." In these last few citations from Husserl's *Ideas* we see the western intellectual, who has left the body out of his methodological schemes, out of that philosophical practice which is supposed to lead the practitioner to a new kind of knowledge, chasing his own tail hopelessly in an irresolvable logical dilemma. Husserl seeks to "disconnect" the ego from its ordinary perceptive existence while ignoring the ego's connection, as a perceptual mechanism, to the bodily foundations, the psychophysical internalizations, in which it takes its origin.

Eastern thought has been successful, largely, in escaping this unfortunate position. "It is not . . . by the mental will in man that [liberation of consciousness] can be wholly [accomplished]," writes Sri Aurobindo (1974, pp. 29–30), "for the mind goes only to a certain point and after that can only move in a circle. A conversion has to be made, a turning of the consciousness by which mind has to change into the higher principle. This method is to be found, [for example], through the ancient . . . discipline and practice of yoga." Husserl's *Ideas,* in the final analysis, moves in the hapless, intellectual circle to which Aurobindo refers. What, then, of the *Cartesian Meditations,* a work that was written late in Husserl's career and that supposedly "breaks new ground" in resolving the issue of "pure Ego" (Lauer 1965, p. 54)?

Pure Ego: Glimmers of Futility

The most memorable thing about the *Cartesian Meditations* ([1929] 1960)[7] is not the new epistemological ground they are supposed to break but the way they indicate Husserl's growing realization that the problem of self-reflection, or "pure" egotic consciousness, is rooted in the problem of the "beginning," the genetic and developmental issues of human existence which Husserl chose to ignore throughout most of his life. When he declares (p. 26) that "just as the reduced Ego is not a piece of the world, so conversely neither the world nor any worldly object is a piece of my ego, to be found in my conscious life as a really inherent part of it," he merely fills us with a renewed sense of the enormous limitations of his "mentalist" approach, which appears to be oblivious of the degree to which the objects of the external world are internalized into the body of the perceiving organism. "Reflection" may "make an object" out of "what was previously a subjective process but not objective" (p. 34), yet "reflection" also leaves the object of the inner world untouched and thus in control, in preventive control, of the modal shift Husserl seeks to induce in his followers. Once and for all let us admit that there is no "pure psychology of consciousness" and hence no "transcendental phenomenology of consciousness" (p. 32) because there is no pure consciousness, no egotic awareness that is not touched by unconscious processes, by those "immortal objects," to use Roy Schafer's expression, that become an integral aspect of the body-mind during the early years (Schafer 1968, p. 220). There is no "a priori self-explication" that "gives the facts their place in the corresponding universe of pure . . . possibilities" (p. 84), for in the sphere of consciousness "possibilities" are never "pure," any more than "forms" are in Kant's "transcendental" sphere. Husserl may deny (p. 86) that his method is Kantian and ultimately carries the old Kantian dilemma of "purity," but all he doth in that methinks is protest too much. The denial bears witness to the persistence of the problem.

When Husserl tries further to justify his position by employing the image of the mirror and by stating that his "monadic very-ownness" is "mirrored" in "his own ego" (p. 94), he calls to mind the psychology of narcissism, the degree to which our "egos" are derived from the initial mirroring relationship with the objects of the early period. Husserl, generally in all his work, is simply not aware that the ordinary self of ordinary consciousness is a derived self, and that the derivation springs from the mother-infant bond. We are "windowless monads" (p. 94) only to the extent that our projective perceptual activities do not constitute a "real," "objective" window, a "real," "objective" way in and out of the "monad," and I mean "objective" here in the old, dualistic sense of the Cartesian dichotomy. Husserl rightly employs "intention" in explanation of the manner in which his "monads" contact one another in interpersonal relations (p. 115), but he does not see that "intentionality" is present in all self-perception too, that "intentionality" harbors the object in the dynamic sense we are developing here. Husserl's special "grasping" perception (p. 101) in which the "ego" is supposedly given to itself merely recalls the emotive grasping of the infant as he sets up his primitive ego by taking the caregiver into his "visceral brain," his responsive, perceiving organism. To declare, as Husserl does, that it is "no longer an enigma how I can constitute myself in another Ego," and that "this identification is no greater [an] enigma than any other identification" (p. 126), obliges us to point out that it is the monumental discovery of unconscious "identification," of the degree to which our earliest and deepest internalizations impinge upon the "identifications" of later years, that has assisted us most profoundly as inhabitants of this century in "grasping" the "enigma" of interpersonal relations.

These references to "identification" and "enigma" put us in an excellent position, I believe, to take up those passages in which Husserl appears to be aware that what is fundamentally wrong with his system has something to do with key psychological issues. As he remarks upon "the parallels" between the "psychology of consciousness" and the "phenomenology of consciousness" (p. 32) he calls to mind similar passages in his *Ideas* ([1913] 1969, p. 18) in which phenomenology's relevance to psychology is stressed. Yet, when he writes that his phenomenological "reduction" and "synthesis," that is, his inadequate method, "equips us with the principle for combining any relatively closed constitutional theory with any other by an incessant uncovering of horizons—not only those belonging to objects of consciousness internally, but also those having an external reference" (p. 54), he seems to reveal a sensitivity to the problem of inner objects similar to the one Freud ([1915] 1971) revealed in his groundbreaking essay on the unconscious.

Nothing comes of this, however; for the spell of the "pure Ego," the faith in the existence of such an entity, and the inability to see a way out of the theoretical difficulty it presents, drive Husserl a few pages later back into the old position of "purity" as well as into philosophical descriptions that become more and more bizarre and unintelligible: "In my synthetic activity, the object becomes constituted originally, perceptively, in the explicit sense-form: 'something identical having its manifold properties,' or 'object as identical with itself and undergoing determination in respect of its manifold properties.' This, my activity of positing and explicating being, sets up a habituality of my Ego, by virtue of which the object as having its manifold determinations, is mine abidingly" (p. 68). I am aware, needless to say, of the difficulties inherent in Husserl's "peculiar" style; yet I must still contend that the only thing "abiding" here is the confusion. Or take this utterance: "The 'ready-made' object that confronts us in life as an existent mere physical thing ... is given, with the originality of the 'it itself,' in the synthesis of a passive experience. As such a thing, it is given beforehand to 'spiritual' activities, which begin with active grasping" (p. 78). There is nothing "spiritual" about the dynamic perceptions of the inner world or about our awareness of them. Husserl makes "spiritual" precisely that which he does not understand.

It is these three items, Husserl's consciousness of the fundamental relationship of phenomenology to psychology, his dim sense of the inner object, and his struggle to connect the question of the ego to matters of cognitive functioning, that cause him to admit in his final pages that his systematic effort to render the essence of human perception feels "keenly" the "problem of genetic constitution" (p. 135), the "problem which leads us" (and here are the decisive words—written with courage and candor) to the "enigmas" concerning that which is "innate" in human "character" (p. 136). Indeed, as he confesses a moment later, not realizing perhaps how his whole edifice is compromised by the point, "the above-indicated genetic problems of birth and death and the generative nexus of psychophysical being have not yet been touched. Manifestly they belong to a higher dimension and presuppose such a tremendous labor of explication pertaining to the lower spheres that it will be a long time before they can become problems to work on" (p. 142). Here at last the issue is fully in the open. It certainly *is* the "genetic problem" that is crucial to our understanding of epistemological matters, the "genetic problem" as it emerges from the analysis of unconscious processes, particularly in the area of internalization.

That Husserl should declare this problem is of a "higher dimension" that has "not yet been touched," presumably in both his work and the work of others, is bewildering, for this man was a contemporary of Freud; he lived in a world where Freud's writings were being read and widely discussed, even by Husserl's "existential" followers (Binswanger, for example). How is it that Husserl fails in his work not only to take up Freud's discovery of the unconscious, but even to mention Freud? To read Husserl is to get the impression that the whole development of modern psychology was not occurring in Europe during the early part of this century. We cannot, of course, answer this question with certainty, but an answer does suggest itself in Husserl's final remarks, in his reference to the "hugeness" of the problem of the "beginning," in his appreciation of the fundamental nature of the "genetic" question. To have explored this in even a preliminary way, and to have attempted to use it at all in his philosophy, would have obliged Husserl to undergo a veritable Copernican revolution as an epistemologist. It would have obliged him to refashion his system. Most of all, perhaps, it would have obliged him to reassess his old philosophical ties to Descartes, Hume, and Kant. This, Husserl simply (and understandably) was not willing to do.

Husserl's system, more obviously and more explicitly than the systems of his predecessors, seeks to provide men and women with a means (the "reduction") to alter their awareness and, through such alteration, to gain a contact with themselves, each other, and the world that is fresher and more acute than that which is provided by "the natural attitude." He ([1913] 1969, p. 166) once wrote that phenomenology is "the secret longing of the whole philosophy of modern times." Yet such a quotation calls to mind not only *the systems* of the pivotal modern philosophers; it calls to mind also the peaceful meditations of Descartes which preceded his intellectual work, Hume's quiet walks along the river, walks in which his mind became "collected," Kant's lengthy, serene contemplation of "pure reason," and Hegel's attempt to absorb himself in the perfection of the Absolute. The "secret longing" of modern philosophy reveals itself as much in these activities, activities designed to achieve a certain relaxation, as in the formal theoretics of the completed writings. Until phenomenology, along with the other "schools" of modern philosophy, opens its theoretical door to the discovery of the unconscious, and more specifically, to the discovery of the degree to which the perceiving ego is fraught with the tensions of the internalized object, that "secret longing" will remain unfulfilled.

Merleau-Ponty: The Centrality of the Body

We have in Merleau-Ponty a thinker who is universally regarded as the finest proponent of phenomenological philosophy to have emerged since the Second World War, a writer of enormous learning and genuine literary gifts, the modern heir to the tradition initiated by Descartes. Moreover, we have in Merleau-Ponty not only a philosopher who is supremely aware of the body's role in epistemological matters, but a theoretician who has familiarized himself with the work of Freud and other recent psychologists. Here, perhaps, we will discover an integrated approach to the problem of self-reflection, to the problem of "objects" and "objectivity" with which we have been dealing.

Merleau-Ponty's reflections upon the body's role in experience frequently occur within Kantian contexts, contexts in which the inadequacies of a transcendental position are underscored. "The thinking ego," we are told, "can never abolish its inherence in an individual subject, which knows all things in a particular perspective. . . . This is why the problem of the knowledge of other people is never posed in Kantian philosophy: the transcendental ego which it discusses is just as much other people's as mine, analysis is from the start located outside me, and has nothing to do but to determine the general conditions which make possible a world for an ego—myself or others equally—and so it never comes up against the question: *who is thinking?*" (Merleau-Ponty 1970, pp. 61–62).[8] It is "the body" that "expresses total existence, not because it is an external accompaniment to that existence, but because existence comes into its own in the body" (*Phen,* 166). The philosopher who adopts a transcendental perspective "describes sensations and their substratum as one might describe the fauna of a distant land—without being aware that he himself perceives, that he is the perceiving subject, and that perception as he lives it belies everything that he says of perception in general" (*Phen,* 207).

Nor is the scientist untouched by this dilemma; on the contrary, he often forgets that "science" itself "is a form of perception" which easily "loses sight of its origins and believes itself complete" (*Phen,* 57). Thus, whether we are doing philosophy or science, or merely existing in everyday consciousness, the "thing" (and we can read "object" here) is "inseparable from a person perceiving it, and can never be actually *in itself* because its articulations are those of our very existence, and because it stands at the other end of our gaze or at the terminus of a sensory exploration which invests it with humanity" (*Phen,* 320). We cannot quarrel with this powerfully expressed position which recalls much of what we have said hitherto about the epistemological issue, but we can suggest in a preliminary way that Merleau-Ponty's insistence that the "thinking ego" can "never abolish its inherence in an individual subject" calls to mind the whole problem of the presence of *the unconscious in the ego,* a problem which is "inseparable," in turn, from an analysis of the *internalizations* that in large measure comprise the unconscious *and* the ego. The ego's "thinking" engages that "other" realm in which the percept is governed not simply by the body out of which it "gazes," but by the psychic "material" that has been taken into the body, that "colors" the percept with an affective "tone," and that constitutes the very "humanity" of which Merleau-Ponty speaks. How can the human aspect of perception be fully grasped if one fails to discover its root in the objects of the early period, with all their ambivalence, tension, and bliss? Perception is an emotive act, and the "thinking ego" is a conflictual entity, always aware of "the beginning."

Merleau-Ponty is careful not to treat the problem of perception in an unsystematic fashion. Only concentration upon the whole organism, upon its characteristic way of being in the world, can hope to offer an accurate psychological and philosophical picture of man. To talk of stimulus and response in a dualistic manner, to divorce the person from his field, to isolate perceptual phenomena artificially through restrictive experimentation, will lead only to a falsification and mechanistic dehumanization of our experience. "The form of the excitant is created by the organism itself to actions from the outside" (1963, p. 13).[9] From the moment of even the "weakest excitation, certain muscular, and consequently nerve, groupings are completely at work. Each wave, even the smallest, clearly seems to run through the whole system" (*B*, 24). In this way, "there is no physiological definition of sensation, and more generally, there is no physiological psychology which is autonomous, because the physiological event itself obeys biological and psychological laws. . . . The elementary is no longer that which by addition will cumulatively constitute the whole" (*Phen*, 9).

It is "no longer" in "pairs" that "mental facts" and "physiological facts" are "brought together," for "it is recognized that the life of consciousness and the life of the organism are not made up of a collection of events external to each other like the grains of sand in a pile, but rather that psychology and physiology are both investigating the modes of organization of behavior and the degrees of its integration" (*B*, 75–76). Once again, we cannot quarrel with this position, one that is particularly timely in a technological age. But we can stress that the "manner" of the organism's "offering itself to actions," the attitude, in short, of the psychological creature, can hardly be understood apart from the affective life of the early period, a life that cannot itself be "separated" from the "field," from the overall "mode" of "behavior." To speak of "integration," of perceptions working together in an ordered fashion, obliges us to see in "integration" a word that calls to mind the way we handle those internalized "things" which, before we can reflect upon anything, come to influence our organizational "system," our "response" to experiential "stimuli" that awaken, along with other potentials, our capacity for defensive physical and psychological posture.

Pure Ego Again

Merleau-Ponty's remarks about the *goal* of phenomenology recall the work of Husserl. "A direct description of our experience as it is," a "return to things themselves," to "that world which precedes knowledge, of which knowledge always *speaks,* and in relation to which every scientific schematization is an abstract and derivative sign-language" (*Phen*, vii, ix), are the expressions Merleau-Ponty employs. As for the method of reaching "things as they are," or the "essences of perception" (*Phen*, vii), that too recalls the work of Husserl. Additionally, it brings us very close to the epistemological limitations of Merleau-Ponty's system as a whole. For we must ask, how can "contact" be "direct" when the mind conditions all that it encounters? How can "reflection" get at "essences" when reflection itself discloses our unique, individual "attitude" toward the world and toward ourselves as a part of the world?

Entering upon what he calls "this ambiguous domain" with the intention of "transforming the phenomenal field into a transcendental one" (*Phen*, 63), Merleau-Ponty tells us that "reflection does not withdraw from the world towards the unity of consciousness as the world's basis; it steps back to watch the forms of transcendence fly up like sparks from a fire; *it slackens the intentional threads which attach us to the world and thus brings them to our notice*; it alone is consciousness of the world because it reveals that world as strange and paradoxical" (*Phen*, xiii, my emphasis). And he goes on, "in order to see the world and grasp it as paradoxical, we must break with our familiar acceptance of it and, also, from the fact that from this break we can learn nothing but the unmotivated upsurge of this world. The most important lesson which the reduction teaches us is the impossibility of a complete reduction. . . . Looking for the world's essence is not looking for what it is as an idea once it has been reduced to a theme of discourse; it is looking for what it is as a fact for us, before any thematization" (*Phen*, xiv, xv). The difficulty emerges in earnest: if we cannot "reduce" completely how can we talk of establishing "direct contact"? And if a complete reduction is "impossible," as Merleau-Ponty says it is, how incomplete is the incomplete part? What is the measure of it? Such a difficulty will not easily go away. Merleau-Ponty, in fact, wrestles with it again and again, just as Husserl does.

Merleau-Ponty tries at one point to analogize the "reduction" by calling to mind a description of mental activity in Kant's *Critique of Judgement:* "Kant . . . shows . . . that there exists a unity of the imagination and the understanding and a unity of subjects *before the object*, and that, in experiencing the beautiful . . . I am aware of a harmony between sensation and concept . . . which is itself without any concept. Here the subject . . . discovers and enjoys his own nature as spontaneously in harmony with the law of the understanding. . . . It is no longer merely the aesthetic judgement, but knowledge too which rests upon this art" (*Phen*, xvii). Yet exactly how we go about achieving this "art" in a hard, methodological way for knowledge remains an issue, in spite of the beautiful analogy. For as Merleau-Ponty tells us in another place, "in no case can consciousness entirely cease to be what it is in perception . . . it cannot take full possession of its operations" (*Phen, 50*). And again, "we are never the unreflective subject that we seek to know; but neither can we become wholly consciousness, or make ourselves into the transcendental consciousness. If we were consciousness, we would have to have before us the world, our history and perceived objects in their uniqueness as systems of transparent relationships" (*Phen, 62–63*). And finally: "Since perception is initiation into the world, and since, as has been said with insight, 'there is nothing anterior to it which is mind,' we cannot put into it objective relationships which are not yet constituted at its level" (*Phen, 257*). Thus the kind of "reflection" that Merleau-Ponty offers us in his pursuit of the reduction must reach into what he calls a "pre-objective realm" (*Phen, 12*), and it must reach into that realm in a very special way, one that resolves the dilemma he has himself revealed. In his own terms, we must attain "a new *cogito*" (*Phen, 50*) which will make the epistemological problem disappear once and for all at the methodological level.

Merleau-Ponty never achieves his goal; his writings failing to offer us a genuine methodology which might lead us to an actual modal shift. His supposedly "new *cogito*" is, in the last analysis, merely an intensive reflection in which internalized materials lurk and in which the individual still views the world through a projective screen. Let me illustrate the problem by, first of all, focusing on a number of Merleau-Ponty's passages which strikingly reveal the psychological shortcomings of his approach, and then, by examining closely his theories of perceptual development and their implications for the achievement of "direct contact."

Intentionality

To suggest, as Merleau-Ponty does, that "our perception ends in objects" (*Phen, 67*), calls to mind the thesis of this entire book. "Perception" must be taken to mean "ordinary perception," perception that is tied transitionally to the internalized objects which enter the "perceptual apparatus" during infancy. Merleau-Ponty writes, "whether a system of motor or perceptual powers, our body is not an object for an 'I think,' it is a grouping of lived-through meanings which moves toward its equilibrium" (*Phen,* 153). But he does not recognize that our "meanings," or "intentions," are connected inextricably to "meanings" that were not simply "lived-through" from the beginning but *taken into the perceiving human organism* from the beginning. At the unconscious level, the internalization *does* give an "objective" existence to the "I think." It obliges us to consider "equilibriums" as attainable either within ordinary consciousness where we can gain at best an anxious balance, a state of persistent, "adaptive" tension and stress, or outside of ordinary consciousness where we can gain some genuine equilibrium through the moderation of perceptual ties to the inner world.

There is no way to "slacken the intentional threads," as Merleau-Ponty puts it, that link us to the universe because in phenomenology "intentionality" is precisely where the internalization dwells. Merleau-Ponty's "threads" constitute a kind of perceptual umbilicus that binds the perceiver to the past at the level of his mind and body. Because reflection, no matter what kind it is, cannot directly touch that mind-body, it is ultimately insufficient as a methodological tool. Indeed, *as* "I think," or *as* "I reflect," I *re-establish* "threads." Thinking and reflecting are ways back to the object of the early time. The reflection *itself* reconfirms a subjective dilemma that will continue to exist until methodology confronts the entire infantile process out of which ordinary consciousness arises, until it engages the internalization in a practical way at the bodily level, until, in a word, it *cuts* the "intentional threads."

Clearly then, the great problem in Merleau-Ponty—and this applies to other recent philosophers such as Paul Ricoeur and Susanne Langer—is his failure to recognize the extent to which the human animal is an internalizing creature. Although Merleau-Ponty has a profound phenomenological understanding of space and time, his analyses lack the full, psychodynamic dimension. "The house itself is not the house seen from nowhere," he writes, "but the house seen from everywhere. The completed object is translucent, being shot through from all sides by an infinite number of present scrutinies which intersect in its depths leaving nothing hidden" (*Phen,* 69). But something *is* left hidden here, namely the extent to which our perception of the house, "infinite" though it is spatially, projects the object of the inner world through which our senses of location and space are formed. While it is true that "to look at an object is to inhabit it" (*Phen,* 68), it is also true that, in ordinary, everyday awareness, "to look at an object" is to be inhabited *by* "the object" associated with spatial representations on the inside. "The object makes its appearance through the medium of time" (*Phen,* 240) in two senses—one phenomenological and one psychoanalytical—which cannot be disassociated. The *internalized* object "makes its appearance" to the infant's "dawning psyche" in close, inextricable connection with the infant's dawning sense of sequential relations that ultimately produce for him/her a continuum of time. "Objective being" certainly does have "its roots in the ambiguities of time" (*Phen,* 333) because "objective being" is "being" rooted in ordinary consciousness and hence in the ambiguous (ambivalent), split internalizations of the primary years, internalizations which give the "objectivity" of being its unconscious signification. Let us probe further into all of this, following Merleau-Ponty closely as he develops his ideas.

Reflection

The "original object" of the perceptual life, writes Merleau-Ponty, is not an "unorganized mass" or chaotic jumble, but "the actions of other human subjects" (*B,* 166), for perception "is a moment of the living dialectic of a concrete subject." When perception is "nascent" it has a "double character"; it is "directed toward human intentions rather than toward objects of nature or the pure qualities (hot, cold, white, black) of which they are the supports." Thus, "infantile perception attaches itself first of all to faces and gestures, in particular to those of the mother" (*B,* 166). But the infant, we must point out at once, is not merely "directed" toward his "human subjects," or even "attached" to them. Such a view reflects the old Freudian notion of "infantile cathexis." The infant "participates" in his "subjects" *literally* by taking them in, by psychically internalizing them into his actual perceiving *body.* What occurs is a genuine psychobiological event of an instinctual, defensive nature, an event that reflects the neotenous emergence of the little simian creature from the mother's womb, as well as the long and precarious period of dependency, full of separation anxiety, that lies ahead of it. Merleau-Ponty declares that it is "out of the question to suppose in children the perception of *objects* defined by the ensemble of visual, tactile, and sonorous properties" (*B,* 167). But what of those *parental objects* which are the "intentional" targets of the infant's internalizing urge, and which come to reside permanently in the "perceptual apparatus" that discovers the "properties" of "objects" later on? No matter how much we would like to, we cannot, at the theoretical level, divorce the perceiving ego from its unconscious aspect.

When Merleau-Ponty states that the "notion of form," or "configuration," or "sensory gestalt," permits us "to describe the mode of existence of the primitive objects of perception" which are "lived as realities" rather than "known as true objects" (*B*, 168), he brings us to a philosophical and psychological crossroad. There *are no* "true objects" in the dualistic sense Merleau-Ponty means, and one is surprised to discover the distinction in his work. The objects of the early period are indeed "lived as realities," but so are *all* "objects" of the perceptual life within ordinary, transitional awareness. Of course there are differences between infantile and adult perception. At one deep emotive and perceptual level, however, there are *not*. It is the purblind, persistent denial of this truth (cf. Flew 1978) which will prevent people from understanding the extent to which irrationality inheres in human development.

By the time the development of language transpires, the "structures" prefigured in the child's consciousness which will allow him to discover the "act of speech," and to construct the ordinary, symbolic world where he will dwell as an adult, have become "structures" in a hard psychobiological sense and not merely in the sense of biological disposition, as Merleau-Ponty indicates (*B*, 168–69). The use of speech and the problem of separation cannot be divorced. The object of the early period is tied not only to early "intentionality" and hence to early human perception, but also to the early structuring of the organism and hence to the structures into which language "enters" as the ordinary world, or "the natural attitude," undergoes its growth in earnest. In this way, "speech and other persons" are not, as Merleau-Ponty suggests, "indecomposable structures," or the "a priori" of human perception (*B*, 171). On the contrary, "other persons" are "decomposable" into the first internalizations, and to that extent they are "objective"; they are the projective and incorporative targets of the infant's anxiety. No mere reflection can "reduce" a "reality" grounded in such psychological factors. The crack of the Zen master's staff on the head has a much better chance. All of this calls to mind Merleau-Ponty's explicit attempt to link his psychological discussion to epistemological matters.

"The radical originality of Cartesianism," Merleau-Ponty writes, "is to situate itself within perception itself. . . . Beyond causal explanations which constitute the appearance of perception as an effect of nature, Descartes, in search of the internal structure, makes its meaning explicit and disengages the grounds which assure naive consciousness that it is acceding to 'things'; that, beyond the transitory appearances, it is grasping a solid being in a piece of wax, for example" (*B*, 195). He goes on, "the Cartesian doubt necessarily carries its solution within itself precisely because it presupposes nothing—no realist idea of knowledge—and because—bringing attention back in this way from the vision or touch which lives in things to the 'thought of seeing and touching' and laying bare the internal meaning of perception and of acts of knowledge in general—it reveals to thought the indubitable domain of significations" (*B*, 195–96). Although Descartes, in this way, comes "very close to the modern notion of consciousness," he "does not follow his path to the end" because he gives us, finally "only the essence of the thing, only the intelligible structure of dream objects or of perceived objects" (*B*, 196). The "experience of a sensible presence is explained by a real presence; the soul, when it perceives is 'excited' to think such and such an existing object by means of a bodily event to which it 'applies itself' and which 'represents' to it an event from the real extension. The body ceases to be what it was vis-a-vis the understanding—a fragment of extension" (*B*, 196–97). The "experience of my body as 'mine' . . . is explained in turn by a real 'mixture' of 'the mind with the body'" (*B*, 197).

Thus "Descartes did not attempt to integrate the knowledge of truth and the experience of reality, intellection and sensation. . . . But after Descartes this integration was to appear. . . . It would permit abandoning the action of the body or of things on the mind and allow them to be defined as *the indubitable objects of consciousness;* it would permit . . . *associating* . . . a transcendental idealism and an empirical realism" (*B*, 197, my emphasis). Here Merleau-Ponty reaches the essence of his position: "the act of knowing is not of the order of events; it is a taking possession of events, even internal ones, which is not mingled with them; it is always an internal 're-creation' of the mental image and . . . a recognizance, a recognition" (*B*, 199). When we focus for a moment on the word "experience," which turns up so frequently in these quotations and which comprises a pivotal term in the distinctions Merleau-Ponty is making, and further, when we recall from our discussion of Hume that we cannot "go beyond" our experience, or "beyond ourselves" and that the object of the inner world lurks within "experience" itself, we begin to discern the fallaciousness, the inadequacy of Merleau-Ponty's conceptualizations.

Merleau-Ponty is suggesting that we can become aware, reflectively aware, of the experiential side of our perceptual behavior, of our inter-relations with the wax. We are able to realize, as Descartes did not, that we are in the bodily perception of the object, perceptually and irreducibly involved therein. This added experiential reflection, this phenomenological entering-in, or grasping, can bring us to the essence of our perceptive behavior, and hence, to the end of the erroneous dualism that haunts our civilization. The matter is expressed even more dramatically in the *Phenomenology of Perception* where Merleau-Ponty maintains, "the core of philosophy is no longer an autonomous transcendental subjectivity, to be found everywhere and nowhere: it lies in the perceptual beginning of reflection, at the point where the individual life begins to reflect on itself. Reflection is truly reflection only if it is not carried outside itself [?], only if it knows itself as reflection-on-an-unreflective-experience, and consequently as a change in [the] structure of our experience" (*Phen,* 62). It is not only the unintelligibility of "reflection" as a methodological tool at the conscious philosophical level that emerges here — the sorry tangle in which the problem of "pure ego" leaves phenomenology as a whole; what also emerges is the way in which our grasp of the internalized object as the basis of perception gets at the root of the problem, as Husserl suspected it might.

It is precisely *because* reflection "knows itself" as reflection that reflection is, in the end, reflection. And it is precisely because reflection is, in the end, an intellectual tool, tied to language, to our ordinary consciousness, to the running on of our thoughts *over* the "unreflective experience," that the "structure" of our existence will not be changed by its application. All that Merleau-Ponty's method will do is leave the object of the inner world residing beneath our supposedly elemental experience. Indeed, without overstating the case, to do what Merleau-Ponty recommends is to do almost nothing in the way of attaining direct contact with "objects." His procedure is simply another mentalist assault upon "the truth," a kind of super-aware *thinking* that cannot touch directly the tissues and the organs whence perception derives; it is a refinement of Husserl's "reduction" or "epoche" that ultimately postulates the existence of "pure ego" and therefore dooms itself to the same contradictions Husserl could not escape. It is not only Descartes who does not "follow" the matter "all the way back"; Merleau-Ponty does not do that either. The "constitutive history" (*B,* 208) of the human organism without which "the essence" of the creature cannot be grasped (is this Merleau-Ponty's concession to Husserl's insistence that phenomenology probe the "enigma of character"?) is a history not merely of "attachment" and "direction," of "intentions" in the phenomenological sense, it is a history of *internalization*. What is always recognized in ordinary consciousness as we go about our acts of "knowing" is the transitional, maternal figure of the early time. Life is not simply "a dream." Within everyday awareness, it is a dream of the absent object.

Contradictions

As he brings his discussions to a close, Merleau-Ponty seems to be aware of the contradiction in his position. "The idea of a transcendental philosophy, that is, the idea of consciousness as constituting the universe before it and grasping the objects themselves in an indubitable external experience, seems to us to be a definitive acquisition as the first phase of reflection," he declares (*B*, 215). He then asks, "but is one not obliged to re-establish a duality within consciousness which is no longer accepted between it and external realities? . . . Every theory of perception tries to surmount [this] . . . contradiction" (*B*, 215). What is the solution? Again, only a kind of *mental* activity: "The antinomy of which we are speaking disappears . . . at the level of reflexive thought . . . which encounters only significations in front of it. The experience of passivity is *not explained* by an actual passivity. But it should have a meaning and be able *to be understood* . . . The perceived is not an effect of cerebral functioning; it is its signification" (*B*, 215–16). We have here the weakest timber in Merleau-Ponty's phenomenological edifice. Ironically, he who recognized in bodily existence a great clue to the essence of perceptual life leaves the body *out* of his methodological schemes. The "understanding" that "grasps" the "perceived" is, rather obviously in fact, a mere heightened cognition in the old intellectual sense. There is no way for Merleau-Ponty to return to the "givens of naïve consciousness," to "things in exactly the sense in which I see them" (*B*, 219), through "understanding" or "reflection" without encountering the dynamic "givens" of the first internalizing relationship, the "objective" structure forged in the defensive requirements of infancy and childhood. As long as philosophy continues to believe that it is "merely an elucidated experience" (*Phen*, 63), and that, having declared its nature thus, it cannot be "any further clarified by analysis" (*Phen*, xviii), not only will it continue to wriggle in the grip of the problem of "pure ego," or "original experience" (*B*, 220), or "objectivity," it will not make any difference in our lives because it will not provide us with a genuine method for change. At this point the question arises, how is it that Merleau-Ponty, with his enormous learning and explicit interest in psychoanalysis, overlooked the issue of internalization and its great significance for human perception and human freedom generally?

Merleau-Ponty and Psychoanalysis

We cannot, of course, answer this question with absolute assurance, but we can point out a few striking possibilities. When Merleau-Ponty refers in his work to psychoanalysis it is not merely of Freud that he is thinking, it is the Freud of "repression, resistance, regression, the Oedipus complex." In short, it is the "classical" Freud with his theory of energic instincts and his nineteenth-century hydraulic models of behavior. Nowhere in Merleau-Ponty's work is there evidence of his having noticed, let alone familiarized himself with, the Freud who came to see an unconscious side to the ego, linked the perceptual life to the development of the inner world, and addressed the Kantian position directly by postulating a realm of inner objects. Merleau-Ponty's discussions of Freud are devoted primarily to demonstrating the degree to which psychoanalysis points us, inadvertently, toward a systemic approach to human conduct in which psychological items may be viewed as parts of a governing gestalt. Thus "the significance of psychoanalysis is less to make psychology biological than to discover a dialetical process in functions thought of as 'purely bodily,' and to reintegrate sexuality into the human being" (*Phen*, 158). Again, as with "Gestalt theory," no "layer of sense-data can be identified as immediately dependent on sense-organs: the smallest sense-datum is never presented in any other way than integrated into a configuration and already 'patterned'" (*Phen*, 159). This emphasis on pattern and system certainly has its strength. Indeed, it calls to mind recent trends in psychoanalysis toward an informational approach to behavior. Too, there is no question that much of Freud's work, particularly the early work, tends to play down the question of "integration," the meaning of the "symptom" to the whole person.

There is, however, a danger in such a gestaltist approach to behavior (a danger that calls to mind, also, the weakness of an informational approach): the emphasis comes to be on "human meaning" and "relevance to the whole person" in a "soft" way, a kind of humanistic way that loses sight of the dynamic, bodily unconscious, of the extent to which early conflictual experience enters into the very musculature, the very chemistry of the organism through the defensive employment of internalizing tendencies. I believe it may be said of Merleau-Ponty's work generally that the perceptual significance of the dynamic unconscious, particularly with reference to its impact on the body, goes unrecognized. As Merleau-Ponty himself declares, "the notion of Gestalt" leads us "back to its Hegelian meaning, that is, to the concept before it has become conscious of itself" (*B*, 210). Do we need to point out at this juncture that such "concepts" are loaded with unconscious materials, with the weight of conflictual developmental events which occur during the phases of infancy and childhood and which leave their "trace" upon the whole perceiving organism?

Merleau-Ponty's confinement to the early Freud—the Freud who had yet to realize the degree to which the perceiving ego reflected the unconscious—as well as his attraction to gestaltist explanations of behavior, stand squarely behind his belief in the "normalcy" of "ordinary humans," his assumption that "integration" can occur naturally, that it is not necessarily a condition which has to be achieved—in a word, his tendency to presume that normal, integrated people are, as it were, walking around in large numbers, everywhere. Merleau-Ponty's writing on this score is not only fascinating in itself but important for our purposes in a way noted below. "In the normal person every event related to movement or sense of touch causes consciousness to put up a host of intentions which run from the body as the centre of potential action either towards the body itself or towards the object" (*Phen*, 109). As we have seen, however, such passages, not only in Merleau-Ponty but in philosophy generally, can no longer be put forward without the word "object" carrying a dynamic signification. Because all "response" is influenced by the objects of the inner world, because the unconscious resides in the ego, the "stimulus" will "cause" the "consciousness" of even the "normal" person to move toward the "object" of the "external world" in a state of stress (frequently unrecognized). As Freud ([1926] 1959, p. 75) stated explicitly, the consciousness of *all* people is fraught with the need to "isolate" events from one another, to cope with persistent and powerful unconscious feelings of an unpleasant nature.

Anxiety, he wrote, is something that accompanies all of us throughout our lives. The "neurotic" differs from the "normal" person only in the *strength* of his anxiety. Thus, while there is certainly justification for distinguishing "normal" and "pathological," there is none for suggesting that "normal" is not burdened with stress, stress deriving from the anxiety, separation, rejection, and narcissistic defeats of the early time. Recent evidence, in fact, indicates that the child's very lack of effectiveness, something he cannot avoid, has a traumatic effect on his development. Merely being "unable to influence the environment" causes us to experience "narcissistic injury" and contributes to the delusional aspect of our conduct, to our compensatory grandiosity, or to our schizoid inclinations to withdraw from the world (Broucek 1979, pp. 311–16).

The point is, when Merleau-Ponty writes that the normal person's "life of consciousness" is "subtended by an intentional arc" which "projects round about" him his "past," his "future," his "human setting," and his "moral situation" (*Phen,* 136), he obliges us to use the term "projects" in a hard psychoanalytic way that captures the presence of the internalization in all the intentional, anxious perceiving that we "normals" do. There may exist in an "animal" activity that is both "normal" and "free" of "conflict" (*B,* 43), but there exists no such activity in the human animal, where "normal" means a certain measure of "conflict." The "integrated" man is not synonymous with the "normal" man, as Merleau-Ponty declares he is (*B,* 180). Integration is something "normals" strive to gain, and unless their striving includes a methodology that is able to touch the perceiving body in a concrete, physical manner that alters the legacy of tension at the actual, somatic level, it will never accomplish its goal. Clearly then, the full significance of Merleau-Ponty's belief in the adequacy of "normal" behavior is at hand: there is an essential connection between that belief, and his reliance on *reflection* as a method of achieving direct contact with objects. Like all phenomenologists, and like all ego psychologists too, Merleau-Ponty simply fails to recognize the degree to which consciousness, forever rooted in the body, hums with the transitional problems of life's first years.

The Alteration of Awareness

As Merleau-Ponty expresses them, the aims of phenomenology are strikingly similar to those of "mystical" detachment. Phenomenology is to "bring the world to light as it is before any falling back on ourselves has occurred" (*Phen,* xvi); it is to achieve a "direct and primitive contact" with the universe of which we form an integral part (*Phen,* vii). Phenomenology is not the reflection of "a pre-existing truth"; it is "the act of bringing truth into being" (*Phen,* xx). It is "an infinite meditation" (*Phen,* xxi). The body, indeed "my body," writes Merleau-Ponty, "has its world, or understands its world, without having to make use of my 'symbolic' or 'objectifying' function" (*Phen,* 140), and phenomenology's purpose is to give the individual a philosophical grasp of this "irreducible" dimension of his existence, a dimension in which knowledge and pure experience become one. It takes but a moment's consideration to realize that such words could as well be coming from the mouth of an accomplished Kabbalist or Zen master as from the pen of a French philosopher, and also that such words make phenomenology, with regard specifically to the reduction, look very much like that realm of perceptive mind-rest toward which psychoanalysis has long expressed a profound ambivalence, or even resistance (Wangh and Galef 1983). I want to explore this further.

Paul Ricoeur (1970, p. 376) has written that "what turns phenomenology directly toward psychoanalysis, prior to any elaboration of a particular theme, is the philosophic act with which phenomenology begins, which Husserl calls the 'reduction.' Phenomenology begins with a methodological displacement that already affords some understanding of [the psychoanalytic] displacement or off-centering of meaning with respect to consciousness." What must be stressed at this stage of the discussion, however, is that any phenomenological reduction which is to be methodologically effective must be "turned toward" a new psychoanalysis of perception, a psychoanalysis that appreciates the need for a methodology capable of achieving a detachment from internalized materials at the bodily level. As suggested earlier, neither "reflexive thought" nor the "talking cure" can alter the emotive, perceptual ground from which ordinary reality, or the natural attitude, arises. Now, to proceed from this perspective is to do precisely what the traditional disciplines, or the non-transitional "schools" of detachment (Zen, Yoga, Sufi) have been doing in an intuitive or "unscientific" way for centuries. It is not merely psychoanalysis and phenomenology that join in what we can call the new reduction; it is psychoanalysis, phenomenology, and *practice* that join.

Which reminds us for a final time that philosophy's deepest unconscious aim — its "secret longing" as Husserl expressed it — has not been simply the attainment of "objectivity" but the accomplishment of a new or renewed sight of the world in which the internalized object no longer rules our perception, killing wonder and joy, and breeding the stressful delusions of projective awareness. Descartes, Hume, Kant, Hegel, Husserl, Merleau-Ponty—all these philosophers have sought not only "truth" but release from "passion," from what Spinoza called "human bondage," from the anxiety and tension of the "parent in the percept." To this extent these philosophers have sought the delight of a full, free, open evolving consciousness. And indeed, it may be suggested that all philosophy, religion, and psychoanalysis is, in the last reckoning, a struggle toward the evolution of a higher awareness, capable of detaching itself from the symbolic, transitional mode of perception which has dominated the life of the species for perhaps 50,000 years.

Merleau-Ponty writes, "how significance and intentionality could come to dwell in molecular edifices or masses of cells is a thing which can never be made comprehensible" (*Phen,* 351). This statement is true enough if we take the word "comprehensible" in the ultimate sense, for who can know the secrets of the universe? But when we recall the manner in which the internalized object comes to reside in the individual, we do see "how" our "molecular edifices" can get the "intentions," the transitional anxieties and aims, which characterize our ordinary consciousness. To suggest that "all inner perception is inadequate because I am not an object that can be perceived" (*Phen,* 383) is to suggest something that is both right and wrong. In the deep psychoanalytic sense, a sense that we may not feel inclined to face, we *are* "objects," the objects that have entered us during the early period. And we will *remain* "objects" until we adopt a methodological "reduction" capable of getting those objects out of our "perceptions." "My body" is indeed "the fabric into which all objects are woven" (*Pen,* 235), objects in the dynamic sense, that is! "Might mechanistic science have missed the definition of objectivity?", Merleau-Ponty asks (*B,* 10). Assuredly it did. But so did phenomenology—by missing the "objectivity" of that inner world first explored by Freud nearly a century ago. Let us accept bravely, now, the need for synthesis among these three fields, psychoanalysis, phenomenology, and what I have chosen to call practice. If the reasoning in the context of this book has some consistency and strength, we can see that such a synthesis is not only of great heuristic and therapeutic value, but of great evolutionary value as well. It might just lead, in fact, to a transformation of the species, to an era in which the old pressures from within no longer make inner peace the possession of so few.

6
EPISTEMOLOGY AND THE
ISSUE OF SOCIAL
ORGANIZATION

It is not only the epistemological issue that psychoanalysis connects to the inner world of objects, to that "portion" of the environment that we "set up" in our "ego" and hence in our perceptual existence (Freud [1940] 1964, p. 205). Psychoanalysis connects the issue of social life, or group life, to that inner world as well. To think about it for a moment is to realize that it could not be any other way. For if our perception of "objects" generally is influenced by internalizations, and thus projectively based, then our perception of social "objects," of social entities and institutions, is bound to be similarly influenced and based.

The orthodox mainstream of psychoanalytic thought is prone to discover the unconscious foundation of the group's cohesiveness in its *identification* with the dominant paternal figure or, as Freud expressed it in his *Group Psychology* ([1919] 1955, p. 127), "the leader" who is "still" the "dreaded primal father." Freud's principal examples here were the church and the army. As we have seen throughout the course of this book, however, such identification, such *bonding,* is itself rooted in the *internalization of the primary caregiver* which marks human development from its inception. Identification is but a "higher" aspect of a more basic defensive manoeuvre. As Schafer (1968, p. 147) renders the matter, "identifications cannot be created out of nothing. They involve selective reorganization of already existing wishes, behavior patterns, capacities, viewpoints, and emphases—and quite possibly earlier identifications too... the *selective reorganization* of these already existing factors is evidenced by the subject's experiencing and expressing them under altered conditions, in a different style, [and] with a changed regard for the object." The point is, to modify psycho-analytic assertions about *the group* in accordance with our under-standing of internalization is to recontact vital insights into the psycho-dynamic nature of *civilization generally* as set forth in Chapter 2, for civilization, or culture, is also grounded in internalization and is as much a version of the "familial situation" as is the group to which Freud addressed his remarks. To cite Roheim's pivotal conclusions again, "civilization originates in delayed infancy and its function is security. It is a huge network of more or less successful attempts to protect mankind against the danger of object-loss, the colossal efforts made by a baby who is afraid of being left alone in the dark" (Roheim 1971, p. 131). Yet the issue goes deeper than this.

To recognize that the individual's tie to civilization is associated in-extricably with his tie to the maternal object is to recognize, in turn, that his tie to civilization is also associated with his tie to *ordinary per-ception,* for as we have seen, his ordinary perception—of time, space, symbol, language—functions in large measure as an avenue back to the mothering figure. Indeed, it originates largely as a defensive reply to the anxieties and disappointments of the early period, a period character-ized not only by the good breast and the good feed but also by helpless-ness, ambivalence, rage, frustration, terror, and splitting. The tension Freud discovers in the relation to the male leader is connected dynam-ically with earlier structural tension inherent in the imperfect relation with the female parent. When Freud ([1919] 1955, p. 128) writes that group "suggestion" is based upon an "erotic tie" and not upon "percep-tion" he reveals precisely the limitation of his approach. Erotic ties are *built into* our "perception" and should not be regarded dualistically. To perceive in ordinary consciousness is to feel the emotive realities of the inner world. Hence, we can no more probe the issue of our economic and political institutions apart from consideration of the internalized object than we can probe the organization of our philosophizing minds apart from such consideration. Our "perceptions" shape the cultural organization that surrounds us; we forge and re-forge it in a psycholog-ical give-and-take which comprises the unconscious side of our history.

The Centrality of Perception in Marx

I would emphasize, above all, that Marx's entire way of thinking, of ap-proaching the problem of economic and political organization and its relation to the individual, is rooted in an explicit epistemological position worked out in reference not merely to Hegel's phenomenology but in reference to Hegel's employment of the word "object" in his philosophical discourse. The essence of the matter is discovered in these brief quotations from Marx's *Critique of Hegel's Doctrine of the State* ([1843] 1975, p. 69):[1] "He has converted into a product, a predicate of the Idea, what was properly its subject. He does not develop his thought from the object, but instead the object is constructed according to a system of thought perfected in the abstract sphere of logic." Marx goes on: "His task is not to elaborate the definite idea of the political constitution, but to provide the political constitution with a relationship to the abstract Idea and to establish it as a link in the life-history of the Idea—an obvious mystification" (*CHDS,* 69–70). Again—and this is crucial—"the soul of an object, in this case the state, is established and predestined prior to its body which is really just an illusion" (*CHDS,* 70). Thus "reality" becomes "concept" (*CHDS,* 73). While Hegel "makes the predicates, the objects, autonomous," he does so "by separating them from their real autonomy, viz. their subject . . . the mystical substance [Idea] . . . becomes the real subject, [and] the actual subject appears as something else, namely as a moment of the mystical substance" (*CHDS,* 80). The "final, solid, distinguishing factor between persons," namely "the body," is lost in the systematic elevation of "universal spirit," or "God" (*CHDS,* 99–100). Now, the fundamental aim of Marx's revolutionary approach to economics and politics, the aim on which all practical measures rest, derives directly from this epistemological clash. I am referring to Marx's attempt to get individuals to look at the world in a specific way, a way opposed to Hegel's way in which the material object is absorbed into a spiritual reality. Important to keep in mind here is Hegel's metaphysical assertion that spiritual (or ideal) objects actually contain the material ones they absorb through a "negation of the negation."

To say that Marx's aim is to get people to look out at the world in a specific way is not to use a figure of speech. The individual must actually alter his mode of perception; he must achieve the ability to penetrate appearances—in short, he must attain that which comprises the traditional goal of all philosophy and sciences: direct contact with things as they are. "To recognize the inner essence and inner structure of [the capitalistic] process," to recognize what lies "behind its outer appearance," the new and revolutionary political economist must gain the capacity to "penetrate" the "phenomena" which surround him and which "strike [his] eye" (Marx [1867] 1967, Vol. 3, p. 168).[2] If one is "to be radical" he must be able "to grasp things by the root" (Marx [1844] 1975, p. 251). Our "programme must be," Marx ([1843a] 1975, p. 209) declares, "the reform of consciousness," a reform accomplished "not through dogmas" but by "analyzing... consciousness" itself, "whether it appears in religious or political form." Needless to say, as we recall for a moment the clash with Hegel's system, "the root" for Marx, or the "essence of phenomena," or "things as they are," means the exploited, suffering, struggling human *body* on whose back rests the bulk of the "establishment" in all its political and economic reality.

The epistemological emphasis carries through with perfect consistency to Marx's exhaustive analysis of capitalism. It cannot be overstressed that his assault on this system, an assault designed to catalyze certain measures of reform, is grounded in a perceptual strategy. Before one does anything else, he must gain a new perception of the economic setup in its underlying, and perhaps even unconscious, actualities. "Blinded" by the chase after riches, and by competition, the capitalist "misperceives" the nature of the organization he relies on. Specifically, he will not *see* the extent to which his "profit" derives from the exploitation of the worker. He has "a special interest in deceiving himself on this score" (*Kap,* Vol. 3, p. 168). Nor is the "labourer" less "mystified" in this regard than the owner. He doesn't *see* what is going on either. It is precisely such "misperception," such "mystification," that "revolutionary economics" must correct. "Vulgar economy," Marx declares (and note how the following sentences apply to such economists of our own day as Milton Friedman and Paul Samuelson), "does no more than interpret, systematize and defend in doctrinaire fashion the conceptions of the agents of bourgeois production who are entrapped in bourgeois production relations. It should not astonish us, then, that vulgar economy feels particularly at home in the estranged outward appearances of economic relations in which... absurd... contraditions appear and that these relations seem the more self-evident the more their internal relationships are concealed... although they are understandable to the popular mind" (*Kap,* Vol. 3, p. 817). And then, going to the heart of the matter and indicating the basis of his radical, penetrative approach: "But all science would be superfluous if the outward appearance and the essence of things directly coincided" (*Kap,* Vol. 3, p. 817). It might be noted parenthetically that few words turn up with more frequency in *Kapital* than the word "appear," in both its nominal and verbal forms. The word runs like a leitmotif throughout the work, announcing the omnipresence of Marx's epistemological intention.

In the *Grundrisse,* or the notebooks Marx used as the theoretical foundation for *Kapital,* the perceptual issue also emerges with striking clarity — this time in close association with his theory of objects. Discussing the manner in which the material object is transformed into a commodity by a productive process based not on direct relations of men to things but on socially manipulated, "alien" behavior, Marx ([1857] 1973, p. 92)[3] writes, "the need which consumption feels for the object is created by *the perception* of it. . . . Production produces consumption (1) by creating the material for it; (2) by determining the manner of consumption; and (3) by creating the products, initially posited by it as objects, in the form of a need felt by the consumer. . . . Consumption likewise produces the producer's *inclination* by beckoning to him as an aim-determining need." What Marx is demonstrating for us here is the integral relationship between the nature of the system and the perception of the system, the manner in which the system grounds its success in inducing a certain kind of perception of the object in the subject, a perception that transforms "things" into "commodities," and "commodities," in turn, into "fetishes."

"A commodity," writes Marx in *Kapital* (Vol. 1, p. 72) is "a mysterious thing," both "perceptible and imperceptible by the senses." He goes on, "in the same way, the light from an object is perceived by us not as the subjective excitation of our optic nerve, but as the objective form of something outside the eye itself. But, in the act of seeing, there is at all events, an actual passage of light from one thing to another . . . there is a physical relation between physical things. But it is different with commodities. There, the existence of the things [as] commodities, and the value-relation between the products of labour which stamps them as commodities, have absolutely no connexion with their physical properties and with the material relations arising therefrom. There it is a definite social relation between men, that assumes, in their eyes, the fantastic form of a relation between things." And then, "in order . . . to find an analogy, we must have recourse to the mist-enveloped regions of the religious world. In that world the productions of the human brain appear as independent beings endowed with life, and entering into relation both with one another and the human race. So it is in the world of commodities with the products of men's hands. This I call the Fetishism which attaches itself to the products of labour." If commodities were able to "speak," Marx declares in a famous, ironic passage which alerts us to the dynamic signification of the word object, "they would say: 'Our use-value may be a thing that interests men. It is no part of us as objects. What, however, does belong to us as objects, is our value. Our natural intercourse as commodities proves it. In the eyes of each other we are nothing but exchange values.' . . . So far no chemist has ever discovered exchange-value either in a pearl or a diamond" (*Kap,* Vol. 1, p. 83). Thus it is the "mind and consciousness" of both the owner and worker that is unable to perceive the "inner nature" of the system, an inner nature which is not "directly perceptible by the senses" (*Kap,* Vol. 1, p. 316). New, revolutionary perception is able to "obtain" a sight of the system's "pure form" after "stripping" its "incidental functions" away (*Kap,* Vol. 3, p. 268). No one, surely, can miss here the similarity between Marx's perceptual "program" and the aims of phenomenology, particularly as they are tied to the concept of "the reduction." The implications of this striking correspondence will soon emerge fully.

Commodities and Transitional Needs

Marx's analysis of "commodities," his postulation of an emotive "fetishism" that people attach to them, his realization that capitalist economics reflect perceptual tendencies identical to those which created the religious universe of projective realities—all of this bears witness to Marx having sensed what can only be called in our own day (following Winnicott) the *transitional* features of the capitalist system. Those features emerge most strikingly, however, from Marx's analysis of money, an economic object that, like "commodity," is perceived in a very special way. "In the form of *money,* all properties of the commodity as exchange value appear as an object distinct from it, as a form of social existence separated from the natural existence of the commodity" (*G,* 145). Again, "money in its final, completed character . . . appears in all directions as a contradiction, a contradiction which dissolves itself, drives towards its own dissolution. As *the general form of wealth,* the whole world of real riches stands opposite it. It is their pure abstraction . . . a mere conceit. Where wealth as such seems to appear in an entirely material, tangible form, its existence is only in my head, it is a pure fantasy. . . . On the other side, *as material representative of general wealth,* it is realized only by being thrown back into circulation, to disappear in exchange for the singular, particular modes of wealth" (*G,* 233).

The capitalist "thirsts" for his "money," his "profit," his "wealth," and he is indifferent to, indeed careless with, the "human material" he must exploit in order to get it (*Kap*, Vol. 3, pp. 86–88). Gold is his "holy grail," his "fetish" (*Kap*, Vol. 1, p. 133), his all-consuming "passion" and aim (*Kap*, Vol. 1, p. 593). Marx portrays the capitalist as the "knight of the woeful countenance" (*Kap*, Vol. 1, p. 598) searching for that stuff which is dearest to his heart. In this way, "celestial need" becomes "self-interest" (Marx [1843a] 1975, p. 241), and money becomes an idol, a god (*Kap*, Vol. 1, pp. 132–33). When we recall the general agreement among scholars (cf. Einzig 1951) that money originated in ancient religious *sacrifice,* that the first monies were the actual instruments and animals used in ceremonies designed to afford an impure mortal communion with a perfect, parental god, we recognize the transitional significance of Marx's assertion that capitalism—which is based upon monetary exchange—comprises "a religion of everyday life" (*Kap*, Vol. 3, p. 830). Profits enhance what I chose to call in Chapter 2 (following Roheim) the "dual-unity" of ordinary consciousness. They reinforce the individual's "hook" onto the internalized caregiver.

As for money's transitional significance as a means of offsetting the narcissistic wounds of infancy, as a means of responding to the bad object's "voice" within, we have this unforgettable passage: "That which exists for me through the medium of *money,* that which I can pay for, i.e. which money can buy, that *am I,* the possessor of money. The stronger the power of my money, the stronger am I. The properties of money are my... properties and [my] powers... I *am* ugly, but I can buy the *most beautiful* woman. Which means to say that I am not *ugly,* for the effect of ugliness, its repelling power, is destroyed by money.... I am *lame,* but money procures me twenty-four legs. Consequently, I am not lame.... Through money I can have anything the human heart desires" (Marx [1844a] 1975, p. 377). The full meaning of this material emerges when we recall that money in capitalist society is for Marx "the direct incarnation" of "human labour" (*Kap*, Vol. 1, p. 92), that it "holds" or "contains" the body of the worker who produces the goods that are exchanged. Hence, at the deep symbolical level where the tie to the internalization is experienced, money makes one the actual master of people, of human bodies. If the cultural world is an extension of the parents, as psychoanalysis teaches us (cf. Schiller 1980), then money permits the individual to control the parents. At both the level of "reality," and the level of one's unconscious existence, money helps to make one "strong." There is no need to continue. The transitional implications of Marx's analysis of capitalism and money are clear enough. We must now explore his depiction of the manner in which capitalism influences the moral or ethical treatment of human beings in society generally. This will point the way toward a synthesis of his humanistic conception of communism and our own grasp of the perceptual problems inherent in his recommendations for change.

The Reform of Consciousness Today

Under capitalism, Marx ([1844b] 1975, p. 266) informs us, "[man's] activity is a torment to him, his own creation confronts him as an alien power, his wealth appears inessential, in fact separation from other men appears to be his true existence, his life appears as the sacrifice of his life, the realization of his essence appears as the de-realization of his life, his production is the production of nothing, his power over objects appears as the power of objects over him." Marx continues ([1844a] 1975, p. 352), "private property has made us so stupid and one-sided that an object is only *ours* when we have it, when it exists for us as capital or when we directly possess, eat, drink, wear, inhabit it, etc., in short, when we *use* it." Under communism, by contrast, where private property has disappeared, "man produces man, himself, and other men. . . . The object, which is the direct activity of his individuality, is at the same time his existence for other men, their existence and their existence for him. . . . The material of labour and man as subject are the starting-point as well as the outcome of the movement. . . . The *social* character is the general character of the whole." Thus communism is, quite simply, "humanism," the "true resolution of the conflict between existence and being, between objectification and self-affirmation." What must be stressed at once here is the impossibility of achieving this kind of human "objectivity" while the inner world remains unaltered. We have seen the manner in which the internalizations of the early period root themselves in the body, in the sensuous, perceptual "apparatus" itself, in the perceiving ego from which the individual's relationship to the environment derives. As long as the individual is left attached at the root, the new and "revolutionary" economies of the day will merely breed (as they have) more transitional madness, more anxiety, more exploitation, more bodily suffering, more aggression. Thus, when we read Marx declaring that under communism man becomes a truly "human object," and when we think on the totalitarian communist regimes of our time, we see not only the historical irony of Marx's statement but its psychological import and hence its potential for change. Man will indeed become a truly human object in both the communist world and the capitalist world, where he is also a "thing" for the corporate exploiters and manipulative "ad men," precisely when he achieves the ability to moderate the influence of the internalizations that prompt his "passionate," transitional desires.

To suggest, as Marx ([1844b] 1975, pp. 269–75) does, that man's "egoism" is dramatically encouraged by private property, that the "object" of capitalistic production is the "objectification of [man's] own *immediate, selfish needs,*" only calls to our minds the unconscious side of the ego, the perceptual system itself which gives to "egoism" its explicitly transitional significance. "Each of us" does indeed only "see" his "objectified self-interest" in the "exchanges of capitalism," but it is an "objectified self-interest" that is unconsciously based upon our transitional manner of "seeing," a manner whose "objectification" derives from perceptual tendencies which are part of our ordinary development. Again, to suggest, as Marx does, that "capital becomes the process of production through the incorporation of labour into capital," and that "capital has exchanged a part of its objective being for labour" (G, 304), only calls to our minds the analytic significance of "incorporation" as a psychophysical feature of the early period. A defensive process which profoundly affects our style of relating to the world around us, "incorporation" leads at the unconscious level to the expanding corporations of our own "democratic" period which have succeeded the factories of the last century. Needless to say, it also leads to the state corporations of the so-called "eastern bloc" which have swallowed whole populations in their transitional quest for control.

All of this, of course, points to one overriding conclusion. The "reform of consciousness" Marx ([1843a] 1975, p. 209) calls for—the penetrative, "reductive," revolutionary awareness he relies on to reach an understanding of "the essence" of the system—must be accomplished in a hard, modal way that touches the "objectivity" of mankind in a deep psychological sense, that discovers and "decathects" through actual bodily practice the internalizations of the early time. According to Marx himself, let us remember, it is our manner of perceiving that perpetuates the objectifying tendencies of the economic system (G, 92),

167

the system that turns the human being into an object of the other's need. A "reform of consciousness" that limits itself to the scientific penetrativeness, or "critical philosophy," of Marx's "program" will not be able to "arouse" the world from its dream of itself" ([1843a] 1975, p. 209) precisely because it will leave the internalization lurking in the "perceptual apparatus." Hence, it will permit the egotic dream of ordinary awareness to continue unabated. The "empirical scientist" of the "revolution" will himself be a part of that dream.

Social Relations and the First Relation

We examined in a previous section Hegel's postulation of a transformational object that actually "absorbs" and "holds" the material object it "negates." Such an object achieves by this process a "negation of the negation," a restoration of the negated "thing" to a "higher" mode of existence. Thus in Hegel a purely spiritual or "psychic" entity—an entity comprised of mind—becomes as real, as actual, as the material object through which it expresses its nature. Marx strives to "correct" Hegel's spiritual emphasis by insisting upon the irreducible materiality of human experience, as we have seen. "What is the final, distinguishing factor between persons?", Marx asks, and the reply is, "the *body*" (*CHDS*, 100). Man is not, as in Hegel, "equivalent to *self-consciousness*." He is, on the contrary, a "directly *natural being*," with natural "dispositions" and "*drives*." A "non-objective being," declares Marx ([1844a] 1975, p. 389) in a memorable sentence, "is a non-being." Yet Marx ([1844a] 1975, pp. 385–87, 395) declares in another place that Hegel, in spite of his idealistic excesses, manages in his philosophy to "grasp" the "self-estrangement" of "man," or man's "alienation" from his "true," essential "nature." Now, the internalizations of the early period stand precisely between the idealism of Hegel and the materialism of Marx. The apparently irreconcilable positions of these men are bridged right here, as we recognize that integration is contingent upon our addressing a feature of our existence which is material and non-material at the same time. The "object" of the inward realm is in a very real sense intangible, immeasurable, invisible, a kind of informational "trace" in the "mental apparatus." Yet it is rooted in the body, in the senses; it is connected inextricably to the physical organism. It cannot be addressed, or touched, or altered, apart from the tissues in which it lives. To a significant degree, it is the perceiving body through which it governs the human being's sensorial feedback system. A crucial ameliorative suggestion emerges from this synthesis.

Marx ([1844a] 1975, p. 385) writes that in Hegel's *Phenomenology* "the philosophical dissolution and restoration of the empirical world is already to be found in latent form." What *we* discover "in latent form," however, as we think on the connection between Hegel's "psychic reality," Marx's material object, and the psychoanalytic world of internalizations, is the "dissolution" of ordinary consciousness that can be achieved through actual methods which engage the bodily domain, and the "restoration" of sound, non-transitional awareness that can result from such practice. Marx ([1846] 1967, p. 141) asserts in one place that mankind taken as a "mental totality," as a "mental fact," is "indeed a product of thinking, of comprehension; but it is by no means a product of the idea which evolves spontaneously and whose thinking proceeds outside and above perception and imagination, but is the result of the assimilation and transformation of perceptions and images into concepts." Thus "the human essence is no abstraction inherent in each single individual. *In its reality it is the ensemble of . . . social relations*" ([1846] 1967, p. 122). We can no longer exclude the *first* relations, the *first* society, the *first* world of the child—in short, the first *object relations,* from this sociological analysis. We must always bear in mind the degree to which perception itself, the "assimilation" and "transformation" of "images" into "concepts," carries the emotive, transitional issues which attach themselves to ordinary consciousness and determine the kind of object one man will become for another.

Again and again Marx ([1844a] 1975, p. 425) insists that our consciousness is invariably affected by the economic and political structures which surround us: "it is not the consciousness of men that determines their existence, but their social existence that determines their consciousness." And even more succinctly, "life is not determined by consciousness but consciousness by life" ([1846] 1967, p. 47). What, then, of Marx's own radical critique of capitalism? What of his own views? Are not they, too, determined by "life"? From a purely philosophical standpoint Marx never addresses this problem directly. As noted earlier, he merely aligns himself with the "scientific" methods of his day and regards his "critical philosophy" as a "scientific tool" capable of "stripping" away "appearances," of getting at the "essence" of things. Thus the problem of "pure ego," the problem of apprehending the environment "objectively," lingers in Marx quite as much as it lingers in the philosophers who preceded him.

The Sociology of Knowledge

The epistemological issue of "objectivity" is directly addressed in the political and economic investigations of our own day. According to Adorno ([1957] 1976, p. 252) the "resurrection of epistemological controversies that were fought out long ago, but which short-winded intellects, pleading the prior claims of present activity, are all too ready to forget," may well have the effect, eventually, of weaning the "social sciences" away from the callow "empirical" assumptions, from their "superstition" that "research has to begin with a *tabula rasa,* upon which data gathered without any preconceived plan are then assembled into some kind of pattern." It may be suggested in a general way that such epistemological concern has come to reside, perhaps maddeningly, at the centre of current political and economic debate. In one form or another, it creeps into all our efforts at examination, evaluation, and revision.

The most dramatic illustration of the point may be found in the work of Karl Mannheim, who strove to develop a "sociology of knowledge," that is, a method of detecting cultural, contextual influences in knowledge itself, in all ideas of a theoretical or practical nature, including those that touch upon questions of social organization. Mannheim writes in his major work, *Ideology and Utopia* (1936, p. 39),[4] that "the discovery of the social-situational roots of thought at first . . . took the form of unmasking." Gradually, "there entered into the public mind the tendency to unmask the unconscious situational motivations in group thinking." Today, however, Mannheim goes on, "we have reached a stage in which this weapon of . . . reciprocal unmasking . . . has become the property not of one group among many but of all of them" (p. 41). Hence, "there is nothing accidental . . . in the fact that more and more people [are taking] flight into scepticism and irrationalism" (p. 41). Keep these remarks closely in focus for the remainder of this book, for my central purpose here is to diminish this dilemma, this loss of confidence in thought, this belief in the radical subjectivity and partiality of all "knowledge," *by shifting the very assumptions of the argument,* by tracing the impasse not to "thought" but to a particular mode of awareness. Accordingly, a solution to the problem of "unmasking" will be found not in still another intellectual position but in a new methodological route. Let me illustrate.

Mannheim has a very good sense of the need for new directions when he addresses himself to the social scientist as follows: "Do not speak of truth as such but show us the way in which our statements, stemming from our social existence, can be translated into a sphere in which the partisanship, the fragmentariness of human vision, can be transcended" (p. 42). Mannheim devotes *Ideology and Utopia* to "showing" precisely this. However, to examine his actual recommendations—and I mean by that to examine them with an appreciation of the human animal's internalizing tendencies in mind—is to realize, unforgettably, the hopelessness of his program. Mannheim declares, "man attains objectivity and acquires a self with reference to his conception of his world not by giving up his will to action and holding his evaluations in abeyance but in confronting and examining himself. The criterion of such self-illumination is that not only the object but we ourselves fall squarely within our field of vision" (p.47). The "opportunity for relative emancipation from social determination," Mannheim goes on, "increases proportionately with insight into this determination" (pp. 47–48). Accordingly, when we hear the "subject" express "ideas" we are to regard them as a "function of his existence. . . . Opinions, statements, propositions, and systems of ideas are not taken at face value but are interpreted in the light of the life-situation of the one who expresses them" (p. 56). Because "historical totality" is "too comprehensive" to be "grasped" by "an individual point of view," all "points of view" are "but partial." However, since "all these points of view emerge out of the same social and historical current, and since their partiality exists in the matrix of an emerging whole, it is possible to see them in juxtaposition, and their synthesis becomes a problem which must continually be reformulated and resolved" (p. 151).

Thus the individual who practises a "sociology of knowledge" will be in a position not only to "unveil hidden motives" but "really to choose" (p. 262). Can anyone fail to see at this juncture that the problem to which Mannheim addresses himself persists in his method, as vigorously as ever? How, we must ask, do individuals achieve the ability to "reformulate points of view" without reflecting in the process their own unconscious inclinations and ideological assumptions? Is being aware of differences—even psychoanalytically and cross-culturally aware of

171

them—sufficient to curb one's own deepest aims? Might not the tendrils of unconscious purpose just extend themselves into all this self-examination and comparison of juxtaposed attitudes? With the context of this book in mind, it may be premature for Mannheim to discover in the "modern period" the "dissolution of the unitary objective world-view" which characterized western thought for many centuries (p. 39). That view may well remain at the unconscious level where, tied to the perceptual system itself, the egotic objectives of the personality make their presence known.

Mannheim declares in one place, "if the problem of the nature of reality were a mere speculative product of the imagination, we could easily ignore it. But as we proceed, it becomes more and more evident that it is precisely the multiplicity of the conceptions of reality which produces the multiplicity of our modes of thought.... Each group seems to move in a separate and distinct world of ideas... which... may be reduced to different modes of experiencing the same 'reality'" (pp. 98–99). What emerges from this statement is not merely its obvious "truth" but its epistemological and psychological inadequacy as well. "Reality" is made not only in a conscious, sociological, anthropological sense; it is also made in a hard psychodynamic sense which reflects the influence of the internalization in the "reality" that exists at the conscious level. In this sense, *all* men and women live in *one* "reality," one ordinary, transitional "reality" in which the perceptual system maintains the purposes that entered the organism during the early periods of development. It is not so much the "realities" of the world that have *variety*—they are all rooted in the object—as the ways in which anxiety and narcissistic preoccupation manifest themselves through cultural symbols. Clearly then, what Mannheim offers us as a method of change—a heightened sensitivity, a heightened consciousness, an intensified version of Marxian awareness itself—is too weak to handle the underlying tensions that reside in the "realities" of "groups." With the unconscious working its will in everyone—including those who know all about it—such a method will fail to accomplish anything genuinely new. It will not touch the *body*, the perceiving body, in which the unconscious is based.

As it turns out, Mannheim is aware of a dilemma and somewhat uneasy in his scheme. Even after "we recognize" the "vanity" of "discovering truth in a form which is independent of an historically and socially determined set of meanings," he writes, we have not solved anything.

We are merely in "a better position to state the actual problems" (p. 80). In another passage he maintains, "the attempts to distill a pure theory out of the sphere of political economy . . . is another instance of the aim to distinguish sharply between 'evaluation' and 'factual content'." And then, "it is not yet certain how far the separation of these two spheres can go. It is by no means impossible that there are domains in which this can be done. The 'non-evaluative' . . . character of these spheres will be fundamentally assured only after we have analysed the body of axioms or the categorical apparatus which we employ with reference to its 'roots' in a *Weltanschauung*" (p. 187). But surely anyone can see that nothing "objective" will be "assured" by such an "analysis" as long as the analyzer remains in an egotic perceptual state that reflects the transitional aims of the unconscious. Mannheim is pushing the method that contains the dilemma as hard as he can in the hope that the dilemma will somehow go away. When he writes that in "the realm of politics . . . there is no such thing as a purely theoretical outlook," that "the purposes a man has give him his vision," and that the "task of sociology" is to "establish" this (p. 170), he merely confirms our doubts.

Actual Detachment

I would not want to suggest that Mannheim's treatise fails to offer us anything of value in the way of resolving this epistemic problem. There are, to be sure, a number of useful passages on this score. But their usefulness emerges fully only as we apply to them insights gained from recent analytic investigations of the psychodynamics of internalization and the transitional features of ordinary consciousness. Mannheim writes, for example, that "to Marxism belongs the credit for discovering that politics does not consist merely in parliamentary parties and the discussions they carry on, and that these . . . are only surface expressions of deeper-lying economic and social situations which can be made intelligible . . . through a new *mode of thought*" (p. 150, my emphasis), through the "gaining" of a genuinely "*detached* perspective" (p. 282, my emphasis). This calls to mind the need for modal change in a concrete sense, a sense that would touch the unconscious directly by actually altering awareness, by *really detaching* the individual from his symbolical world, from his transitional feedback system, so that he might *return* to social concerns from another "sphere" in which the "partisanship [and] the fragmentariness of human vision" have been "transcended" (p. 42).

We desperately require, Mannheim asserts, "a new conception of objectivity" (p. 47). It is precisely such a new conception that our psychoanalytic epistemology gives us, a conception which sees the internalized object "defused" within the perceptual system, which sees the egotic attitude toward the environment lessened through "objective," bodily practice. Mannheim is indeed correct in declaring that "our revision of epistemology" has not "up to now . . . taken the social nature of thought sufficiently into account" (p. 50). But *we* must take *this* statement to include (as we did with Marx) the "social nature" of infantile existence itself, the period in which the "perceptual apparatus" absorbs the "good" and "bad" stimulations which invariably attend its development. If our "purposes" reside "in our perceptions" rather than "in addition" to them, as Mannheim claims (p. 295), then to achieve the kind of "unattachedness" (p. 157) Mannheim considers to be healthy for the future we must adopt a method of change that permits us to purge those perceptions of the old, unconscious "purposes" that inform them, purposes which discovered their origin in the anxieties of life's first years.

Considering that such a method calls to mind the "mystical" techniques of the world's transcendent "schools" (Zen, Yoga, Sufi), I find it ironic, and very instructive, that Mannheim, like Marx and Freud before him, discovered in mysticism only an ecstatic "longing" for the "world of the beyond" (p. 215). It is a world "beyond" the transitional madness of *this one* that the practice of perceptive mind-rest may afford us.

Habermas and the Frankfurt School

Mannheim's influence upon the members of what has come to be known as the Frankfurt school of sociological research—Adorno, Marcuse, Horkheimer, Habermas—is considerable. Of these critical thinkers it is Habermas who addresses his work most directly to the kinds of perceptual and epistemological issues with which we have been dealing. Concerned with modifying the influence of a growing technological revolution that may appear to be ideologically neutral but that shapes our world along lines which correspond to the wishes of those in power, Habermas drives home his thesis with uncompromising insistence: mindless devotion to the advancement of technology furthers particular interests and aims. It fosters an irrational world of dangerous material expansion and greed. To regard it as somehow divorced or removed from the political-ideological sphere is not merely to be blind and irresponsible, it is actually to support those who strive to dominate and exploit their fellows. The perils Marx discovered in the classic capitalist system Habermas discovers in the vast technological network of corporate control that, with the aid of governments, spreads itself across the so-called democratic societies of the west.

To offset this tendency, Habermas ([1963] 1974, p. 51)[5] declares in one of his earliest books that the modern obsession with "mastering nature" must rediscover the ancient purpose of all political and social organization — namely, living in compliance with the natural order. For centuries western cultures considered not simply the goals and directions of action, but the question of rightful goals and just directions. If our world is going to progress in a humane, moral way it requires more than the "methodological rigor" of "modern science"; it requires a "clarification of consciousness" as well (*TP*, 79). From Aristotle and Plato, to More, Locke, and Marx, says Habermas, there has always been a theoretical connection between our methods of social development and the *aims* of our society (*TP*, 115). Today, however, "the claim by which theory was once related to praxis has become dubious. Emancipation by means of enlightenment is replaced by instruction over . . . objectified processes" (*TP*, 254). Yet the "positivistic adaptation to a basic philosophy of . . . pure control" cannot "take the place" of traditional moral and philosophic concerns without damaging severely the well-being of mankind (*TP*, 115). What, then, are we to do? How are we to end the "peculiar domination of the external over the internal" (*TP*, 235)? How are we to halt the "false consciousness," the "evil," of an "infinity of material progress (*TP*, 234), the march of a mindless "technical control" which encourages "the growth of a mass of irrationality" (*TP*, 265)?

Habermas's solution to this problem is epitomized in the words "reason" and "reflection." "Reason," he writes, "takes up a partisan position in the controversy between critique and dogmatism, and with each new stage of emancipation it wins a further victory. In this kind of practical reason, insight and the explicit interest in liberation by means of reflection converge. The higher level of reflection coincides with a step forward in the progress toward the autonomy of the individual" (*TP*, 254). Western societies, indeed all societies, must attempt "to attain a rational consensus on the part of citizens concerning the practical control of their destiny." For only an "interested reason" can end the "confusion" of "control with action," the positivistic view of society as merely "a nexus of behavioral modes" available to "sociotechnical control" (*TP,* 255). In this way, like Marx and Mannheim before him, Habermas cries out for not less than "a change in the state of consciousness itself," a change in which "reason will attain power over dogmatism... because it has incorporated the will of reason in its own interest" (*TP,* 256–57). "Today," he asserts, "the convergence of reason and commitment, which the philosophy of the [Enlightenment] considered to be intimately linked, must be regained.... The demythification which does not break the mythic spell but merely seeks to evade it will only bring forth new witch doctors. The enlightenment which does not break the spell dialectically, but instead winds the veil of a halfway rationalization only more tightly around us, makes the world divested of deities itself into a myth" (*TP,* 281).

There is no need at this point in the discussion to dwell upon the inadequacy of all this. The call for reason, for a change of consciousness, for enlightenment in the traditional western sense, means little in relation to a creature in whom perception itself is fraught with irrational aims. What Habermas misses here is precisely what Freud discovered in *The Ego and the Id,* namely, the presence of the dynamic unconscious in everyday, egotic existence, the *normative* connection between conscious, "rational" processes and the projective realm of deeply buried anxieties. What Habermas also misses is what Freud's followers discovered, namely the degree to which our perceiving *bodies* contain and express the transitional desires of the early period, the period in which our internalizing minds become defensively operative. To call for "reason" in a creature that is by virtue of his normal development not reasonable is to provide a solution that is no solution at all.

Psychoanalytic Hermeneutics

In his subsequent efforts to strengthen his rationalistic position Habermas, like other members of the Frankfurt school, relies upon what can be termed a psychoanalytic hermeneutics, a methodological tool designed to interpret the "texts" of individual and cultural expression in a way that calls to mind the specialized theologian's attempt to interpret the religious texts of the past—but with an added sensitivity, derived from Freud, to the unconscious dimension of symbols and words. According to Ricoeur ([1965] 1976, p. 194), hermeneutics comprises, on the one hand, "the manifestation and restoration of a meaning addressed to me in the manner of a message, a proclamation, or as is sometimes said, a kerygma." On the other hand, it comprises "a demystification," a "reduction of illusion." And then, "psychoanalysis... aligns itself with the second understanding of hermeneutics."

There are, of course, philosophical problems in this approach. Wilhelm Dilthey himself, the pivotal figure in the rise of hermeneutics as an historical and sociological tool, was supremely aware of them. "The whole of a work," he wrote (Dilthey [1900] 1975, p. 115) toward the turn of the century, "must be understood from the individual words and their combinations, and yet the full comprehension of the details presupposes the understanding of the whole. This circle is repeated in the relationship of the individual work to the disposition and development of its author, and once again in the relationship of the individual work to its literary genre.... Theoretically one comes up against the limits of all exegesis here; it always completes its task only up to a certain point." Later writers such as Gadamer ([1965] 1976, pp. 121–32), however, have traced the problem not merely to the matter of the whole and the part but to the matter of self-reflection, subjectivity, the unconscious. "The prejudices and fore-meanings in the mind of the interpreter are not at his free disposal. He is not able to separate in advance the productive prejudices that made understanding possible from the prejudices that hinder understanding and lead to misunderstandings." Because "knowledge of oneself can never be complete," one must continually "test his prejudices" in order to provide his interpretations with a measure of "objectivity." It is precisely this issue, this interpretative, epistemological issue expressed in hermeneutic and psychoanalytic terms, which takes us to the heart of Habermas's most crucial suggestions, and through those suggestions, to an understanding of the Frankfurt approach to social issues as it has expressed itself during recent years (cf. Keat 1981, p. 207).

"Whether dealing with contemporary objectivations or historical traditions," writes Habermas (1968, p. 181),[6] "the interpreter cannot abstractly free himself from his hermeneutic point of departure. He cannot simply jump over the open horizon of his own life activity and just suspend the context of tradition in which his own subjectivity has been formed in order to submerge himself in a subhistorical stream of life that allows the pleasureable identification of everyone with everyone else." Nevertheless, Habermas goes on, hermeneutic understanding "can arrive at objectivity" to the extent that "the understanding subject learns . . . to comprehend itself in its own self-formative process. An interpretation can only grasp its object and penetrate it in a relation in which the interpreter reflects on the object and himself *at the same time* as moments of an objective structure that likewise encompasses both and makes them possible" (*KHI,* 181). Indeed, declares Habermas, "the pursuit of reflection knows itself as a movement of emancipation. Reason is at the same time subject to the interest in reason. We can say that it obeys an *emancipatory cognitive interest,* which aims at the pursuit of reflection" (*KHI,* 198). In this way, "a new stage of self-reflection in the self-formative process of the species" (*KHI,* 213) is not only within our reach, it is the "only possible dynamic" through which "enlightenment" may be gained, the "only possible dynamic" through which the steady advance of technological irrationality may be halted (*KHI,* 288). Habermas proceeds to work out in great detail the practical and theoretical processes involved in the development of his emancipatory scheme.

His efforts are based on the belief that human communication is, at least in part, biologically rooted in the individual's desire to communicate actualities, to indicate what is *there,* to express correctly his observations of the world. In Habermas's own words (1976, p. 98),[7] human communication is a "structure of rationality," a structure that can be purged, through stringent intellectual analysis and discipline, of its tendency to distort the "objects" of its "experience" (*CES,* 23). Habermas reminds us that "the *concept of ego development,* ontogenesis, can be analyzed in terms of the capability for cognition, speech, and action" (*CES,* 99–100). From "Hegel through Freud, to Piaget," he goes on, "the idea has developed that subject and object are reciprocally constituted, that the subject can grasp hold of itself only in relation to and by the way of construction of an objective world. This nonsubjective is, on the one hand, an 'object' in Piaget's sense—a cognitively objectified and manipulable reality; on the other hand, it is an object in Freud's sense—a domain of interaction opened up by communication and secured through identification" (*CES,* 100). Such distinctions prompt Habermas to offer us—as opposed to "purposive-rational action"—what he calls "*communicative action,*" action that is "oriented to observing intersubjectively valid norms that link reciprocal expectations" (*CES,* 118).

Here, "the validity basis of speech is presupposed. The universal validity claims (truth, rightness, truthfulness), which participants at least implicitly raise and reciprocally recognize, make possible the consensus that carries action in common. . . . The consensual presuppositions of communicative actions can secure motivations" (*CES*, 118). By closely examining our development along the lines laid down by Freud, Piaget, Eric Erikson, G. H. Mead, H. S. Sullivan, and others (*CES*, 73), we can *see* where the ego goes astray in its communicative actions, and we can guide it toward a communicative norm in which all participants share their deepest needs and goals. Thus we can gain control over "those relations of force that are inconspicuously set in the very structures of communication," those "relations of force" that "prevent conscious settlement of conflicts" (*CES*, 119). There is no need for sociology to bid a "melancholy farewell" to psychoanalysis because the dynamics of individual neurosis cannot explain the ills of society (*CES*, 71). On the contrary, the work of the psychologists just mentioned—Erikson, Sullivan, Mead, and Freud—can help us to grasp the communicative significance of ego development and hence the method for achieving genuine inter-societal and cross-cultural communication in the service of rationality.

The overwhelming problem here resides in Habermas's attempt to mix the psychoanalytic and "Piagetian" positions, to employ an intellectually re-educated ego as the vehicle for achieving "objectivity." Piaget's notion of the "cognitive object" (*CES*, 98–102) guts human development in a way that cannot be reconciled with the findings of those who explore object relations along psychodynamic lines. As Wilden (1972, p. 349) expresses it, "Piaget seems quite honestly afraid to discover the irrationality of what passes for reason in western culture." There is no cognitive development among humans that occurs apart from affective development, affective development that is integrally connected to cognition at the perceptual, bodily level. It is not "identification" but internalization that must be introduced conceptually in order to grasp the psychoanalytic nature of the ego's growth. "Identification" invariably contains a history of object relations which bear significantly upon cognitive processes in a hard, structural way from the inception of human life. Habermas is attempting to get around the epistemological dilemma by offering us a patched-up dualism in which the ego is all right over here (Piaget) and disturbed over there (Freud), and in which we attain to "reason" when the disturbance is cleared away. This will not do. No matter how much re-education the ego undergoes at the cognitive level it will not relinquish its irrational purpose. Indeed, within ordinary consciousness, *language itself,* the "communicative action" itself, is tied to the ego's ambivalent, transitional aims, is but an aspect of perception, a continuous unconscious arousal of the individual's deep-seated fears. There is simply no way to leave us firmly in the grip of the linguistic-symbolic mode of awareness without encountering an unreason solidly based in the imperfection of the early years. To escape unreason, to be free, the individual must achieve the ability to put language and symbol *off,* to moderate the tie to the "objects" within, the internalized presences *from which* the inclination to use language takes its *affective and cognitive* origin. The security of words is an ancient illusion for which the world has paid a huge price of suffering.

Habermas has no sense of the perceptual import of psychoanalytic structures. When he declares, following Marx, that "man" is an "ensemble of social relationships" (*CES,* 133) and that by the age of six or seven his basic ego structures have established his communicative potential; and when he declares, further, that a reflective grasp of these structures along hermeneutic-psychoanalytic lines can dispel the irrationality which vitiates human communication (*CES,* 146), he discloses, just as Marx does, his failure to appreciate the significance of the *first* "social relationship" in which the parental "object" enters the psyche. For Habermas "structure" is essentially mental and linguistic; the "ego" is tied cerebrally and through "identification" to the "elements" of "language" and "communication." Thus, Habermas refers to our "internal nature" (*CES,* 146) in a kind of Durkheimean manner that misses what might be called the other side of our experience, the *bodily side* in which the first internalizations are taken into the perceiving organism to be linked thereafter with all "communicative action." The "deep structures" that individuals follow "nonintentionally in generating observable cultural formations" are indeed related to the "psychoanalytic theory of language" (*CES,* 167, 169), but related to that theory as it understands and discloses the word as an avenue back to the parental figure and language as originating in the defensive reply to the fear of separation and loss.

What is the upshot? Habermas's methodology, rooted in Piaget, hermeneutics, Freud, and a group of ego psychologists who have still to really confront Freud's revolutionary discovery of the ego's irrational

180

nature, leaves the unconscious "object" lurking in the "cognitive structure," stimulating the organism from within, and preventing human beings from behaving in an enlightened fashion, a fashion that does not
betray at every crucial turn the press of transitional anxieties and
wishes. Which prompts me to offer the following, "radical" conclusion:
the epistemological issue should be closed. It cannot be rationally resolved. It is a feature, even a quirk, of ordinary consciousness. In a
strict sense, it is not a philosophical issue at all, but a modal, ontological one; its origin is not in "reality" but in our symbol-making, reflective, mirror-like brains. Which calls to mind a further observation: nowhere in Habermas's work is there a single syllable that attests to his
recognition of "reality" as a made and hence alterable category dependent for its existence on the individual's bodily, organismic perception.

As in Hegel, the body is almost totally absent in Habermas's writings.
Hermeneutics, reflection, communication, words—these are the central items in his revisionist program. His elaborate charts and graphs
(*CES*, 40,89) stand as a final, sad reminder of the futility of purely western methodologies, the futility of attempting to touch and change an internalizing animal through his head alone. Far from being the "only
dynamic" capable of allowing us to attain "enlightenment" (*KHI*, 288),
"reflection" merely reflects the dynamic tensions and imperfections of
the first mirror-relationship, the relationship that ultimately prevents
our "enlightenment" by encouraging the expression of unconscious
aims and their derivatives. We must look on the word "enlightenment"
as a guide to the future not only in the rationalist, eighteenth century
sense, but also in the traditional eastern sense. In *that* meaning of the
term resides not only the notion, but the *method* of "objectivity" or
detachment, the actual means of changing the individual's projective
perception of the world—including, of course, his projective perception of other human beings.

Technological Development: Computational Machines and Psychoanalysis

The Frankfurt school's most valuable contribution to our economic
and political awareness derives not from its methodological recommendations for change but from its dynamic, "running" depiction of
the current capitalistic setup, the system as it has developed from
Marx's time to our own. Far from being "vulgar Marxists" attempting

to apply old terms to new problems, the Frankfurt writers are acutely aware of the singular manner in which the modern industrial order has learned to cope with resistance, to prevent genuine reform in the distribution of wealth—in a word, to preserve its power base intact. Overwhelmingly, the shift in the organization of control has witnessed the interweaving of private business and governmental institutions, institutions which work to fulfil the system's "classical" purpose, namely profit, yet, at the same time, strive to protect the social structure on which the system rests. It is not merely enlightened self-interest that stands behind this protective function ("who needs a revolution?"), it is ideological commitment as well ("our democratic heritage"). Advanced capitalist societies, Claus Offe (1980, p. 13) points out, "appear to generate mass values and concerns which have high priorities for individuals for the sake of the expression of their individual and collective identity, but which, at the same time, are inaccessible to the established forms of articulation and resolution of political conflict and the definition of the concrete use of state power."

In this way, while significant changes have occurred, while conflict has softened into uneasy integration, while "consensus" provides a degree of protection for everyone, the old transitional aims of power and profit continue to express themselves as fervently as ever. In the words of Habermas (1971, p. 109), it is "not that class antagonisms have been abolished but that they have become latent. . . . The generalized interest in perpetuating the system is still anchored today . . . in a structure of privilege. . . . The political system has incorporated an interest . . . in preserving the compensatory distribution facade." Taken together, the recent productions of the Frankfurt school depict a huge, political-economic machine, a "one-dimensional" industrial state, steadily expanding and refining its influence upon the creatures through whom it derives its existence. Which returns us to Habermas's critical emphasis upon the role of technology in the origination and perpetuation of economic "realities."

The problem of technology, and the sciences related to it, cannot be genuinely grasped apart from the transitional dynamics associated generally with the industrial state. Technology and science, like business investment and consumerism, are related integrally to the "objects" of the inner world, to the issue of ordinary as opposed to altered perception, to the problems of anxiety, separation, and conversion that characterize the early, internalizing period of human life. Where Marx confronted the task of revealing the underlying nature of commodity and exchange, we confront the task of revealing the underlying nature — and by that I mean the underlying *psychoanalytical* nature — of our current devotion to technological objects and development.

Technology's transitional implications are revealed most arrestingly through analysis of the machine that resides at the centre of the current industrial and political order, namely the *computer*: it offers itself to its manipulator as a powerful little world, a powerful little universe, a kind of microcosm, that can be totally mastered, totally controlled, in such a way as to offset, at the unconscious level, early narcissistic wounds experienced in the failure to master, to control, the primary caregiver or "object." Writes Daniel Stern (1977, p. 68): "the mother's enormous flexibility in her capacity to perform infant-elicited behaviors with different distribution in time provides her with potentially exquisite control over the infant's attention, excitement, and affect." This "exquisite control" *can itself* constitute a narcissistic injury, create a feeling of inadequacy and powerlessness, attest to the enormous influence, the *omnipotence,* of the significant other person.

According to Broucek (1979, p. 315), the infant undergoes "trauma" when he is merely "unable to influence" an "event" he expected "to be able to control." *All* children, writes a reviewer of Dorothy Bloch's *So the Witch Won't Eat Me,* "find the parental power over life and death highly threatening. Since children find it too dangerous to direct anger and terror at their parents, those emotions are displaced onto witches, goblins and other fantasy figures."[8] In "adults," such anger and terror persist as an aspect of ordinary consciousness, of the normative, transitional, projective, perceptual system (cf. Rinsley 1983). Such emotions are involved in the attraction to the "wonder machine," the "fantasy figure" that promises *exquisite control* of the environment. Because the internalized object's rule is over our sensorial "knobs" and "adjusters," our organismic feedback system, *our perception itself,* because we do not possess in ordinary consciousness *the freedom to manage our perceptual lives,* we compensate by handling other "knobs," other "controls," other "stimulus-response systems." We master the environment by mastering machines that are projective models of our own narcissistic strivings — mechanical, inhuman versions of our own grandiose aspirations or deeply buried hostilities. When the researcher puts his information, his equations, his models, his precious intellectual creations, into his "switched on" computing machine, writes Harry Kleinberg (1977, p. 176), a computer expert, he "suddenly" finds himself in possession of a "mythical world whose fate he totally controls."

Like the maternal object herself, the computer is integrally associated with problems of *feeding*. Information derived from the perceptual life is fed into it, and it, in turn, feeds back information symbiotically. It may be said, in fact, that all questions bound up with the control of the computer and its control of us are directly related to metaphors of feeding and feedback, metaphors with genuine psychoanalytical import. One of the first lessons psychoanalysis taught us was that of the unconscious meaning of words. We must not forget that lesson here. Again, the computer, like the maternal object of the early time, cannot be manipulated without careful consideration of its positive and negative poles, its tendency to operate through simple oppositions inherent in terms such as "and," "not," "or" — in a word, its split, binary nature. If one feeds the machine appropriately along the positive and / or negative channels it "accepts" what one offers; if one feeds the machine wrongly it "rejects" one's offering and will not "come 'round" until the feeder has determined the correct "input," the input that will be incorporated into the "guts" of the creature so that it may work its transformative processes upon it, eventually feeding back the desired "response." The unconscious significance of this material is completed, of course, as we recall the current, widespread tendency to present the computer in art, literature, and film as a quasi-human entity, an object in the psychological sense of the term. As is often the case, the creative, imaginative expressions of the species—a species whose emotional life is determined by the manner in which it processes the information of the early years—harbor its deep, unrecognized wishes and fears.

This brings us to the issue of what Mortimer Taube (1961)[9] has called "the myth of the thinking machine," the question of whether or not the computer can "actually" be made to think, to fully adopt human powers of reception and response. The chief objections to this idea— and they strike me as irrefutable—derive from three directions: the nature of language, the ultimately informal character of mathematics, and the problem of the original programming itself.

With reference to the first point, "language as a system of meaningful symbols spoken or written is not a formal process and cannot be reduced to one without destroying its very nature. . . . When language is formalized it ceases to be language and becomes a code. Even those linguists who emphasize the primacy of speech as a physical phenomenon must use the nonformal notion of similarity in order to classify distinct physical events as constituting the *same* phoneme" (*CCS,* 7). Important to note here for its relation to subsequent points is the inextricable connection between affect and language development, between verbal communication and the internalizing of the primary object. The attempt to make the computer think, through the employment of a universal language, is an attempt to dominate the object of the inner world by transferring communication to a substitute that can be mastered by the programmer who controls the system, the programmer who now becomes the omnipotent feeder.

As for the problem of formalizing mathematics, it does not reside merely in the tedium of the business. Indeed, "if the objection to the difficulty of a purely formal treatment of mathematics lay only in its tedium, the advent of the electronic computer would have led to the complete formalization of mathematics. As it was, many problems which had resisted formal treatment because of the number of steps involved became amenable to formal solution with computers. . . . Success in this regard was so striking that many people began to assume that every mathematical problem could be formalized, that is, solved mechanically" (*CCS,* 6). However, "this goal . . . is not attainable. The formalization of mathematics requires that all mathematical statements be derivable from logical statements; but logical truth itself is informal" (*CCS,* 7). Transitional significances reside in these considerations just as they reside in considerations of spoken and written "phonemic" language, for the development of the numerical sense is also tied to the object of the early period. "Mathematics is a language," writes Anotol Rapoport (1974, p. 297), "not a set of facts about the external world . . . the objects of modern mathematical discussion are neither numbers of oranges nor rotations of cubes, nor flights of projectiles, but certain contentless relations." In this way, mathematics must be viewed in the general context of human communication, a context that cannot be divorced from the internalizations of life's first years without distorting seriously our understanding of what it means to be a person. "The deepest assumption underlying work in artificial intelligence," Hubert Dreyfus (1979, p. 203) reminds us, is "that the world can be exhaustively analyzed in terms of context-free data or atomic facts." It is precisely because people internalize "the world," or the "data" which "reach" the "perceptual apparatus"—and this includes the mathematical data—that human intelligence is characteristically contextual.

185

Machines, by contrast, do not internalize anything. They are fed. Hence they have no "understanding" — an ingredient of "intelligence" as we presently comprehend it.

The history of mathematics is fraught with doubts about the nature of infinity, doubts which reveal an underlying transitional dilemma. The "notion of potential infinity — that for any line there is always a longer line — ," writes Allan Calder (1979, p. 146), "is a reasonable extrapolation from natural experience. The concept of completed, or actual, infinity — that there are actually infinitely long lines — is metaphysically quite different, and it requires a daunting leap of the imagination when it is first encountered. . . . It was some time before the undeniable utility of the calculus forced mathematicians into an uneasy acceptance of it and of the actual infinity it implied." After carefully charting the struggle of modern mathematicians to "restore certainty" to their discipline, to remove from it all "theological" tendencies and "ideal objects," Calder (1979, p. 171) writes as follows: "to believe that mathematical truth exists independently of man's knowledge of it is an act of faith that most mathematicians enter into unconsciously." Like the scientist with his faith in the "paradigm" that happens to be current, the mathematician is not immune to projecting into his "pure" considerations affective material rooted in his dynamic unconscious. The endless, heated squabble over the "actual" or "potential" nature of infinity derives in large measure from that *ontological place* where one's basic doubts and insecurities about the nature of the universe are rooted: "the infinite normally inspires such feelings of helplessness, fatality, and despair that the natural human impulse is to reject it out of hand" (Rucker 1982, p. 51). And *that* place, we have come by this time to recognize, cannot *itself* be grasped apart from consideration of one's developing sense of time, space, boundary, extension, causality — in short, one's developing sense of existence as it grows through the primary influence of the maternal figure.

Now, the development of mathematics is tied to the rise of capitalism explicitly. "The new form of universal accountancy," writes Mumford (1966, Vol. 1, p. 278), "isolated from the tissue of events just those factors that could be judged on an impersonal, quantitative scale. Counting numbers began here and in the end numbers alone counted. . . . Wherever the capitalist spirit took hold, people became familiar with the abstractions of the counting house. . . . This order has been smoothly translated into automatic machines and computers, even more incapable of exercising humane judgement and discretion than a trained clerk." Thus the transitional feelings inherent in the employment of number as language are transferred to the capitalistic system — to its technological structure and the computing device (now quasi-human) on which it rests. The power of the industrial order is linked to that of a machine which reflects the power of the internalized object over the individuals who serve the irrational system.

Computers as Thinkers: Cognition and the Inner World

The notion of the original programmer is tied to "infinity" through the problem of infinite regression: if one goes back far enough, will he not always discover a human intelligence behind a mechanical device, even a device of unlimited complexity? Who sets the "omniscient" system into motion? "If it is possible to conceive a machine capable of constructing and programming another which is more complex and more efficient than itself," writes Errol Harris (1962, p. 481), "we could hold that such a process of reproduction of machines might be revolutionary. But nowhere in the series, however far back, could we presume a machine to come into existence out of disorganized parts. . . . Just as for St. Thomas the regress of causes cannot be infinite because the infinite regress never provides an *adequate* cause, so the regress of programming cannot be infinite because it provides no programmer who is logically complete and independent." Harris (1962, p. 476) then reminds us that "purposive activity" is "directed by the awareness of an order of life constructed by ourselves in the course of our experience in the effort to satisfy ourselves as total personalities. . . . It is the awareness of an order of life . . . which makes possible the exercise of deliberate choice." In this way, "although machines do effect processes of organization, although their activities are systematic and their functioning dependent upon structural interrelation of parts and operations, the medium in which they work is not consciousness, their objects are not feelings, and they have no means of *self*-expression for the communication of emotion or the avowal of *self*-awareness. These are the products of mental activity, and of that alone and where they are not actually or potentially present in some degree there is no mind."

When Harris writes that the machine's "objects" are not "feelings," and when he alludes to the mind as an emotive, sensorial, living entity,

187

he calls forth the psychoanalytic meaning of "object" and hence provides a clue to the unconscious side of the problem. I am referring here to the unconscious significance of the notion that what is produced by a complete system of awareness and is but a partial expression of it can at the same time become that system, that "mind," although by definition it (the part) does not contain the "mind" that created it in the first place. The issue recalls the dilemma of the "object" and the "Absolute" in Hegel. Indeed, the issue is essentially one of whether or not a material object can become, in the strict sense, ideal.

Hegel's transformation of an "object" into an "ideal object" which actually contains the material object and thus leads, logically, to the necessity for further transformation ad infinitum, is completed by fiat. The transformed object, says Hegel, approximates an Absolute which is pure spirit, and that is that. By contrast, the current belief in a "thinking machine" that somehow transcends the "mind" that produces it is rationalized through specific modern concepts such as "evolution" and "reproduction." Errol Harris (1962, p. 481) informs us, for example, that Professor J. J. C. Smart "boldly asserts that he believes human beings to be nothing but very complex machines. . . . The fact that artifacts cannot sign a document, he maintains, is purely accidental. They could do this . . . if they belonged to a society of machines that had evolved social rules about such matters." And again, "F. H. George draws attention to the fact that human organisms are, like artifacts, also constructed, but by a different sort of process, the biological process; and he hints that the construction of one machine by another would be no different in principle from animal procreation."

Thus, where Hegel can terminate the infinite regression by calling forth the Absolute in an orthodox theological fashion, the scientist must rely upon his belief in the nature of the machine itself. The machine becomes the Absolute, an object that possesses the features of "the creator." The machine, in a word, becomes that into which one places his absolute faith. The *transitional* significances are obviously embedded in the scientist's unconscious religious attitude, his "material Hegelianism." Mumford (1966, Vol. 2, p. 70) writes, the "machine" in "technological civilization" is the "Supreme Power, an object of religious adoration and worship." Additionally, the narcissistic wound of being derived from another, of not having produced oneself, and the unconscious wish to be one's own progenitor (Freud called this the "causa-sui project"), are also transferred to a machine that not only has the ability to produce itself but to make us omnipotent through our identification with its reproductive characteristics. The anxiety that stems from the inner world of objects and that is usually resolved through reliance upon a deity, is resolved in our own day by devotion to a computational device capable of controlling the world.

Many of the fears and fantasies surrounding the computer are delusional and speak clearly for the machine's ability to arouse the primitive unconscious: computers run mad, take over the world, devour and enslave human beings, and so on. Other fears, however, have ground, ground that cannot be appreciated apart from specific political and economic issues. "Dartmouth College President John G. Kemeny, an eminent mathematician, envisions great benefits from the computer, but in his worst-case imaginings he sees a government that would possess one immense, interconnecting computer system: Big Brother. The alternative is obviously to isolate government computers from one another, to decentralize them, to prevent them from possibly becoming dictatorial."[10] When we recall the work of Habermas (1971) and Offe (1980) in which the monetary fate of neo-capitalism is shown to be linked directly to governmental participation in business we see the full economic and ideological implications of the growth of a centralized computer service which spans the so-called public and private sectors.

What Mumford (1966, Vol. 1, p. 262) terms the "megamachine" — the business-government complex based upon computational, technological expansion — allows "the king in person to be overthrown and removed, only to return again in more gigantic and dehumanized form as the Sovereign State." Tying the issue directly to the matter of energy control, to the use of energic resources on which the welfare of the current economic order depends, Marvin Harris (1977, pp. 193–94) maintains that "the fuel revolution has opened the possibility for a more direct form of energy despotism" than existed in the past. In those countries in which nuclear power is emerging as an ultimate source of energy supply, "there already exists the electronic capability for the tracking of individual behavior by centralized networks of surveillance and record-keeping computers. It is highly probable that the conversion to nuclear energy production will provide precisely those basic material conditions for using the power of the computer to establish a new and enduring form of despotism."

The point is, when we unmask the technological developments of our own day depicted in Habermas, Offe, Mumford, Marvin Harris,

189

and others, when we relate the style of control and exploitation discovered in the industrial state to the technological object upon which the order rests, namely the computer, we discover the same kind of unconscious dynamics, the same preoccupation with narcissistic issues, the same fascination with mastery, with power, the same religious commitment to substitute divinities, in a word, the same transitional obsessions that Marx discovered in his unmasking of the "classical" capitalist system with its fetishes, gods, grails. And just as Marx held perception to be the central issue in perpetuation of that system, just as he realized the machine was driven by the manner in which the owners and workers perceived it, so we must recognize in our own perception the crucial factor in the maintenance and expansion of our own megamachine. The technological order of the day reflects the extent to which the internalized object enters our awareness to evoke our transitional mode of existence. The subtlety and pervasiveness of this influence makes it very difficult to detect. Indeed, in ordinary consciousness the perceptual system itself serves a defensive purpose and thus carries the transitional aims which find their way, quite naturally, into the economic sphere.

Accordingly, the revisionist call for a new man, a new consciousness, a new science, a new technology, is not, as Habermas (1971, p. 43) suggests, a "symptom" of our disturbance; it is the vital solution to the issue of where our burgeoning technology is taking us. The attainment of *reason* upon which Habermas pins his hopes will not come about until the rule of the internalized object, which persists *in consciousness,* in the egotic, "perceptual apparatus," in *reason itself as we know it,* is ended. Adorno ([1957] 1976, p. 245) has written, "only an insight into the genesis of the present patterns of response and their relationship to the intrinsic meaning of what is experienced would permit a true interpretation of the phenomenon registered." Marcuse (1969, pp. 37, 53) for his part has declared, "the revolution must be . . . in perception. . . . Radical change in consciousness is the beginning." Such remarks are related in a fundamental way. The new psychoanalytic epistemology, that is, the wedding of mind-body detachment to the discoveries of object relations theory, provides us not only with an understanding of the "genesis" of the "response" to the registered "phenomenon" of which Adorno writes, it also provides us with a concrete *method* for accomplishing that "revolution of consciousness," that "beginning," to which Marcuse refers.

Nor is it an accident that the machine to which our present economic and political development is tied is an information-processing machine keyed to a feedback mechanism: the anxious human organism which produced that machine is also (in part, of course) an information processing system whose perceptual feedback is governed by the unconscious presence of the internalized other. The machine is a sensorial extension and reflection of its maker, a technological mirror of the inner world. Which calls to mind another crucial point. We do not currently need—as the modern myth says—a variety of significant symbols to "live by" (Epstein 1981, p. 162). We always have significant symbols: our very mode of consciousness is symbolic. When the old symbols fade we immediately find others, such as the machine. What we need, rather, is to attain a perceptive mind-rest that permits us to *put off* our symbolic mentation—our transitional attachment to objects—and that allows us thereby to free our perceptual channels from the internalized presences that govern them.

Mumford (1966, Vol. 1, p. 4) writes of our attitude toward the machine that it is rooted in our misperception of history, and he goes on to develop an interpretation which is sensitive to our struggle to find an outlet for the "overcharge of psychical energy" placed at our disposal by our "large brains." There is much in that. But could it not also be that our devotion to the machine derives from our failure to grasp the transitional tendencies of our internalizing minds, our inclination as bigbrained, anxious animals to outwardly project, in our most sophisticated creations, the dynamic tensions of the inner world? The ability to *get away* from that world, to moderate the tie to the internalized object, offers not merely release from tension and an actual change of consciousness in a positive, individual sense; it offers as well an opportunity to create a future in which "civilization" becomes not an oppressive, technological nightmare but the expressive vehicle for a sensuous being whose "perceptual apparatus" is open to receive, at all levels, the wondrous stimulations of life.

The belief that machines are "like" people derives from individuals who are asleep in ordinary awareness and hence unable to feel deeply the immediacy, the spontaneousness, of their sensorial nature. The machines *are* "like" *those individuals* who believe that the machines are *like people,* since *both* those individuals *and* the machines are not yet fully alive. Just as the laboratory psychologist who is inclined to see men and women as rats reveals his deep ambivalence toward becoming

191

fully human, so the technician, or scientist, or intellectual, or layman, who would put an equal sign between people and computers, or even elevate the computer as the master race of the future (cf. Jastrow 1978, p. 47), reveals a similar ambivalence—a tendency to prefer artificial feeding situations that can be entirely controlled to the life of the human body, including, of course, its emotional dimension. No wonder the western scientist has had, at least until very recently, little more than contempt for those eastern disciplines which stress harmonious relations with the universe, as well as inner mastery, as opposed to technical control of the environment through the development of mechanical devices. The whole anxious machinery of the occident is threatened by such an emphasis. "Intimate love, and mysticism," declares Bharati (1976, p. 202), "are the real dangers" to the "establishmentarians," for they "alienate a man's mind and body from the king." It is time now to detach ourselves from the kings, and queens, of the *inner* world. Emancipation from the machine will only follow *that.*

CONCLUSION

For perhaps 2,000 years western thinkers have been preoccupied with ocular metaphors. Theories of knowledge were modeled upon the act of vision, and "truth" was figuratively expressed as that which appeared in the "mirror" of the mind when "error" was removed through study, or faith. The "mind of man," wrote Francis Bacon ([1605] 1863, Vol. 6, p. 276), "far from the nature of a clear and equal glass, wherein the beams of things should reflect according to their true incidence . . . is rather like an enchanted glass, full of superstition and imposture, if it be not delivered and reduced." The unavoidable consequence of such metaphorical tendencies has been, in Dewey's words, "a spectator theory of knowledge" with the image of the "mirror" at the centre (Dewey 1929, p. 22).

It seems that things are changing. Physiological studies of the brain and psychological analyses of perception have exposed the old "spectator theory" for what it is, a poetical imposition on the epistemic realities of our nature. Such studies and analyses have had profound, somewhat predictable effects upon philosophers. Richard Rorty (1980, p. 295), for example, has recently outlined procedures whereby one may approximate a "truth without mirrors," and John Heil (1983, p. 228) has announced the "philosopher's task" in the face of the growing insight into "perception and cognition" to be "simply that of exposing as much of what is below the surface as possible." The main intention of this book has been to bring the "mirror relationship" between the infant and the caregiver squarely into the developing picture. While our grasp of

193

"truth" may no longer be affected by the metaphor of the mirror at the *conscious* level, our understanding of ourselves, our perception, our cognition, our whole manner of relating to and being in the world, will remain tragically incomplete until we integrate the psychoanalytic "data" on the dynamic origins of our "mental apparatus" into our theoretical schemes. How can the philosopher, or anyone else, responsibly attend to "what is going on below the surface" if he refuses to look at the internalized roots of human awareness as they take shape during the primary years? All of our subsequent "perception and cognition"—*all of it*—is inextricably bound up with these events.

Like philosophy, science has also recently experienced a disruptive awakening to the underlying import of its workaday assumptions. Less prone to declare its "objective" grasp of "the facts" than it was thirty or forty years ago, science has come to recognize not only that the very terms it employs at the foundation of its enterprise—space, distance, time, number, matter—are fraught with an ineluctable trace of human "subjectivity," but that its very *effort* to be perfectly "objective," to describe the world "as it is," comprises a defence against the anxiety engendered by the perception of the unknown and inexplicable. "There is an essential human element in even the coldest, most objective and external of scientific concepts," writes the physicist Roger Jones (1982, p. 15), and then, the "cardinal metaphors" of science such as "space, time, matter, and number . . . deal with our deepest questions and fears about our existence. They express our elemental needs for extension, distinction, identity, stability, endurance, variation, movement, and meaning. Even their quantitative character seems to fortify us with a deceptive measure of . . . existence."

Beyond these "metaphors and illusions," however, is the world of "chaos and death" (Jones 1982, pp. 171–72). By focusing psychoanalytical light on the origins of space, time, extension, stability, endurance, and identity as they emerge from the first relationship, and further, by exploring the commencement of our fears of death and chaos as they are bound integrally to the internalizations of the caregiver in her/his negative or "bad" aspect, we gain precious insight into the emotive situation that *leads* to the cult of "objectivity." Such insight can help us to ease the anxiety that feeds our attempts to remove the human element from our descriptions of the universe. And when we link that insight to an actual technique designed to diminish infantile terror and stress at the somatic, *bodily* level we put ourselves in a position to counter the technological consciousness that, wittingly or unwittingly, spreads its schizoid, dehumanized, and ultimately destructive view of creation and creatures across the face of the planet.

That there is a paradoxical or irrational aspect to the methodological side of this study, that detachment should mean, in the end, a better understanding of and closer connection to the world than that which derives from our ordinary mentation, must not frighten us or hold us back. As Gregory Bateson (1980, pp. 158–59) expresses it, "change will require various sorts of relaxation or contradiction within the system of presuppositions. . . . We must pass through the threat of that chaos where thought becomes impossible." From its opening pages, this book has attempted to pin down the *unconscious, perceptual* meaning of such "change" as it emerges from our philosophical heritage, as well as the concrete sources of such "change" as they emerge, "contradictorily," from the realms of psychoanalysis and mind-altering practice.

Taken as a whole, then, this discussion suggests that a fresh, salubrious, and evolutionarily significant "participation" in the world is possible. However, such "participation" will not be brought about by a reliance on "imagination" (Barfield n.d.), or "faith," or "mysticism," or the "talking cure" of psychoanalysis as these are usually conceived. What the situation requires is, on the one hand, a courageous examination of the ways in which our elemental internalizations have come to determine our perceptions of the environment—including other people therein, and, on the other hand, the regularized employment of a bodily procedure designed explicitly to diminish the stress that spread through the organism during the mirror and separation phases. To examine thus, and to practise thus, is to moderate the tie to the object within, which means in alternative terms to *play* with the substitutive, symbolical universe that was forged initially by the child in his magical effort to retain his connection to the parent. When it comes right down to it, the disease of "man" will end only as "man" develops the capacity to *let go*. Until that happens, we will simply have more madness, more disturbed, projective views of "reality" such as our latest one in which the wondrous cosmos is reduced to "bits" of "information" and the human animal to a mere "processor" of the "bits" (cf. Rifkin 1983). How unrelaxed and unhappy at the deepest levels of his existence must be the individual who would succumb to such a vision.

NOTES AND REFERENCES

PREFACE

Faber, M. D. 1973. Analytic Prolegomena to the Study of Western Tragedy. *Hartford Studies in Literature* 5: 31–60.

—. 1981. *Culture and Consciousness: The Social Meaning of Altered Awareness.* New York: Human Sciences Press.

CHAPTER ONE: PSYCHOANALYSIS AND THE CENTRAL PROBLEM OF PHILOSOPHY

Althusser, Louis. 1971. *Lenin and Philosophy,* trans. Ben Brewster. New York: Monthly Review Press.

Bateson, Gregory. [1956] 1978. Toward a Theory of Schizophrenia, in *Steps to an Ecology of Mind.* New York: Ballantine.

Compton, Allan. 1983. The Current Status of the Psychoanalytic Theory of Drives. *PQ* 52: 402–26.

de Levita, David J. 1983. A Few Remarks on H. Segal's "Some Clinical Implications of Melanie Klein's Work." *IJP* 64: 277–80.

Descartes, René. 1969. *The Essential Descartes,* ed. Margaret D. Wilson. New York: New American Library.

Freud, Sigmund. [1915] 1971. The Unconscious, in *Collected Papers,* ed. Joan Riviere. London: Hogarth, Vol. 4.

Jones, Roger S. 1982. *Physics as Metaphor.* New York: New American Library.

Miller, Alice. 1981. *The Drama of the Gifted Child,* trans. Ruth Ward. New York: Basic Books.

Müller, Anton. 1974. *Quantum Mechanics: A Physical World Picture,* trans. Eva Rona. Oxford: Pergamon.

Ogden, Thomas H. 1983. The Concept of Internal Object Relations. *IJP* 64: 227–42.

Peterfreund, Emanuel. 1971. *Information, Systems, and Psychoanalysis.* New York: International Universities Press (in collaboration with J. T. Schwartz).

Schafer, Roy. 1968. *Aspects of Internalization.* New York: International Universities Press.

Wilden, Anthony. 1972. *System and Structure.* London: Tavistock.

Wilson, Edgar. 1979. *The Mental as Physical.* London: Routledge and Kegan Paul.

CHAPTER TWO: THE PSYCHODYNAMIC ORIGINS OF HUMAN PERCEPTION

1. I regard the recent concentration of ego psychology on the psychodynamics of infancy and childhood largely as an outgrowth of tendencies rooted in the Kleinean approach and in the activities of the British school generally. The valuable work of Margaret Mahler, for example, has been fed significantly by those streams, and not simply by the endeavors of Heinz Hartmann and Anna Freud.

2. Further citations from this work will be followed immediately in the text by a page reference.

Abraham, Ruth. 1982. Freud's Mother Conflict and the Formulation of the Oedipal Father. *PR* 69: 441–53.

Almansi, Renato J. 1983. On the Persistence of Very Early Memory Traces in Psychoanalysis, Myth, and Religion. *JAPA* 31: 391–421.

Andresen, Jeffrey J. 1980. Why People Talk to Themselves. *JAPA* 28: 499–518.

Bachelard, Gaston. 1969. *The Poetics of Space.* Boston: Beacon.

Basch, Michael F. 1981. Psychoanalytic Interpretation and Cognitive Transformation. *IJP* 62: 151–74.

Becker, Ernest. 1973. *The Denial of Death.* New York: The Free Press.

Beres, David. 1960. Perception, Imagination, and Reality. *IJP* 41: 327–34.

Berman, Morris. 1981. *The Reenchantment of the World.* Ithaca: Cornell University Press.

Blackburn, Thomas R. 1973. Sensuous–Intellectual Complementarity in Science, in *The Nature of Human Consciousness,* ed. Robert Ornstein. San Francisco: W. H. Freeman, 27–40.

Blanck, Gertrude and Robin Blanck. 1979. *Ego Psychology II.* New York: Columbia University Press.

Bleich, David. 1970. New Considerations of the Infantile Acquisition of Language and Symbolic Thought. Presented to Psychological Center for the Study of the Arts. State University of New York, Buffalo, pp. 1–28.

Bloch, Dorothy. 1979. *So the Witch Won't Eat Me*. New York: Harper and Row.

Broucek, Francis. 1979. Efficacy in Infancy. *IJP* 60: 311–16.

Coen, Stanley J. 1981. Notes on the Concepts of Selfobject and Preoedipal Selfobject. *JAPA* 29: 395–411.

Colarusso, Calvin. 1979. The Development of Time Sense. *IJP* 60: 243–52.

Compton, Allan. 1980. A Study of the Psychoanalytic Theory of Anxiety. *JAPA* 28: 739–74.

Dinnerstein, Dorothy. 1977. *The Mermaid and the Minotaur*. New York: Harper and Row.

Dowling, Scott. 1981. From the Literature on Neonatology. *PQ* 50: 290–95.

Dupont, M. A. 1974. A Provisional Contribution to the Psychoanalytic Study of Time. *IJP* 60: 483–84.

Erikson, Erik H. 1958. *Young Man Luther*. New York: Norton.

Fagen, Jeffrey W. and Carolyn K. Rovee-Collier. 1982. A Conditioning Analysis of Infant Memory, in *The Expression of Knowledge*, ed. Robert L. Isaacson and Norman E. Spear. New York: Plenum Press, 67–106.

Freud, Sigmund. [1894] 1959. The Defence Neuro-Psychoses, in *Collected Papers*, ed. Joan Riviere. New York: Basic Books. Vol. 1.

—. [1895] 1950. Extracts from the Fliess Papers. *The Standard Edition*, ed. James Strachey, Vol. 1.

—. [1896] 1959. Further Remarks on the Defence Neuro-Psychoses. Ed. cit.

—. [1923] 1974. *The Ego and the Id*, trans. Joan Riviere. London: Hogarth.

—. [1930] 1975. *Civilization and Its Discontents*, trans. Joan Riviere. London: Hogarth.

—. [1940] 1964. An Outline of Psychoanalysis. *The Standard Edition*, ed. James Strachey, Vol. 23.

Gedo, John. 1979. *Toward a Revised Theory of Psychoanalysis*. New York: International Universities Press.

Grotstein, James. 1978. Inner Space: Its Dimensions and Coordinates. *IJP* 59: 53–61.

Gruen, Arno. 1974. The Discontinuity in the Ontogeny of the Self. *PR* 61: 557–69.

Hagglund, Tor-Bjorn. 1980. The Inner Space of the Body Image. *PQ* 49: 256–83.

Hartmann, Heinz. [1939] 1958. *Ego Psychology and the Problem of Adaptation*, trans. David Rapoport. New York: International Universities Press.

Hartocollis, Peter. 1974. Origins of Time. *PQ* 43: 243–61.

James, William. 1890. *The Principles of Psychology*. New York: Holt, Vol. 1.

Jones, Roger S. 1982. *Physics as Metaphor.* New York: New American Library.

Katan, Maurits. 1979. Further Exploration of the Schizophrenic Regression to the Undifferentiated State. *IJP* 60: 145–76.

Korbin, Jill E. 1981. *Child Abuse and Neglect.* Berkeley: University of California Press.

Lax, Ruth. 1977. The Role of Internalization in the Development of Female Masochism. *IJP* 58: 289–300.

Lichtenstein, Heinz. 1961. Identity and Sexuality. *JAPA* 9: 179–260.

McCall, Robert B. 1979. *Infants.* New York: Vintage.

Mahler, Margaret S., Fred Pine, and Anni Bergman. 1975. *The Psychological Birth of the Human Infant.* New York: Basic Books.

Melito, Richard. 1983. Cognitive Aspects of Splitting. *JAPA* 31: 515–34.

Meissner, W. W. 1976. Internalization as Process. *PQ* 45: 374–93.

Menaker, Esther. 1978. A Kohut Symposium. *PR* 65: 615–29.

Mushatt, Cecil. 1975. Mind-Body Environment: Toward Understanding the Impact of Loss on Psyche and Soma. *PQ* 44: 84–107.

Neubauer, Peter C. 1980. The Life Cycle as Indicated by the Nature of the Transference. *IJP* 61: 137–44.

Neumann, Erich. 1970. *The Great Mother.* Princeton: Princeton University Press.

Ornston, Darius. 1978. On Projection: A Study of Freud's Usage. *The Psychoanalytic Study of the Child,* Vol. 33.

Piaget, Jean. 1968. *Six Psychological Studies,* trans. Anita Tenzer. New York: Vintage.

Pine, Fred. 1979. On the Pathology of the Separation-Individuation Crisis. *IJP* 60: 225–42.

Pines, Dinora. 1980. Skin Communication. *IJP* 61: 315–24.

Rank, Otto. 1929. *The Trauma of Birth.* London: Kegan, Paul.

Reynolds, Peter C. 1981. *On the Evolution of Human Behavior.* Berkeley: University of California Press.

Rheingold, Joseph C. 1964. *The Fear of Being a Woman.* New York: Grune and Stratton.

Rizzuto, Ana-Maria. 1979. *The Birth of the Living God.* Chicago: University of Chicago Press.

Roheim, Geza. 1962. *Magic and Schizophrenia.* Bloomington: Indiana University Press.

—. 1971. *The Origin and Function of Culture.* New York: Doubleday.

Ross, John M. and Peter B. Dunn. 1980. Notes on the Genesis of Psychological Splitting. *IJP* 61: 335–50.

Roth, David and Sidney Blatt. 1974. Spatial Representations and Psychopathology. *JAPA* 55: 854–72.

Roustang, François. 1976. *Dire Mastery: Discipleship from Freud to Lacan,* trans. Ned Lukacher. Baltimore: Johns Hopkins.

Schiffer, Irvine. 1978. *The Trauma of Time.* New York: International Universities Press.

Slater, Philip. 1974. *Earthwalk.* New York: Doubleday.

Southwood, H. M. 1973. The Origin of Self-Awareness and Ego Behavior. *IJP* 54: 235–39.

Spitz, Rene. 1965. *The First Year of Life.* New York: International Universities Press.

Steinzor, Bernard. 1979. Death and the Construction of Reality. *Omega: Journal of Death and Dying* 9: 97–124.

Stern, Daniel. 1977. *The First Relationship: Mother and Infant.* Cambridge, Mass.: Harvard University Press.

Taylor, Gordon R. 1981. *The Natural History of the Mind.* London: Granada.

Vygotsky, L. S. [1934] 1979. *Thought and Language,* trans. E. Hanfmann and G. Vakar. Cambridge, Mass.: M.I.T. Press.

Weil, Annemarie. 1978. Maturational Variations and Genetic-Dynamic Issues. *JAPA* 26: 461–92.

Winnicott, D. W. 1953. Transitional Objects and Transitional Phenomena. *IJP* 34: 89–97.

—. 1966. The Location of Cultural Experience. *IJP* 48: 368–72.

—. 1971. *Playing and Reality.* London: Penguin.

CHAPTER THREE: PERCEPTIVE MIND-REST

1. Horton plays it both ways. He maintains in one place, following Winnicot (p. 373), that mystical experiences are "irreducible." He then goes on to declare in another place (p. 374) that they are "transitional." Needless to say, the term "transitional" is loaded with suggestions of infantilism.

2. The research of Frank Putnam at NIMH has established electronically that the bodies of people with multiple personalities undergo physiological changes as one personality succeeds another. See "Bodies Change with Personality" in *Brain-Mind Bulletin,* 3 October 1983, p. 1.

3. The examples to follow are from Lecture XVI.

4. Some psychoanalytic writers, such as Emanuel Peterfreund and Jacob T. Schwartz, do not find the terms "primary and secondary process" to be useful any longer. See their *Information, Systems, and Psychoanalysis* (New York: International Universities Press 1971), p. 370. Robert Rogers, on the other hand, considers the terms to be useful still. Rogers summarizes the theoretical controversy in his paper, "Psychoanalytic and Cybernetic Modes of Mentation," presented to the Psychological Center for the Study of the Arts, Amherst, New York, February 1980, pp. 2–6.

Aronson, Gerald. 1977. Defence and Deficit Models. *IJP* 57: 11–16.

Bateson, Gregory. 1980. *Mind and Nature.* New York: Bantam.

Bertalanffy, Ludwig von. 1952. *Problems of Life.* New York: Wiley.

—. 1968. *General Systems Theory.* New York: Braziller.

Blofeld, J. 1962. *The Zen Teaching of Hui Hai.* London: Rider.

Bohm, David and John Welwood. 1980. Issues in Physics, Psychology, and Metaphysics. *JTP* 12: 25–36.

Bonaparte, Marie. 1940. Time and the Unconscious. *IJP* 21: 427–68. Freud's remarks appear in a footnote written specifically for this paper.

Brain-Mind Bulletin. Bodies Change with Personality. 3 October 1983, pp. 1–2.

Brown, Daniel P. and Jack Engler. 1980. The Stages of Mindfulness Meditation. *JTP* 12: 143–92.

Brown, Norman O. 1959. *Life against Death.* New York: Vintage Books.

Campbell, Anthony. 1975. *The Mechanics of Enlightenment.* London: Gollancz.

Carrington, Patricia. 1982. Meditation Techniques in Clinical Practice, in *The Newer Therapies: A Sourcebook,* ed. Lawrence E. Abt and Irving R. Stuart. New York: Van Nostrand Reinhold, 60–78.

Dean, Stanley. 1975. *Psychiatry and Mysticism.* Chicago: Nelson-Hall.

Deikman, Arthur. 1973. Deautomatization and the Mystic Experience, in *The Nature of Human Consciousness,* ed. Robert Ornstein. San Francisco: W. H. Freeman, 216–23.

Delgado, José. 1971. *Physical Control of the Mind.* New York: Harper and Row.

Dicara, Leo. 1972. Learning in the Autonomic Nervous System, in *Altered States of Awareness,* ed. Timothy Teyler. San Francisco: W. H. Freeman, 74–85.

Earle, Jonathan. 1981. Cerebral Laterality and Meditation: A Review of the Literature. *JTP* 13: 155–73.

Eccles, John. 1972. The Physiology of Imagination, in *Altered States of Awareness,* ed. Timothy Teyler. San Francisco: W. H. Freeman, 31–40.

Eisendrath, C. R. 1971. *The Unifying Moment: The Psychological Philosophy of William James and Alfred North Whitehead.* Cambridge, Mass.: Harvard University Press.

Ellis, Havelock. [1898] 1961. Mescal: A New Artificial Paradise, in *The Drug Experience,* ed. David Ebin. New York: Grove Press, 225–36.

Fisher, David J. 1976. Sigmund Freud and Romain Rolland: The Terrestrial Animal and His Great Oceanic Friend. *AI* 33: 1–59.

Freud, Sigmund. [1930] 1975. *Civilization and Its Discontents,* trans. Joan Riviere. London: Hogarth.

GAP (Group for the Advancement of Psychiatry). 1976. What Mysticism Is, in *Consciousness: Brain, States of Awareness, and Mysticism,* ed. Daniel Goleman and Richard Davidson. New York: Harper and Row, 187–90.

Garfield, Charles. 1975. Consciousness Alteration and Fear of Death. *JTP* 7: 147–75.

Gimello, Robert M. 1978. Mysticism and Meditation, in *Mysticism and Philosophical Analysis*, ed. Steven T. Katz. New York: Oxford.

Goleman, Daniel. 1977. *The Varieties of Meditative Experience*. New York: E. P. Dutton.

—. 1981. Buddhist and Western Psychology: Some Commonalities and Differences. *JTP* 13: 125–36.

Greeley, Andrew and William McReady. 1979. Are We a Nation of Mystics?, in *Consciousness: Brain, States of Awareness, and Mysticism*, ed. Daniel Goleman and Richard J. Davidson. New York: Harper and Row, 178–83.

Halevi, Z'ev Ben Shimon. 1976. *The Way of Kabbalah*. New York: Samuel Weiser.

Heron, W. 1972. The Pathology of Boredom, in *Altered States of Awareness*, ed. Timothy Teyler. San Francisco: W. H. Freeman, pp. 60–64.

Herrick, C. J. 1949. *George Ellet Coghill*. Chicago: University of Chicago Press.

Horton, Paul. 1974. *The Mystical Experience. JAPA* 22: 364–80.

Huber, Jack. 1967. *Through an Eastern Window*. Boston: Houghton, Mifflin.

Huizinga, Johan. 1950. *Homo Ludens*. Boston: Beacon.

Huxley, Aldous. 1974. *The Doors of Perception*. London: Penguin.

—. 1970. *The Perennial Philosophy*. New York: Harper and Row.

Huxley, Laura. 1971. *This Timeless Moment*. New York: Ballantine. Huxley's remark is cited here by his wife.

James, William. [1902] 1958. *The Varieties of Religious Experience*. New York: New American Library.

Kapleau, Philip. 1973. Zen Meditation, in *The Nature of Human Consciousness*, ed. Robert Ornstein. San Francisco: W. H. Freeman, 237–41.

—. 1965. *The Three Pillars of Zen*. Boston: Beacon.

Kleitman, Nathaniel. [1960] 1972. Patterns of Dreaming, in *Altered States of Awareness*, ed. Timothy Teyler. San Francisco: W. H. Freeman, 44–50.

Kohler, Ivo. 1972. Experiments with Goggles, in *Altered States of Awareness*, ed. Timothy Teyler. San Francisco: W. H. Freeman, 108–18.

Kornfield, Jack. 1979. Intensive Insight Meditation. *JTP* 11: 41–58.

Langer, Susanne. 1942. *Philosophy in a New Key*. New York: Mentor.

Lashley, K. S. [1951] 1969. The Problem of Serial Order in Behavior, in *Brain and Behavior*, ed. K. H. Pribram. London: Penguin, Vol. 2, 515–40.

M. 1928. *Gospel of Sri Ramakrishna*. Mylapore, India: Sri Ramakrishna Math.

Maharishi Mahesh Yogi. 1969. *On the Bhagavad Gita*. Baltimore: Penguin.

—. 1966. *The Science of Being and the Art of Loving*. Los Angeles: SRM Publications.

Mayhew, Christopher. [1956] 1961. Peyote, in *The Drug Experience,* ed. David Ebin. New York: Grove Press, 293–306.

Meissner, W. W. 1980. The Problem of Internalization and Structure Formation. *IJP* 61: 237–48.

Mumford, Lewis. 1967. *The Myth of the Machine.* New York: Harcourt, Brace, Jovanovich.

Mushatt, Cecil. 1975. Mind-Body Environment: Toward Understanding the Impact of Loss on Psyche and Soma. *PQ* 44: 84–107.

Neisser, Ulric. 1973. The Processes of Vision, in *The Nature of Human Consciousness,* ed. Robert Ornstein. San Francisco: W. H. Freeman, 195–210.

Ornstein, Robert and Claudio Naranjo. 1972. *On the Psychology of Meditation.* New York: Viking.

Pelletier, Kenneth. 1978. *Toward a Science of Consciousness.* New York: Delta.

Penfield, Wilder and T. Rasmussen. 1950. *Cerebral Cortex of Man.* New York: Macmillan.

— and Lamar Roberts. 1959. *Speech and Brain Mechanisms.* Princeton: Princeton University Press.

Peterfreund, Emanuel and Jacob T. Schwartz. 1971. *Information, Systems, and Psychoanalysis.* New York: International Universities.

Pietsch, Paul. 1972. Shuffle Brain. *Harper's Magazine,* May 1972, 41–48.

Pribram, Karl H. 1982. What the Fuss Is All About, in *The Holographic Paradigm,* ed. Ken Wilber. Boulder: Shambhala.

Rogers, Robert. 1978. *Metaphor: A Psychoanalytic View.* Berkeley: University of California Press.

—. 1980. Psychoanalytic and Cybernetic Modes of Mentation. Presented to the Psychological Center for the Study of the Arts, Amherst, N.Y., February 1980, 1–60.

Shah, Indries. 1971. *Wisdom of the Idiots.* New York: E. P. Dutton.

Shannon, William H. 1981. *Thomas Merton's Dark Path.* New York: Farrar, Straus, Giroux.

Shibayama, Zenkei. 1974. Zen Comments on the Mumonkan. New York: New American Library.

Speeth, Kathleen. 1982. On Psychotherapeutic Attention. *JTP* 14: 141–60.

Stevens, Leonard. 1966. *Neurons: Building Blocks of the Brain.* New York: Crowell.

Suzuki, Shunryu. 1973. *Zen Mind, Beginner's Mind.* New York: Weatherhill.

Treurniet, N. 1980. On the Relation between the Concepts of Self and Ego. *IJP* 61: 325–34.

Wallace, Robert and Herbert Benson. 1972. The Physiology of Meditation, in *Altered States of Awareness,* ed. Timothy Teyler. San Francisco: W. H. Freeman, 125–32.

Wilson, Edgar. 1979. *The Mental as Physical*. London: Routledge and Kegan Paul.

Walsh, Roger. 1982. A Model for Viewing Meditation Research. *JTP* 14: 69–84.

—. 1979. Emerging Cross-Disciplinary Parallels: Suggestions from the Neuro-Sciences. *JTP* 11: 175–84.

Wangh, Martin and Harold R. Galef. 1983. Narcissism in Our Time. *PQ* 52: 321–24.

Welwood, John. 1979. *The Meeting of the Ways*. New York: Schocken.

Wilber, Ken. 1977. *The Spectrum of Consciousness*. Wheaton: Theosophical Publishing.

—. 1982. *The Holographic Paradigm*. Boulder: Shambhala.

Winnicott, D. W. 1971. *Playing and Reality*. London: Penguin.

CHAPTER FOUR: FREUD, THE STRUCTURAL THEORY, AND PERCEPTION

1. Further citations from *The Ego and the Id* will be followed in the text by a page reference to this edition.
2. Further citations from *Inhibitions, Symptoms, and Anxiety* will be followed in the text by a page reference to this edition.

Freud, Sigmund. [1895] 1966. *Project for a Scientific Psychology*. Standard Edition, ed. James Strachey, Vol. 1, pp. 295–343.

—. [1914] 1971. On Narcissism, in *Collected Papers*, trans. Joan Riviere. London: Hogarth, Vol. 4, pp. 30–59.

—. [1915] 1971. The Unconscious, in *Collected Papers*, trans. Joan Riviere. London: Hogarth, Vol. 4, pp. 98–136.

—. [1917] 1968. *A General Introduction to Psychoanalysis*, trans. Joan Riviere. New York: Washington Square.

—. [1920] 1959. *Beyond the Pleasure Principle*, trans. James Strachey. New York: Bantam.

—. [1923] 1974. *The Ego and the Id*, trans. Joan Riviere. London: Hogarth.

—. [1925] 1959. A Note upon the Mystic Writing Pad, in *Collected Papers*, ed. James Strachey. London: Hogarth, Vol. 5, pp. 175–80.

—. [1926] 1959. *Inhibitions, Symptoms, and Anxiety*, ed. James Strachey. New York: Norton.

—. [1927] 1953. *The Future of an Illusion*, trans. W. D. Robson-Scott. New York: Doubleday.

—. [1932] 1953. *New Introductory Lectures on Psychoanalysis*, ed. James Strachey. The Standard Edition, Vol. 22, pp. 5–182.

—. [1938] 1959. Some Elementary Lessons in Psycho-Analysis, in *Collected Papers*, ed. James Strachey. London: Hogarth, Vol. 5, pp. 376–82.

Gill, Merton and Karl Pribram. 1976. *Freud's 'Project' Reassessed*. New York: Basic Books.

Harrison, Irving. 1979. On Freud's View of the Mother-Infant Relationship and of the Oceanic Feeling. *JAPA* 27: 399–423.

Mahler, Margaret. 1968. *On Human Symbiosis and the Vicissitudes of Individuation.* New York: International Universities.

Ornston, Darius. 1978. On Projection: A Study of Freud's Usage. *The Psychoanalytic Study of the Child.* New Haven: Yale, Vol. 33, pp. 117–66.

Pribram, Karl and Merton Gill. 1976. *Freud's 'Project' Reassessed.* New York: Basic Books.

Rapoport, David. 1960. *The Structure of Psychoanalytic Theory.* New York: International Universities.

Regan, David. 1979. Electrical Responses Evoked from the Human Brain. *Scientific American* 241: 134–46.

Ricoeur, Paul. 1970. *Freud and Philosophy.* New Haven: Yale.

Schiffer, Irvine. 1978. *The Trauma of Time.* New York: International Universities.

Stoller, Robert J. 1974. Facts and Fancies: An Examination of Freud's Concept of Bisexuality, in *Women and Analysis,* ed. Jean Strouse. New York: Dell, pp. 391–415.

Strachey, James. 1966 Introduction, in *Project for a Scientific Psychology* (Freud). *The Standard Edition,* Vol. 1, pp. 290–93.

Sulloway, Frank. 1983. *Freud: Biologist of the Mind.* New York: Basic Books.

Wilson, Edgar. 1979. *The Mental as Physical.* London: Routledge and Kegan Paul.

CHAPTER FIVE: EPISTEMOLOGY AND THE QUESTION OF PURE EGO

1. My citations in this and subsequent sections are from Descartes' *Rules for the Direction of the Mind, Discourse on the Method, Meditations on First Philosophy,* and *Principles of Philosophy,* as each appears in Wilson (1969). All citations will be accompanied by a page reference to Wilson. References to pages between 35 and 105 are to *Rules,* between 106 and 153 are to *Discourse,* between 154 and 223 are to *Meditations,* and between 301 and 352 are to *Principles.*

2. Further citations from Hume ([1739] 1975) will be followed immediately in the text by a page reference to the *Treatise.*

3. Further citations from Kant ([1787] 1950) will be followed immediately in the text by a page reference to the *Critique.*

4. Heinrich von Kleist, the German dramatist, is a famous example of someone who was made melancholy by Kant's conclusions shortly after the *Critique* appeared.

5. Further citations from Hegel ([1806] 1967) will be followed immediately in the text by a page reference to the *Phenomenology.*

6. Further citations from Husserl's *Ideas* ([1913] 1969) will be followed immediately in the text by a page reference.
7. Further citations from Husserl's *Cartesian Meditations* ([1929] 1960) will be followed immediately in the text by a page reference.
8. Further citations from Merleau-Ponty's *Phenomenology* (1970) will be followed immediately in the text by a page reference and the abbreviation *Phen.*
9. Further citations from Merleau-Ponty's *Structure of Behavior* (1963) will be followed immediately in the text by a page reference and the abbreviation *B.*

Aurobindo, Sri. 1974. *The Essential Aurobindo,* ed. R. A. McDermott. New York: Schocken.

Brainerd, Charles. 1979. *The Origin of the Number Concept.* New York: Praeger.

Broucek, Francis. 1979. Efficacy in Infancy. *IJP* 60: 311–16.

Chessick, Richard D. 1980. The Problematical Self in Kant and Kohut. *PQ* 49: 456–73.

Descartes, Rene. [1627] 1969. Rules for the Direction of the Mind, in *The Essential Descartes,* ed. Margaret D. Wilson. New York: New American Library.

Dussinger, John A. 1980. David Hume's Denial of Personal Identity. *AI* 37: 334–50.

Fink, Eugen. [1939] 1981. The Problem of the Phenomenology of Edmund Husserl, in *A Priori and World,* ed. W. McKenna, R. M. Harlan, and L. E. Winters. The Hague: Martinus Nijhoff, pp. 21–55.

Flew, Anthony. 1978. Transitional Objects and Transitional Phenomena, in *Between Fantasy and Reality: Transitional Objects and Phenomena,* ed. Simon A. Grolnick and Leonard Barkin. New York: Jason Aronson.

Freud, Sigmund. [1925] 1959. A Note upon the Mystic Writing Pad, in *Collected Papers,* ed. James Strachey. London: Hogarth. Vol. 5, pp. 175–80.

—. [1938] 1959. Some Elementary Lessons in Psycho-Analysis, in *Collected Papers,* ed. James Strachey. London: Hogarth, Vol. 5, pp. 376–82.

—. [1915] 1971. The Unconscious, in *Collected Papers,* trans. Joan Riviere. London: Hogarth, pp. 98–136.

—. [1926] 1959. *Inhibitions, Symptoms, and Anxiety,* trans. Alix Strachey. New York: Norton.

Habermas, Jurgen. 1971. *Knowledge and Human Interest,* trans. J. J. Shapiro. Boston: Beacon.

Hegel, G. W. F. [1806] 1967. *The Phenomenology of Mind,* trans. J. B. Baillie. New York: Harper and Row.

—. [1821] 1967. *Philosophy of Right,* trans. T. M. Knox. Oxford: Oxford University.

Hume, David. [1739] 1975. *A Treatise of Human Nature.* Oxford: Oxford University.

Husserl, Edmund. [1911] 1965. *Phenomenology and the Crisis of European Philosophy,* trans. Quentin Lauer. New York: Harper and Row.

—. [1913] 1969. *Ideas: General Introduction to Pure Phenomenology,* trans. W. R. B. Gibson. London: Collier-Macmillan.

—. [1929] 1960. *Cartesian Meditations.* trans. Dorian Cairns. The Hague: Martinus Nijhoff.

Kant, Immanuel. [1787] 1950. *Critique of Pure Reason,* trans. J. M. Meiklejohn. London: Dent.

Lacan, Jacques. 1966. *Ecrits.* Paris: Editions du Seuil.

Lauer, Quentin. 1965. Introduction, in *Phenomenology and the Crisis of European Philosophy* (Husserl). New York: Harper and Row.

Mahoney, Michael S. 1980. The Beginnings of Algebraic Thought in the Seventeenth Century, in *Descartes: Philosophy, Mathematics and Physics,* ed. Stephen Gaukroger. New Jersey: Barnes and Noble, pp. 141–55.

Merleau-Ponty, Maurice. 1963. *The Structure of Behavior,* trans. Alden Fisher. Boston: Beacon.

—. 1964. *The Primacy of Perception,* ed. James Edie. Evanston: Northwestern.

—. 1970. *The Phenomenology of Perception,* trans. Colin Smith. New York: Humanities Press.

Ricoeur, Paul. 1970. *Freud and Philosophy,* trans. Denis Savage. New Haven: Yale.

Schafer, Roy. 1968. *Aspects of Internalization.* New York: International Universities.

Stern, Karl. 1965. *The Flight from Women.* New York: Farrar, Straus, and Giroux.

Wangh, Martin and Harold R. Galef. 1983. Narcissism in Our Time. *PQ* 52: 321–24.

Weitz, Morris. 1983. Descartes' Theory of Concepts, in *Midwest Studies in Philosophy,* ed. P. French, T. Veling, and H. Wettstein. Minneapolis, University of Minnesota, Vol. 8, pp. 89–104.

Wilden, Anthony. 1972. *System and Structure.* London: Tavistock.

Wilson, Margaret D., ed. 1969. *The Essential Descartes.* New York: New American Library.

CHAPTER SIX: EPISTEMOLOGY AND THE ISSUE OF SOCIAL ORGANIZATION

1. Subsequent citations will be followed immediately in the text by a page reference to this edition and by the abbreviation *CHDS*.

2. Subsequent citations will be followed immediately in the text by a page reference to this edition and by the abbreviation *Kap*.

3. Subsequent citations will be followed immediately in the text by a page reference to this edition and by the abbreviation *G*.

4. Further citations from this work will be followed immediately in the text by a page reference to this edition.

5. Subsequent citations will be followed immediately in the text by a page reference to this edition and by the abbreviation *TP*.

6. Subsequent citations will be followed immediately in the text by a page reference to this edition and by the abbreviation *KHI*.

7. Subsequent citations will be followed immediately in the text by a page reference to this edition and by the abbreviation *CES*.

8. The review of Bloch's book is called "Terrible Tales: Coping with Fear of Infanticide," and may be found in *Time,* 5 February 1979, p. 62.

9. Subsequent citations will be followed immediately in the text by a page reference to this edition and by the abbreviation *CCS*.

10. Kemeny's remarks appear in an article titled "The Age of the Miracle Chips." See *Time,* 20 February 1978, p. 28.

Adorno, Theodor. [1957] 1976. Sociology and Empirical Research, in *Critical Sociology,* ed. Paul Connerton. London: Penguin, pp. 237–57.

Bharati, A. 1976. *The Light at the Center: Context and Pretext of Modern Mysticism.* Santa Barbara: Ross-Erikson.

Broucek, Francis. 1979. Efficacy in Infancy. *IJP* 60: 311–16.

Calder, Allan. 1979. Constructive Mathematics. *Scientific American,* Vol. 241 (October), pp. 146–71.

Dilthey, Wilhelm [1900] 1976. The Rise of Hermeneutics, in *Critical Sociology,* ed. Paul Connerton. London: Penguin, pp. 104–16.

Dreyfus, Hubert. 1979. *What Computers Can't Do.* New York: Harper and Row.

Einzig, Paul. 1951. *Primitive Money.* Oxford: Pergamon.

Epstein, Gerald. 1981. *Waking Dream Therapy.* New York: Human Sciences Press.

Freud, Sigmund. [1940] 1964. An Outline of Psychoanalysis. The Standard Edition, ed. James Strachey. Vol. 23.

—. [1919] 1955. Group Psychology and the Analysis of the Ego. The Standard Edition, ed. James Strachey. Vol. 18.

Gadamer, Hans-George. [1965] 1976. The Historicity of Understanding, in *Critical Sociology,* ed. Paul Connerton. London: Penguin, pp. 117–33.

Habermas, Jürgen. [1963] 1974. *Theory and Practice,* ed. John Viertel. Boston: Beacon.

—. 1968. *Knowledge and Human Interests,* ed. J. J. Shapiro. Boston: Beacon.

—. 1971. *Toward a Rational Society,* ed. J. J. Shapiro. Boston: Beacon.

—. 1976. *Communication and the Evolution of Society,* ed. Thomas McCarthy. Boston: Beacon.

Harris, Errol. 1962. Mind and Mechanical Models, in *Theories of the Mind,* ed. J. M. Scher. New York: The Free Press.

Harris, Marvin. 1977. *Cannibals and Kings: The Origins of Culture.* New York: Random House.

Jastrow, Robert. 1978. Toward an Intelligence beyond Man's. *Time,* 20 February, p. 47.

Keat, Russell. 1981. *The Politics of Social Theory.* Oxford: Blackwell.

Kleinberg, Harry. 1977. *How You Can Learn to Live with Computers.* Philadelphia: Lippincott.

Mannheim, Karl. 1936. *Ideology and Utopia,* ed. Louis Wirth and Edward Shils. New York: Harcourt, Brace, and World.

Marcuse, Herbert. 1969. *An Essay on Liberation.* Boston: Beacon.

Marx, Karl. [1843] 1975. Critique of Hegel's Doctrine of the State, in *Early Writings,* ed. L. Coletti. New York: Vintage, pp. 57–198.

—. [1843a] 1975. Letters from the Franco-German Yearbooks, in *Early Writings,* ed. L. Coletti. New York: Vintage, pp. 199–209.

—. [1844] 1975. Critique of Hegel's Philosophy of Right, in *Early Writings,* ed. L. Coletti. New York: Vintage, pp. 243–57.

—. [1844a] 1975. Economic and Philosophic Manuscripts, in *Early Writings,* ed. L. Coletti. New York: Vintage, pp. 279–400.

—. [1844b] 1975. Excerpts from James Mill's Elements of Political Economy, in *Early Writings,* ed. L. Coletti. New York: Vintage, pp. 259–78.

—. [1846] 1967. *The German Ideology,* ed. C. J. Arthur. New York: International Publishers.

—. [1857] 1973. *Grundrisse,* ed. Martin Nicolaus. New York: Vintage.

—. [1867] 1967. *Das Kapital,* ed. Frederick Engels. New York: International Publishers, 3 vols.

Mumford, Lewis. 1966. *The Myth of the Machine.* New York: Harvest Books, 2 vols.

Offe, Claus. 1980. The Separation of Form and Content in Liberal Democratic Politics. *Studies in Political Economy* (Carleton University) 3: 5–16.

Rapoport, Anotol. 1974. *Fights, Games, and Debates.* Ann Arbor: Michigan.

Ricoeur, Paul. [1965] 1976. Hermeneutics: Restoration of Meaning or Reduction of Illusion?, in *Critical Sociology,* ed. Paul Connerton. London: Penguin, pp. 194–203.

Rinsley, Donald B. 1983. *Borderline and Other Self Disorders.* New York: Aronson.

Roheim, Geza. 1971. *The Origin and Function of Culture.* New York: Doubleday.

Rucker, Rudy. 1982. *Infinity and the Mind.* Boston: Birkhauser.

Schafer, Roy. 1968. *Aspects of Internalization.* New York: International Universities.

Schiller, Jon R. 1980. Psychoanalysis, Ideology and Language. *Canadian Journal of Political and Social Theory* 4: 9–22.

Stern, Daniel. 1977. *The First Relationship: Mother and Infant.* Cambridge, Mass.: Harvard.

Taube, Mortimer. 1961. *Computers and Common Sense.* New York: Columbia University.

Wilden, Anthony. 1972. *System and Structure.* London: Tavistock.

CONCLUSION

Bacon, Francis. [1605] 1863. The Advancement of Learning, in *Works,* ed. James Spedding, Robert Ellis, and Douglas Heath. Cambridge, Eng.: The Riverside Press. 15 vols.

Barfield, Owen. n.d. *Saving the Appearances.* New York: Harcourt, Brace, Jovanovich.

Bateson, Gregory. 1980. *Mind and Nature.* New York: Bantam.

Dewey, John. 1929. *The Quest for Certainty.* New York: Minton, Balch.

Heil, John. 1983. *Perception and Cognition.* Berkeley: University of California.

Jones, Roger. 1982. *Physics as Metaphor.* New York: New American Library.

Rifkin, Jeremy. 1983. *Algeny.* New York: Viking.

Rorty, Richard. 1980. *Philosophy and the Mirror of Nature.* Princeton, N.J.: Princeton University Press.

BIBLIOGRAPHY

Abraham, Ruth
1982
Freud's Mother Conflict and the Formulation of the Oedipal Father. *Psychoanalytic Review* 69: 441–53.

Adorno, Theodor
[1957] 1976
Sociology and Empirical Research. In *Critical Sociology,* edited by Paul Connerton, 258–76. London: Penguin Books.

Almansi, Renato J.
1983
On the Persistence of Very Early Memory Traces in Psychoanalysis, Myth, and Religion. *Journal of the American Psychoanalytic Association* 31: 391–421.

Althusser, Louis
1971
Lenin and Philosophy. Translated by Ben Brewster. New York: Monthly Review Press.

Andresen, Jeffrey J.
1980
Why People Talk to Themselves. *Journal of the American Psychoanalytic Association* 28: 499–518.

Aronson, Gerald
1977
Defence and Deficit Models. *International Journal of Psychoanalysis* 57: 11–16.

Aurobindo, Sri
1974
The Essential Aurobindo. Edited by R. A. McDermott. New York: Schocken Books.

Bachelard, Gaston
1969
The Poetics of Space. Translated by Maria Jolas. Boston: Beacon Press.

Bacon, Francis
[1605] 1863
The Advancement of Learning. In *Works,* edited by James Spedding, Robert Ellis, and Douglas Heath. 15 vols. Cambridge, Eng.: Riverside Press.

Barfield, Owen
n.d.
Saving the Appearances: A Study in Idolatry. New York: Harcourt, Brace, Jovanovich.

Basch, Michael F.
1981

Psychoanalytic Interpretation and Cognitive Transformation. *International Journal of Psychoanalysis* 62: 151–74.

Bateson, Gregory
[1956] 1978

Toward a Theory of Schizophrenia. In *Steps to an Ecology of Mind,* 201–27. New York: Ballantine Books.

1980

Mind and Nature. New York: Bantam Books.

Becker, Ernest
1973

The Denial of Death. New York: Free Press.

Beres, David
1960

Perception, Imagination, and Reality. *International Journal of Psychoanalysis* 41: 327–34.

Berman, Morris
1981

The Reenchantment of the World. Ithaca: Cornell University Press.

Bertalanffy, Ludwig von
1952

Problems of Life. New York: John Wiley and Sons.

1968

General Systems Theory. New York: George Braziller.

Bharati, A.
1976

The Light at the Center: Context and Pretext of Modern Mysticism. Santa Barbara: Ross-Erikson.

Blackburn, Thomas R.
1973

Sensuous–Intellectual Complementarity in Science, in *The Nature of Human Consciousness,* ed. Robert Ornstein, 27–40. San Francisco: W. H. Freeman.

Blanck, Gertrude
and
Blanck, Robin
1979

Ego Psychology II. New York: Columbia University Press.

Bleich, David
1970

New Considerations of the Infantile Acquisition of Language and Symbolic Thought. Presented to Psychological Center for the Study of the Arts. State University of New York, Buffalo, 1970, 1–28.

Bloch, Dorothy
1979

So the Witch Won't Eat Me. New York: Harper and Row.

Blofeld, J.
1962

The Zen Teaching of Hui Hai. London: Rider.

Bohm, David
and
Welwood, John
1980

Issues in Physics, Psychology, and Metaphysics. *Journal of Transpersonal Psychology* 12: 25–36.

Bonaparte, Marie
1940

Time and the Unconscious. *International Journal of Psychoanalysis* 21: 427–68.

Brain Mind Bulletin
1983
Bodies Change with Personality. 3 October, 1–2.

Brainerd, Charles
1979
The Origin of the Number Concept. New York: Praeger Publishers.

Broucek, Francis
1979
Efficacy in Infancy. *International Journal of Psychoanalysis* 60: 311–16.

Brown, Daniel P.
and
Engler, Jack
1980
The Stages of Mindfulness Meditation. *Journal of Transpersonal Psychology* 12: 143–92.

Brown, Norman O.
1959
Life against Death: The Psychoanalytic Meaning of History. New York: Vintage Books.

Calder, Allan
1979
Constructive Mathematics. *Scientific American* (October) 241: 146–71.

Campbell, Anthony
1975
The Mechanics of Enlightenment. London: Victor Gollancz.

Carrington, Patricia
1982
Meditation Techniques in Clinical Practice. In *The Newer Therapies: A Sourcebook,* edited by Lawrence E. Abt and Irving R. Stuart, 60–78. New York: Van Nostrand-Reinhold.

Chessick, Richard D.
1980
The Problematical Self in Kant and Kohut. *Psychoanalytic Quarterly* 49: 456–73.

Coen, Stanley J.
1981
Notes on the Concepts of Selfobject and Preoedipal Selfobject. *Journal of the American Psychoanalytic Association* 29: 395–411

Colarusso, Calvin
1979
The Development of Time Sense. *International Journal of Psychoanalysis* 60: 243–52.

Compton, Allan
1980
A Study of the Psychoanalytic Theory of Anxiety. *Journal of the American Psychoanalytic Association* 28: 739–74.

1983
The Current Status of the Psychoanalytic Theory of Drives. *Psychoanalytic Quarterly* 52: 402–26.

Dean, Stanley
1975
Psychiatry and Mysticism. Chicago: Nelson-Hall.

Deikman, Arthur
1973
Deautomatization and the Mystic Experience. In *The Nature of Human Consciousness,* edited by Robert Ornstein, 216–23. San Franciso: W. H. Freeman.

de Levita, David J.
1983
A Few Remarks on H. Segal's "Some Clinical Implications of Melanie Klein's Work." *International Journal of Psychoanalysis* 64: 277–80.

Delgado, José
1971
Physical Control of the Mind. New York: Harper and Row.

Descartes, Rene 1969 — *The Essential Descartes.* Edited by Margaret D. Wilson. New York: New American Library.

Dewey, John 1929 — *The Quest for Certainty.* New York: Minton, Balch.

Dicara, Leo 1972 — Learning in the Autonomic Nervous System. In *Altered States of Awareness,* edited by Timothy Teyler, 74–85. San Francisco: W. H. Freeman.

Dilthey, Wilhelm [1900] 1976 — The Rise of Hermeneutics. In *Critical Sociology,* edited by Paul Connerton, 104–16. London: Penguin Books.

Dinnerstein, Dorothy 1977 — *The Mermaid and the Minotaur.* New York: Harper and Row.

Dreyfus, Hubert 1979 — *What Computers Can't Do.* New York: Harper and Row.

Dowling, Scott 1981 — From the Literature on Neonatology. *Psychoanalytic Quarterly* 50: 290–95.

Dupont, M. A. 1974 — A Provisional Contribution to the Psychoanalytic Study of Time. *International Journal of Psychoanalysis* 60: 483–84.

Dussinger, John A. 1980 — David Hume's Denial of Personal Identity. *American Imago* 37: 334–50.

Earle, Jonathan 1981 — Cerebral Laterality and Meditation: A Review of the Literature. *Journal of Transpersonal Psychology* 13: 155–73.

Eccles, John 1972 — The Physiology of Imagination. In *Altered States of Awareness,* edited by Timothy Teyler, 31–40. San Francisco: W. H. Freeman.

Einzig, Paul 1951 — *Primitive Money.* Oxford: Pergamon Press.

Eisendrath, C. R. 1971 — *The Unifying Moment: The Psychological Philosophy of William James and Alfred North Whitehead.* Cambridge, Mass.: Harvard University Press.

Ellis, Havelock [1898] 1961 — Mescal: A New Artificial Paradise. In *The Drug Experience,* edited by David Ebin, 225–36. New York: Grove Press.

Epstein, Gerald 1981 — *Waking Dream Therapy.* New York: Human Sciences Press.

Erikson, Erik H. 1958 — *Young Man Luther.* New York: W. W. Norton.

Faber, M. D. 1973 — Analytic Prolegomena to the Study of Western Tragedy. *Hartford Studies in Literature* 5: 31–60.

1981   *Culture and Consciousness: The Social Meaning of Altered Awareness.* New York: Human Sciences Press.

Fagen, Jeffrey W. and Rovee-Collier, Carolyn K. 1982   A Conditioning Analysis of Infant Memory. In *The Expression of Knowledge,* edited by Robert L. Isaacson and Norman E. Spear, 67–106. New York: Plenum Press.

Fink, Eugen [1939] 1981   The Problem of the Phenomenology of Edmund Husserl. In *A Priori and World,* edited by W. McKenna, R. M. Harlan, and L. E. Winters, 21–55. The Hague: Martinus Nijhoff.

Fisher, David J. 1976   The Terrestrial Animal and His Great Oceanic Friend. *American Imago* 33: 1–59.

Flew, Anthony 1978   Transitional Objects and Transitional Phenomena. In *Between Fantasy and Reality: Transitional Objects and Phenomena,* edited by Simon A. Grolnick and Leonard Barkin, 483–502. New York: Jason Aronson.

Freud, Sigmund [1894] 1959   The Defense Neuro-Psychoses. In *Collected Papers,* translated by Joan Riviere, Vol. 1, 59–75. New York: Basic Books.

[1895] 1950   Extracts from the Fliess Papers. In *The Standard Edition,* edited by James Strachey, Vol. 1, 175–278. London: Hogarth Press.

[1895] 1966   Project for a Scientific Psychology. In *The Standard Edition,* edited by James Strachey, Vol. 1, 295–243. London: Hogarth Press.

[1896] 1959   Further Remarks on the Defense Neuro-Psychoses. In *Collected Papers,* translated by Joan Riviere, Vol. 1, 155–82. New York: Basic Books.

[1914] 1971   On Narcissism. In *Collected Papers,* translated by Joan Riviere, Vol. 4, 30–59. London: Hogarth Press.

[1915] 1971   The Unconscious. In *Collected Papers,* translated by Joan Riviere, Vol. 4, 98–136. London: Hogarth Press.

[1917] 1968   *A General Introduction to Psychoanalysis,* translated by Joan Riviere. New York: Washington Square Press.

[1919] 1955   Group Psychology and the Analysis of the Ego. In *The Standard Edition,* edited by James Strachey, Vol. 18, 67–144. London: Hogarth Press.

[1920] 1959 *Beyond the Pleasure Principle.* Translated by James Strachey. New York: Bantam Books.

[1923] 1974 *The Ego and the Id.* Translated by Joan Riviere. London: Hogarth Press.

[1925] 1959 A Note upon the Mystic Writing Pad. In *Collected Papers*, edited by James Strachey, Vol. 5, 175–80. London: Hogarth Press.

[1926] 1959 *Inhibitions, Symptoms, and Anxiety.* Edited by James Strachey. New York: W. W. Norton.

[1927] 1953 *The Future of an Illusion.* Translated by W. D. Robson-Scott. New York: Doubleday.

[1930] 1975 *Civilization and Its Discontents.* Translated by Joan Riviere. London: Hogarth Press.

[1932] 1953 New Introductory Lectures on Psychoanalysis. In *The Standard Edition*, edited by James Strachey, Vol. 22, 5–182. London: Hogarth Press.

[1938] 1959 Some Elementary Lessons in Psycho-Analysis. In *Collected Papers*, edited by James Strachey, Vol. 5, 376–82. London: Hogarth Press.

[1940] 1964 An Outline of Psychoanalysis. In *The Standard Edition*, edited by James Strachey, Vol. 23, 139–208. London: Hogarth Press.

Gadamer, Hans-George [1965] 1976 The Historicity of Understanding. In *Critical Sociology*, edited by Paul Connerton, 117–33. London: Penguin Books.

GAP (Group for the Advancement of Psychiatry) 1979 What Mysticism Is. In *Consciousness: Brain, States of Awareness, and Mysticism*, edited by Daniel Goleman and Richard Davidson, 187–90. New York: Harper and Row.

Garfield, Charles 1975 Consciousness Alteration and Fear of Death. *Journal of Transpersonal Psychology* 7: 147–75.

Gedo, John 1979 *Toward a Revised Theory of Psychoanalysis.* New York: International Universities Press.

Gill, Merton and Pribram, Karl 1976 *Freud's "Project" Reassessed.* New York: Basic Books.

Gimello, Robert M. 1978 Mysticism and Meditation. In *Mysticism and Philosophical Analysis*, edited by Steven T. Katz, 170–99. New York: Oxford University Press.

Goleman, Daniel 1977 *The Varieties of Meditative Experience.* New York: E. P. Dutton.

1981 Buddhist and Western Psychology. *Journal of*

Transpersonal Psychology 13: 125–36.

Greeley, Andrew and McReady, William 1979 — Are We a Nation of Mystics? In *Consciousness: Brain, States of Awareness, and Mysticism,* edited by Daniel Goleman and Richard Davidson, 178–83. New York: Harper and Row.

Grotstein, James 1978 — Inner Space: Its Dimensions and Coordinates. *International Journal of Psychoanalysis* 59: 53–61.

Gruen, Arno 1974 — The Discontinuity in the Ontogeny of the Self. *Psychoanalytic Review* 61: 557–69.

Habermas, Jürgen [1963] 1974 — *Theory and Practice.* Edited by John Viertel. Boston: Beacon Press.

1968 — *Knowledge and Human Interest.* Edited by J. J. Shapiro. Boston: Beacon Press.

1971 — *Toward a Rational Society.* Edited by J. J. Shapiro. Boston: Beacon Press.

1976 — *Communication and the Evolution of Society.* Edited by Thomas McCarthy. Boston: Beacon Press.

Hagglund, Tor-Bjorn 1980 — The Inner Space of the Body Image. *Psychoanalytic Quarterly* 43: 243–61.

Halevi, Z'ev Ben Shimon 1976 — *The Way of Kabbalah.* New York: Samuel Weiser.

Harris, Errol 1962 — Mind and Mechanical Models. In *Theories of the Mind,* edited by J. M. Scher, 464–89. New York: Free Press.

Harris, Marvin 1977 — *Cannibals and Kings: The Origins of Culture.* New York: Random House.

Harrison, Irving 1979 — On Freud's View of the Mother-Infant Relationship and the Oceanic Feeling. *Journal of the American Psychoanalytic Association* 27: 399–423.

Hartmann, Heinz [1939] 1958 — *Ego Psychology and the Problem of Adaptation.* Translated by David Rapoport. New York: International Universities Press.

Hartocollis, Peter 1974 — Origins of Time. *Psychoanalytic Quarterly* 43: 243–61.

Hegel, G. W. F. [1806] 1967 — *The Phenomenology of Mind.* Translated by J. B. Baillie. New York: Harper and Row.

[1821] 1967 — *Philosophy of Right.* Translated by T. M. Knox. Oxford: Oxford University Press.

Heil, John 1983 — *Perception and Cognition.* Berkeley: University of California Press.

217

Heron, W.
1972

The Pathology of Boredom. In *Altered States of Awareness*, edited by Timothy Teyler, 60–64. San Francisco: W. H. Freeman.

Herrick, C. J.
1949

George Ellet Coghill. Chicago: University of Chicago Press.

Horton, Paul
1974

The Mystical Experience. *Journal of the American Psychoanalytic Association* 22: 364–80

Huber, Jack
1967

Through an Eastern Window. Boston: Houghton-Mifflin.

Huizinga, Johan
1950

Homo Ludens. Boston: Beacon Press.

Hume, David
[1739] 1975

A Treatise of Human Nature. Oxford: Oxford University Press.

Husserl, Edmund
[1911] 1965

Phenomenology and the Crisis of European Philosophy. Translated by Quentin Lauer. New York: Harper and Row.

[1913] 1969

Ideas: General Introduction to Pure Phenomenology. Translated by W. R. B. Gibson. London: Collier-Macmillan.

[1929] 1960

Cartesian Meditations. Translated by Dorian Cairns. The Hague: Martinus Nijhoff.

Huxley, Aldous
1970

The Perennial Philosophy. New York: Harper and Row.

1974

The Doors of Perception. London: Penguin Books.

Huxley, Laura
1971

This Timeless Moment. New York: Ballantine Books.

James, William
1890

The Principles of Psychology, 2 vols. New York: Henry Holt.

[1902] 1958

The Varieties of Religious Experience. New York: New American Library.

Jastrow, Robert
1978

Toward an Intelligence beyond Man's. *Time,* Feb. 20, p. 47.

Jones, Roger S.
1982

Physics as Metaphor. New York: New American Library.

Kant, Immanuel
[1787] 1950

Critique of Pure Reason. Translated by J. M. Meiklejohn. London: J. M. Dent.

Kapleau, Philip
1965

The Three Pillars of Zen. Boston: Beacon Press.

1973

Zen Meditation. In *The Nature of Human Consciousness,* edited by Robert Ornstein, 237–41. San Francisco: W. H. Freeman.

Katan, Maurits
1979

Further Exploration of the Schizophrenic Regression to the Undifferentiated State. *International*

Journal of Psychoanalysis 60: 145–76.

Keat, Russell
1981
The Politics of Social Theory. Oxford: Basil Blackwell.

Kleinberg, Harry
1977
How You Can Learn to Live with Computers. Philadelphia: J. B. Lippincott.

Kleitman, Nathaniel
[1960] 1972
Patterns of Dreaming. In *Altered States of Consciousness,* edited by Timothy Teyler, 44–50. San Francisco: W. H. Freeman.

Kohler, Ivo
1972
Experiments with Goggles. In *Altered States of Awareness,* edited by Timothy Teyler. San Francisco: W. H. Freeman.

Korbin, Jill E.
1981
Child Abuse and Neglect. Berkeley: University of California Press.

Kornfield, Jack
1979
Intensive Insight Meditation. *Journal of Transpersonal Psychology* 11: 41–58.

Lacan, Jacques
1966
Ecrits. Paris: Editions du Seuil.

Langer, Susanne
1942
Philosophy in a New Key. New York: Mentor Books.

Lashley, K. S.
[1951] 1969
The Problem of Serial Order in Behavior. In *Brain and Behavior,* edited by K. H. Pribram, vol. 2, 515–40. London: Penguin Books.

Lauer, Quentin
1965
Introduction. In *Phenomenology and the Crisis of European Philosophy* (Husserl). New York: Harper and Row.

Lax, Ruth
1977
The Role of Internalization in the Development of Female Masochism. *International Journal of Psychoanalysis* 58: 289–300.

Lichtenstein, Heinz
1961
Identity and Sexuality. *Journal of the American Psychoanalytic Association* 9: 179–260.

M.
1928
Gospel of Sri Ramakrishna. Mylapore, India: Sri Ramakrishna Math.

Maharishi Mahesh Yogi
1966
The Science of Being and the Art of Loving. Los Angeles: SRM Publications.

1969
On the Bhagavad Gita. Baltimore: Penguin Books.

Mahler, Margaret
1968
On Human Symbiosis and the Vicissitudes of Individuation. New York: International Universities Press.

Mahler, Margaret,
Pine, Fred,
and
Bergman, Anni
1975
The Psychological Birth of the Human Infant. New York: Basic Books.

Mahoney, Michael S.   The Beginnings of Algebraic Thought in the Sev-
1980   enteenth Century. In *Descartes: Philosophy, Mathematics and Physics,* edited by Stephen Gaukroger, 141–55. New Jersey: Barnes and Noble.

Mannheim, Karl   *Ideology and Utopia.* Edited by Louis Wirth and
1936   Edward Shils. New York: Harcourt, Brace, and World.

Marcuse, Herbert   *An Essay on Liberation.* Boston: Beacon Press.
1969

Marx, Karl   Critique of Hegel's Doctrine of the State In *Early*
[1843] 1975   *Writings,* edited by L. Colletti, 57–198. New York: Vintage Books.

[1843a] 1975   Letters from the Franco-German Yearbooks. In *Early Writings,* edited by L. Colletti, 199–209. New York: Vintage Books.

[1844] 1975   Critique of Hegel's Philosophy of Right. In *Early Writings,* edited by L. Colletti, 243–57. New York: Vintage Books.

[1844a] 1975   Economic and Philosophic Manuscripts. In *Early Writings,* edited by L. Colletti, 279–400. New York: Vintage Books.

[1844b] 1975   Excerpts from James Mill's Elements of Political Economy. In *Early Writings,* edited by L. Colletti, 259–78. New York: Vintage Books.

[1846] 1967   *The German Ideology.* Edited by C. J. Arthur. New York: International Publishers.

[1857] 1973   *Grundrisse.* Edited by Martin Nicolaus. New York: Vintage Books.

[1867] 1967   *Das Kapital.* Edited by Frederick Engels, 3 vols. New York: International Publishers.

Mayhew, Christopher   Peyote. In *The Drug Experience,* edited by David
[1956] 1960   Ebin, 293–306. New York: Grove Press.

McCall, Robert B.   *Infants.* New York: Vintage Books.
1979

Meissner, W. W.   Internalization as Process. *Psychoanalytic Quar-*
1976   *terly* 45: 374–93.

1980   The Problem of Internalization and Structure Formation. *International Journal of Psychoanalysis* 61: 237–48.

Melito, Richard   Cognitive Aspects of Splitting. *Journal of the*
1983   *American Psychoanalytic Association* 31: 515–34.

Menaker, Esther A Kohut Symposium. *Psychoanalytic Review* 65:
1978 615–29.

Merleau-Ponty, Maurice *The Structure of Behavior.* Translated by Alden
1963 Fisher. Boston: Beacon Press.

1964 *The Primacy of Perception.* Translated by James
Edie. Evanston: Northwestern University Press.

1970 *The Phenomenology of Perception.* Translated
by Colin Smith. New York: Humanities Press.

Miller, Alice *The Drama of the Gifted Child.* Translated by
1981 Ruth Ward. New York: Basic Books.

Müller, Anton *Quantum Mechanics: A Physical World Picture.*
1974 Oxford: Pergamon Press.

Mumford, Lewis *The Myth of the Machine,* 2 vols. New York:
1967 Harcourt, Brace, Jovanovich.

Mushatt, Cecil Mind-Body Environment: Toward Understand-
1975 ing the Impact of Loss on Psyche and Soma. *Psychoanalytic Quarterly* 44: 84–107.

Neisser, Ulric The Processes of Vision. In *The Nature of Hu-
1973 man Consciousness,* edited by Robert Ornstein,
195–210. San Francisco: W. H. Freeman.

Neubauer, Peter C. The Life Cycle as Indicated by the Nature of the
1980 Transference. *International Journal of Psychoanalysis* 61: 137–44.

Neumann, Erich *The Great Mother.* Princeton: Princeton Univer-
1970 sity Press.

Offe, Claus The Separation of Form and Content in Liberal
1980 Democratic Politics. *Studies in Political Economy*
(Carleton University) 3: 5–15.

Ogden, Thomas H. The Concept of Internalized Object Relations.
1983 *International Journal of Psychoanalysis* 64: 227–
42.

Ornstein, Robert *On the Psychology of Meditation.* New York:
and Viking Press.
Naranjo, Claudio
1972

Ornston, Darius On Projection: A Study of Freud's Usage. *The
1978 Psychoanalytic Study of the Child,* vol. 33,
117–66. New Haven: Yale University Press.

Pelletier, Kenneth *Toward a Science of Consciousness.* New York:
1978 Delta Books.

Penfield, Wilder *Cerebral Cortex of Man.* New York: Macmillan.
and
Rasmussen, T.
1950

Penfield, Wilder and Roberts, Lamar 1959 — *Speech and Brain Mechanisms.* Princeton: Princeton University Press.

Peterfreund, Emanuel 1971 — *Information, Systems, and Psychoanalysis.* New York: International Universities Press (in collaboration with J. T. Schwartz).

Piaget, Jean 1968 — *Six Psychological Studies.* Translated by Anita Tenzer. New York: Vintage Books.

Pietsch, Paul 1972 — Shuffle Brain. *Harper's Magazine,* May, 41–48.

Pine, Fred 1979 — On the Pathology of the Separation-Individuation Crisis. *International Journal of Psychoanalysis* 60: 225–42.

Pines, Dinora 1980 — Skin Communication. *International Journal of Psychoanalysis* 61: 315–24

Pribram, Karl H. 1982 — What the Fuss Is All About. In *The Holographic Paradigm,* edited by Ken Wilber, 27–34. Boulder: Shambhala.

Pribram, Karl H. and Gill, Merton 1976 — *Freud's "Project" Reassessed.* New York: Basic Books.

Rank, Otto 1929 — *The Trauma of Birth.* London: Kegan, Paul.

Rapoport, Anotol 1974 — *Fights, Games, and Debates.* Ann Arbor: University of Michigan Press.

Rapoport, David 1960 — *The Structure of Psychoanalytic Theory.* New York: International Universities Press.

Regan, David 1979 — Electrical Responses Evoked from the Human Brain. *Scientific American* 241: 134–46.

Reynolds, Peter C. 1981 — *On the Evolution of Human Behavior.* Berkeley: University of California Press.

Rheingold, Joseph C. 1964 — *The Fear of Being a Woman.* New York: Grune and Stratton.

Ricoeur, Paul [1965] 1976 — Hermeneutics: Restoration of Meaning or Reduction of Illusion? In *Critical Sociology,* edited by Paul Connerton, 194–203. London: Penguin Books.

1970 — *Freud and Philosophy.* Translated by Denis Savage. New Haven: Yale University Press.

Rifkin, Jeremy 1983 — *Algeny.* New York: Viking Press.

Rinsley, Donald B.
1983
Borderline and Other Self Disorders. New York: Jason Aronson.

Rizzuto, Ana-Maria
1979
The Birth of the Living God. Chicago: University of Chicago Press.

Rogers, Robert
1978
Metaphor: A Psychoanalytic View. Berkeley: University of California Press.

1980
Psychoanalytic and Cybernetic Modes of Mentation. Presented to the Psychological Center for the Study of the Arts. Amherst, N.Y. (February) 1–80.

Roheim, Geza
1962
Magic and Schizophrenia. Bloomington: Indiana University Press.

1971
The Origins and Function of Culture. New York: Doubleday.

Rorty, Richard
1980
Philosophy and the Mirror of Nature. Princeton: Princeton University Press.

Ross, John M. and Dunn, Peter B.
1980
Notes on the Genesis of Psychological Splitting. *International Journal of Psychoanalysis* 61: 335–50.

Roth, David and Blatt, Sidney
1974
Spatial Representations and Psychopathology. *Journal of the American Psychoanalytic Association* 55: 854–72.

Roustang, François
1976
Dire Mastery: Discipleship from Freud to Lacan. Translated by Ned Lukacher. Baltimore: Johns Hopkins University Press.

Rucker, Rudy
1982
Infinity and the Mind. Boston: Birkhauser.

Schafer, Roy
1968
Aspects of Internalization. New York: International Universities Press.

Schiffer, Irvine
1978
The Trauma of Time. New York: International Universities Press.

Schiller, Jon R.
1980
Psychoanalysis, Ideology, and Language. *Canadian Journal of Political and Social Theory* 4: 9–22.

Shah, Indries
1971
Wisdom of the Idiots. New York: E. P. Dutton.

Shannon, William H.
1981
Thomas Merton's Dark Path. New York: Farrar, Straus, and Giroux.

Shibayama, Zenkei
1974
Zen Comments on the Mumonkan. New York: New American Library.

Slater, Philip
1974
Earthwalk. New York: Doubleday.

Southwood, H. M.
1973
The Origin of Self Awareness and Ego Behavior. *International Journal of Psychoanalysis* 54: 235–39.

Speeth, Kathleen
1982
On Psychotherapeutic Attention. *Journal of Transpersonal Psychology* 14: 141–60.

Spitz, Rene
1965
The First Year of Life. New York: International Universities Press.

Steinzor, Bernard
1979
Death and the Construction of Reality. *Omega: Journal of Death and Dying* 9: 97–124.

Stern, Daniel
1977
The First Relationship: Mother and Infant. Cambridge, Mass.: Harvard University Press.

Stern, Karl
1965
The Flight from Women. New York: Farrar, Straus, and Giroux.

Stevens, Leonard
1966
Neurons: Building Blocks of the Brain. New York: Thomas Y. Crowell.

Stoller, Robert J.
1974
Facts and Fancies: An Examination of Freud's Concept of Bisexuality. In *Women and Analysis,* edited by Jean Strouse, 391–415. New York: Dell.

Strachey, James
1966
Introduction. In *Project for a Scientific Psychology* (Freud). *The Standard Edition of Freud's Works,* Vol. 1, 290–93. London: Hogarth Press.

Sulloway, Frank
1983
Freud: Biologist of the Mind. New York: Basic Books.

Suzuki, Shunryu
1973
Zen Mind, Beginner's Mind. New York: Weatherhill.

Taube, Mortimer
1961
Computers and Common Sense. New York: Columbia University Press.

Taylor, Gordon R.
1981
The Natural History of the Mind. London: Granada.

Treurniet, N.
1980
On the Relationship between the Concepts Self and Ego. *International Journal of Psychoanalysis* 61: 325–34.

Vygotsky, L. S.
[1934] 1979
Thought and Language. Translated by E. Hanfmann and G. Vakar. Cambridge, Mass.: M.I.T. Press.

Wallace, Robert
and
Benson, Herbert
1972
The Physiology of Meditation. In *Altered States of Awareness,* edited by Timothy Teyler, 125–32. San Francisco: W. H. Freeman.

Walsh, Roger
1979
Emerging Cross-Disciplinary Parallels: Suggestions from the Neuro-Sciences. *Journal of Transpersonal Psychology* 11: 175–84.

1982	A Model for Viewing Meditation Research. *Journal of Transpersonal Psychology* 14: 69–84.
Wangh, Martin and Galef, Harold R. 1983	Narcissism in Our Time. *Psychoanalytic Quarterly* 52: 321–24.
Weil, Annemarie 1978	Maturational Variations and Genetic-Dynamic Issues. *Journal of the American Psychoanalytic Association* 26: 461–92.
Weitz, Morris 1983	Descartes' Theory of Concepts. In *Midwest Studies in Philosophy,* edited by P. French, T. Veling, and H. Wettstein, Vol. 8, 89–104. Minneapolis: University of Minnesota Press.
Welwood, John 1979	*The Meeting of the Ways.* New York: Schocken Books.
Wilber, Ken 1977	*The Spectrum of Consciousness.* Wheaton: Theosophical Publishing.
1982	*The Holographic Paradigm.* Boulder: Shambhala.
Wilden, Anthony 1972	*System and Structure.* London: Tavistock.
Wilson, Edgar 1979	*The Mental as Physical.* London: Routledge and Kegan Paul.
Wilson, Margaret D. 1969	*The Essential Descartes.* New York: New American Library.
Winnicott, D. W. 1953	Transitional Objects and Transitional Phenomena. *International Journal of Psychoanalysis* 34: 89–97.
1966	The Location of Cultural Experience. *International Journal of Psychoanalysis* 48: 368–72.
1971	*Playing and Reality.* London: Penguin Books.

INDEX